→ en
plein
air

→ Ethnographies
of the Digital

→ Edited by Pujan Karambeigi,
Anneliese Ostertag, Tabea Rossol,
Pierre Schwarzer, Lukas Stolz
→ Spector Books

en plein air

→ The book is published on the occasion of the *warehouse* project
→ www.warehouse.industries

beginning

stranded

entropy

pray

adobe

soft-fiction

home

end

beginning

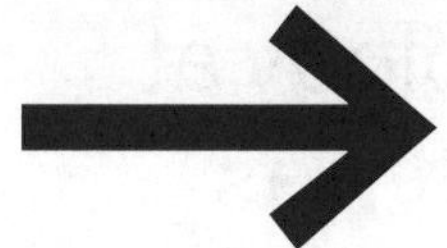

Anneliese Ostertag and
Tabea Rossol

Researchers charged with the task of determining what it was really like do not come back; they do not retrieve, they do not report, they pause and delight with the details.[1]

When Claude Monet packed his tubes for painting outside, his aspiration was the immediate observation of nature, capturing the closeness and likeness of an outside setting at a specific moment in time.[2] *en plein air*—literally painting outdoors—was a revolution; a polemic

1 → Niklas Luhmann, *Ideenevolution: Beiträge zur Wissenssoziologie*, ed. André Kieserling, trans. authors (Frankfurt: Suhrkamp, 2009), 234.

2 → Fred S. Kleiner, *Gardner's Art through the Ages: A Global History*, 15th ed. (Boston: Cengage Learning, 2015).

against the white walls of the studio. The same exercise of leaving the atelier in order to observe was formulated by ethnologist Bronisław Malinowski as the most fundamental requirement of ethnology at the end of the nineteenth century. It was a dissociation of the narrative and stylized studio depiction, countering the models of the laboratory and the Gedankenexperiment 'of' the office. The so called 'armchair-ethnologists' used to form their theories about unknown cultures depending on second hand sources e.g. through lively correspondence with missionaries or other colonial residents. Malinowski's call for participant observation—the personal involvement with the studied people, including learning their languages and trying to understand their worldview by sharing a life—became the paradigm of modern ethnology.[3]

Being in the field, however, the office walls did not leave: the ethnographers carried the models of the laboratory with them. Inspired by the natural sciences, the ideal of a neutral scientist speaking with

3 → Eberhard Berg and Martin Fuchs, "Phänomenologie der Differenz. Reflexionsstufen ethnographischer Repräsentation," in *Kultur, soziale Praxis, Text*, ed. Eberhard Berg and Martin Fuchs, 5th ed. (Frankfurt: Suhrkamp, 2016).

an omniscient voice of authority prevailed in the discipline. Using a formal and allegedly unambiguous language to describe the studied societies, ethnographers still invoked a universal gaze that feigned to be capable of capturing the 'real essence' of a culture. Observations were put into categories following the chimera of pure objectivity. This form of abstraction, eradicating the individual other, converting every particularity into comparable, and thereby manageable entities, is itself—under the guise of scientific research—a part of colonial oppression.[4]

The illusion that ethnography means sorting alien and disordered facts into familiar and clear categories—this is magic, that is technology—has long been destroyed.[5]

But how to represent observations made in the field? How to translate a particular encounter into a scientific discourse? Admitting that ethnographers are neither able to take up an outside position for observation, nor

4 → Anna Echterhölter, "Schöner berichten: Alexander von Humboldt, Hubert Fichte und Daniel Kehlmann in Venezuela," in *Kultur und Gespenster*, ed. Textem, 73–83 (Hamburg: Textem, 2006), 82. And: Lila Abu Lughod, "Writing against Culture," in *Recapturing Anthropology: Working in the Present*, ed. G. Fox Richard, 137–162 (Santa Fe: University of Washington Press, 1991).

5 → Clifford Geertz, *Die künstlichen Wilden: der Anthropologe als Schriftsteller*, provisional translation by the authors (Frankfurt: Fischer Taschenbuchverlag, 1993), 11.

leave their conventions of narration, reflections on their bodily involvement during the research as well as their own cultural background were integrated in academic writing towards the end of the last century. Scientists revealed the biases of their perspectives, exposing their own operations and assumptions knowing well that they were not only depicting but also manifesting certain discourses. Subjective experiences were no longer suppressed but served as a seismograph for reflecting one's own and other's worldviews; self-reflection became an acknowledged methodological tool.

Carrying this further, some ethnographers engaged in writing narrative so as to make clear that their writing was not a representation of true facts, but a representation of their individual experiences. Others emphasized dialogue as a primary source of knowledge and tried to soften the separation between their conversations in the field and the textual representation. Polyphone ethnography opposed conventional monographs to share the authorship and let many voices speak.

Yet, ethnographers were still in power, confronted by the problems of representation that they could—at best—skilfully react to but never dissolve. Being aware of this dilemma, some scientists even chose to stop writing.

Joining these lines of thoughts— without giving up on writing—the aim of this book is to engage with the digital *en plein air*; not only browsing the library, but trying to *engage* with the research object; and, at the same time, not subduing it under one single representational form: approaching the digital from different angles by using various modes of report.

There will be no definition of the digital in the beginning. Instead, there will be disparate definitions, forms, and enquiries. Neither does the digital constitute itself in opposition to the analogue, nor does it simply form an algorithmic architecture. Its boundaries are constantly in flux, digital practices are re-inventing themselves continuously. The unity of the digital—its seemingly homogeneous character—is more a fiction than a reality, more a model of the laboratory than the experience in the field.

There are over thirty people speaking in this book: scientists, performance artists, art critics, essayists, video artists, and poets each providing their own narrative of their encounter with the digital. The book includes different forms of writing such as essayistic texts, interviews and recordings, poems and collages working on semi-fiction, as well as scientific texts. Thereby, different fields of research collide. Some of the texts address the digital explicitly, suggesting definitions that question its structure or consider the dissolution of the term. Others set bodies in relation to media and new technologies, depicting transformations in the relations between human and environment, between observer and observed. Certain texts rather engage in ethnographic questions: how to put thoughts into form, what does it mean to engage in the field, and how much of a distance to keep? Artistic contributions turn observations into fiction, while interviews engage in problems of representation, operations of the gaze, and prospects of intimacy.

A remaining question pertains to how the texts are arranged. A book forms a structured unit. It is an object with a beginning and an end. Organized in different chapters it suggests a sequence unfolding in time connecting different texts with one another.[6] The chapters push content into form, cut them off, highlight a very specific side, arrange them in distinct figures. They violate the texts, forcing them into a certain shape and at the same time they might add something.

soft-fiction, pray, entropy, adobe, home and *stranded* are the titles of the six chapters in this book. Each of these terms is defined by a short text. The chapters try to stay silent and let texts pass by, though, at the same time they open up new spaces for reading and encountering the texts. Remaining permeable they still function as categories that remind us of the illusion of the ethnographic task.

6 → Ulises Carrión, *The New Art of Making Books* (Amsterdam: VOID Distributors, 1980).

stranded

stranded → It is not just being aground on some beach, not just being unsure about the next step, not just running out of money, not just Tom Hanks in *Cast Away* falling in love with a volleyball. Being stranded is more than being lonely or bored or both at the same time. It is about being in a space that is not yet cartographed, in a time that still has no fixed chronology. Or rather, being stranded means to dedicate oneself to revising the map.

On Disappearances
→ Reflections on the Techno-poetics of Invisible Machines →

Felix Maschewski and
Anna-Verena Nosthoff

"The internet will disappear." This statement was made in 2015 by former Google-CEO Eric Schmidt at the World Economic Forum. He did not seek to proclaim its death, but on the contrary, stress the omnipresence of the net to come. According to Schmidt, with so many IP-addresses and smart sensors along with rooms so dynamic and interactive, universal connectivity will go unnoticed: "It will be part of your presence all the time."

While Schmidt's vision mainly focused on smart environments and the internet of things, mars-visionary Elon Musk articulated an even more radical form of digital disappearance. His start-up Neuralink recently started researching the connection of mind, medium, and machine via direct cortex-interfaces.[1] Only by short-circuiting it with technology could the deficient human keep up with the development of artificial intelligence; otherwise, claims Musk, we would become pets of robots.[2]

What is occurring presently was recently made clear by Slavoj Žižek: Musk's plans force the disappearance of the difference between consciousness and reality, between the internal and the external—an "operation both ambiguous and possibly dangerous."[3] The enforced conformity of man and machine touches upon crucial questions: who controls the new techno-organic space and who decides in the end? Is it the fallible human or possibly the 'more objective' algorithm fed with streams of data? Maybe it is something in-between those or a talented hacker. It remains unclear what exactly could still be qualified as a consciousness considering the connection of man and machine. Musk, approaching these questions in a terse manner, explains that we are already "cyborgs"[4] per se through our continuous use of smartphones. He might not even be wrong.

The Cybernetic Hypothesis

The disappearance of the internet postulated by Schmidt is not solely related to the ambivalence of the medium itself—i.e. that the medium itself disappears behind what it renders visible. Like Musk's vision, the prophecy of the Alphabet company's chairman rather attests to a form of erasure and annulment: with the disappearance of the web a 'beyond,' an 'elsewhere' away from the omnipresent devices disappears. If everything is communicating with everything, the internet becomes ineluctable.

The collective Tiqqun described such developments years ago, suggesting a specific world-view: the "cybernetic hypothesis." The cybernetic view presupposes the entirety of "biological, physical, and social behaviors as something integrally programmed and reprogrammable,"[5] while it conceives of the human itself as some sort of machine one would only need to inform correctly through the simple adjustments of communicative feedback-loops.[6]

In this context, Tiqqun describes a cybernetic "modernization of power"—what they call the "visible production of Adam Smith's 'invisible hand.'" The collective therefore recognizes that through the steady establishment of cybernetic concepts and their gradual materialization in the form of forced computerization processes, "the mystical keystone of liberal experimentation" is no longer a mere fiction. The common good, they claim, is no longer based on the blind belief in the somewhat transcendental mechanics of Smith's metaphor. In the processing of computers, its functions become rather visible with the transactions rendered transparent and malleable through the "rational coordination of the flows of information and decisions." According to Tiqqun, thus, "communications systems would be the nerve system of societies, the source and destination of all power."[7]

In this vein, Eric Schmidt's more or less direct reliance on the cybernetic hypothesis is not surprising. In his cyber-pamphlet *The New Digital Age* he candidly mentions that the "importance of the guiding human hand"[8] is on the rise in the dematerialized digital age. He ascribes its growing influence to the rise in connectivity, the massive increase of stored data, and, last but definitely not least, the culturally recognized striving for quantification and the successive metrics of scores, rankings, likes, shares, etc.[9]

Digital 'World Destruction'

Schmidt's vision of converting the entirety of social processes and epistemes into the digital, and of shedding light on the back-room-mentality of antiquated institutions mainly marks a socio-political consequence. In the end, it leads to what Philip Howard recently called "final interconnectedness" (Beth Noveck called it "smart governance" and Parag Khanna "direct technocracy").[10] All those technologically upgraded concepts—dreams of replacing politicians with experts, public discourse with algorithmic regulation, and evidence-based data systems or parliamentary democracy with a fluid technocratic order—focus on continuing the cybernetic program of transparency in the sphere of politics up until a "politics of 'the end of politics.'"[11]

In this regard, digital machines mark a pervasive effect: they inhale matter, thus leading to what Martin Burckhardt describes as "world destruction," meaning, "for no matter which object is to be digitalized, it is to be stripped of its specific quality." Each thing loses its unchangeable idiosyncrasies throughout the process of digital doubling. The latter covers up the real, like a second skin, or a shadow, to finally emancipate itself from its stubborn insufficiencies and design new freedoms. Thus, an almost poetic "moment of symbolic destruction" seems to be characteristic of programming itself.[12] It brings us closer to the "second world,"[13] the world of the fantastic, which it realizes by expanding the realm of the virtual, allowing it to experience a new dignity. Yet, such digital seductions and promises of freedom rely on an ambiguous ground. For the digital questions all stabilities in a disruptive manner, it liquefies institutions, which gives them the sense of being replaceable. Thus, it creates an essential indifference, homogenization or flattening. Finally, the digital logic of programming leads everything to the binary play between 1 and 0.

Regimes of (In-)Visibility

The manifold processes of disappearance—of the internet, of an outside, of politics— are based on an elementary paradox: for the digital machines that so thoroughly demand transparency are they themselves extremely un-transparent. While their panoptic sensors see through both society and its subjects, they are most often incomprehensible (especially artificial intelligence that is elusive even for programmers), ungraspable, complex, and remarkably opaque to us. As media philosopher Wendy Chun explains, digital machines become metaphors for "everything we believe is invisible yet generates powerful effects."[14]

In this ambiguous optical relation Alexander Galloway accentuates "blackness," a specific form of darkness. He thereby sketches the opaque as a condition of possibility of cybernetic programming itself, whereby the logic of the "black box"[15]—a machine rendering visible only its input and output but its functioning remaining hidden—is immanent to modernity. Indeed, its history can be traced back to Leibniz's monad, Smith's formerly mentioned invisible hand, and Marx's definition of a commodity. In today's cybernetic societies of control this "blackness" forms a questionable preference. For if one follows Frank Pasquale, this cybernetic darkness has created a "Black Box Society"[16] ranging from shadow banks over delirious secret services and the well-hidden algorithms of the Facebook feed and Google Search to idiomatic expressions such as 'unknown unknowns.' This Black Box Society has created entirely new relations of power.

The pursuit of open profiles, generalized datafication, and the generalization of the network, all of which put cybernetic surveillance capitalism to work,[17] are only comprehensible via an a-priori opacity—a hidden source code. Through this, the digital age, which mainly accelerates a technological optimization of governmental relations of visibility, marks at least two overarching tendencies. On the one hand, it models a "democratized panoptism" through establishing a "non-hierarchic model of reciprocal visibility"[18] in the service of efficiency and mutual evaluation—with the quantified self being the self-referential variant of everything and everyone. On the other hand, this totalized transparency presupposes new invisibilities—a 'black box-ization.' The profiled visibility of social networks is only possible through the opaque machinery of a finely pixelated flat surface-aesthetics.

In the end, we guess that there are further 'black swans' in such models, that there are various 'deep secrets' in state apparatuses and all kinds of other uncertainties. Thus, we often cautiously request even more data, transparency, and demand light in the dark. Oftentimes however it is forgotten that each beam of light casts a shadow. For with every medium promising more visibility—from Galilei's telescope up to the smartphone—there "appears a dark background of invisibility, deeply intruding into the presentation of the visible."[19] Only through this interplay of Foucauldian 'coverings and un-coverings' can one recognize how the mode of transparency seeps ever more deeply into the flesh of society; how it informs the social; how it installs this maelstrom which in turn installs digitization, including its rather absolute cybernetic feedback logic.

Although both perspectives—opaque and transparent—seem to differ in their functioning, they are inseparably linked. It seems almost necessary to define social constellations of power via both concepts and their mutual dependence. If power is, in a Foucauldian sense, an "acting influence on action, on possible and real, futural, or present action,"[20] then the new agents and agencies pursue their sunny postulate of transparency by the widening of their own spheres of power—which is why national exceptions such as intended by the former German minister of justice Maas are to no avail. Turned into an anecdote, the self-censuring imperative of Schmidt, "if you have something that you don't want anyone to know, maybe you shouldn't be doing it in the first place,"[21] reveals not only the almost religious status[22] of the value of trans-parency in our times, but also a questionable regime of (in-)visibility that certainly carries totalitarian traits.

New Weapons

While Dieter Mersch seems to recognize diverse forms of impotence in the face of the new (in-)visibility and the "celebration of the techno-logical,"[23] Tiqqun suggests looking for new weapons. It is in their interest to extend *the background interference that imposes itself when the feedback loops are triggered, and which makes the recording of behavioral discrepancies by the ensemble of cybernetic apparatuses costly.*"[24] Only the indeterminacy of the inscrutable—of another beyond that tran-scends the dichotomy of transparency and opacity—seems to escape from the generalized processes of disappearance. According to Tiqqun, only a form of opaque fog can "shatter all known coordinates of perception:" "It makes it indiscernible what is visible and what is invisible, what is information and what is an event. This is why it represents one of the conditions for the possibility of events taking place. *Fog makes revolt possible.*"[25]

It however seems doubtful whether one can cloud the senses within the external omnipresence of the internet (Schmidt) and the concurrent subcutaneous installation (Musk), and how the internalized feedback loops could be disrupted. Perhaps a first step would be to recognize that networks, algorithms, as well as digital technologies are not revolutionary as such; that they do not carry emancipatory potentials by themselves, but would far better be understood as mere means to an end.[26] If we leave them in their neoliberal autopilot-mode, they indeed do change the world—but toward a world without us. In that case, following Baudrillard, there will remain nothing but a specter, "narcissistic double, more or less as the Cat left its grin hovering."[27]

1 → That Mark Zuckerberg has had similar plans for some time should not surprise. Facebook has been testing to what extent it is possible for users to be fed their facebook-feeds directly via cranial interfaces.

2 → Felix Maschewski and Anna-Verena Nosthoff "Das Netz ist nie neutral," *Neue Züricher Zeitung*, accessed on June 27, 2017, https://www.nzz.ch/feuilleton/kuenstliche-intelligenz-digitale-technik-ist-nie-neutral-ld.1302959. Neuralink's first goal is the battle against Parkinson's disease or depression. However, as emphasized by Musk, healthy humans should "naturally" be allowed invasive access to the internet within 8 to 10 years.

3 → Slavoj Žižek quoted in RT interview "Who will control this digital space merged with our brain? — Slavoj Zizek on Elon Musk's AI venture," accessed July 01, 2017, https://www.youtube.com/watch?v=kZJSmUExU6M.

4 → Elon Musk at the Code Conference 2016, accessed on July 03, 2017,https://www.youtube.com/watch?v=ZrGPuUQsDjo.

5 → Tiqqun, "The Cybernetic Hypothesis," accessed July 20, 2017, https://theanarchistlibrary.org/library/tiqqun-the-cybernetic-hypothesis.

6 → Historically this logic of the program stems less from La Mettries *Man a Machine* than from Norbert Wiener's *Cybernetics: Or Control and Communication in the Animal and the Machine*, modern game theory (John von Neumann) and behaviorist models of behavior (Gregory Bateson etc.). Those concepts had already subscribed to communicative interconnectivity (the social generalization of models of information, recursivity, and especially feedback loops) in the 1940s.

7 → Tiqqun, "The Cybernetic Hypothesis."

8 → Eric Schmidt and Jared Cohen, *The New Digital Age* (New York: Vintage Books, 2012), 24.

9 → Steffen Mau, *Das metrische Wir. Über die Quantifizierung des Sozialen* (Berlin: Suhrkamp, 2017).

10 → Felix Maschewski and Anna-Verena Nosthoff "Wo ist das egalitäre Internet geblieben?" *Neue Züricher Zeitung*, May 08, 2017, https://www.nzz.ch/feuilleton/machtsphaere-silicon-valley-wo-ist-das-egalitaere-internet-geblieben-ld.1290918. As well as: "Order From Noise. On Cambridge Analytica, Cybernetic Governance and the Technopolitical Imaginary," *Public Seminar*, March 20, 2017, http://www.publicseminar.org/2017/03/order-from-noise.

11 → Tiqqun, "The Cybernetic Hypothesis."

12 → Martin Burckhardt, *Digitale Renaissance, Manifest für eine neue Welt*, trans. editors (Berlin: Metrolit, 2014), 125.

13 → Robert Pfaller, *Zweite Welten und andere Lebenselixiere*, trans. editors (Frankfurt: S. Fischer, 2012).

14 → Wendy Chun, *Programmed Visions: Software and Memory* (Cambridge: MIT Press, 2014), 2.

15 → Alexander Galloway, "Black Box, Black Bloc," Lecture at the New School in New York City, April 12, 2010, http://cultureandcommunication.org/galloway/pdf/Galloway,%20Black%20Box%20Black%20Bloc,%20New%20School.pdf.

16 → Frank Pasquale, *The Black Box Society* (Cambridge: Harvard University Press, 2015).

17 → A thorough overview is offered by Wolfie Christl's Study "Corporate Surveillance in Everyday Life," accessed on July 10, 2017, http://crackedlabs.org/en/corporate-surveillance/ see also the forthcoming book of Shoshana Zuboffs in German: *Herren oder Knechte*.

18 → Ulrich Bröckling, "Totale Mobilmachung. Menschenführung im Qualitäts- und Selbstmanagement," in *Gouvernementalität der Gegenwart. Studien zur Ökonomisierung des Sozialen*, ed. Ulrich Bröckling et al., trans. editors (Frankfurt: Suhrkamp, 2000), 152.

19 → Joseph Vogl, "Medien-Werden: Galileis Fernrohr," in *Archiv für Mediengeschichte 1*, ed. Friedrich Balke, Bernhard Siegert and Joseph Vogl, trans. editors (Paderborn: Wilhelm Fink, 2001), 120.

20 → Michel Foucault, *Subjekt und Macht*, trans. editors (Frankfurt: Suhrkamp, 2005), 285.

21 → Eric Schmidt in an interview with CNBC when he was still CEO of Google, https://www.cnbc.com/2016/05/24/alphabets-eric-schmidt-admits-hes-an-iphone-user-but-says-samsung-is-better.html.

22 → Christopher Hood, "Transparency in Historical Perspective" in *Transparency: The Key to better Governance?*, ed. Christopher Hood und David Heald (Oxford: Oxford University Press, 2006), 3.

23 → Dieter Mersch, *Ordo ab chao-Order from Noise* (Berlin: Diaphanes, 2013), 49.

24 → Tiqqun, "The Cybernetic Hypothesis," (emphasis in original).

25 → Tiqqun, "The Cybernetic Hypothesis," (emphasis in original).

26 → Geert Lovink, *Social Media Abyss, Critical Internet Cultures and the Force of Negation* (Cambridge and Malden: Polity, 2016).

27 → Jean Baudrillard, *Why Hasn't Everything Already Disappeared?* (Chicago: The University of Chicago Press, 2009).

sext: → Ängste zur Kunst and whee.gif

sext is a Twitter meme, in which various text fragments are combined with the premise of *sext:*. This is how you end up with "*sext:* so do you wish you never met me." Or "*sext:* pretend harder." Obvious and not so obvious constellations break with normative, normal sexting— by shifting through diverse tonalities: ironic and bitter, then supersoft and summertime sadness, then again conceptually complex, across diverse languages, even beyond classical Broken European English. The two Twitter accounts *Ängste zur Kunst* and *whee.gif* create a text performance with these memes, reframing their own former tweets into a new context.

sext: 03.09.2017

passion is a disease.
die.
use this to your advantage.
tell me more about your advantage.
connect me with random printers.
, bitch.
your printer is fine tho.
your printer is hot.
you don't have to like this.
volunteer harder.
pretend harder.
wear my dress.
your dress is very black.
I can hardly see it.
represent yourself.
with one hand.
you shouldn't skip this.
skip yourself harder.
your result is fine.
yourself.
do you bring your identity to a conversation?
your font is hot.
typography kills.
you will see a leg 7 days after you read this.
you can totally try this out.
ungender my drone.
send screenshots.
send socks.
you don't need to be part of this.
this won't work but you will.
I want to send you cotton balls.
things you can buy.
I don't think matthew mcconaughey is hot.
sigh.
slowly.
soft af.
you r a beautiful flower from a chair.
aspirin postcomplex.
lol.
3 emojis for the rest of the year.

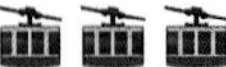

sex scenes in scandinavian movies/series are the worst.
yes all my dreams are movies.

try not to.
you are the fluffiest fleece.
soon.

sext: 09.10.2017

you escaped death this time.
ur dm didn't try very hard.
it is very hard.
use this to your advantage.
send rocks.
memes cannot be made unseen.
never think of this unicorn or its son ever again.
your emoji is blank.
with one hand.
the other one.
now your good foot.
you r a beautiful flower growing from a chair.
, lovely.
stay harder.
with one hand.

I can't write a to-do-list that includes looking at my to-do-list.
do something!
I'm gonna take notes for you.
closely.
lol.
oh.
you might want to change this.
change into something more fluffy.
changes into that one fluff you thought was very fluffy
your result is fine.
thing is: you're beautiful and terrifying.
this is fine.
you cannot afford singularity university.
I'm german.
may I decorate you with text?
yes yes yes yes yes pleaaaasssse.
your machine is universal.
I'm scared of your machine.
send screenshots.
I want to touch your screen.

Malinowski's Kiss →
Notes Toward a Critique of Digital Resistance → Guilel Treiber

The following text has been written at the bequest of the warehouse *project. The aim of the text was defined in advance as a critique of a short manifesto written by the project members. The text online, containing no more than three paragraphs is rich in theoretical positions. The original manifesto since then has been reworked and the name of the project changed from "an ethnography of digital resistance" into "an ethnographic archive of digital distribution." I tried to engage with it properly in the text you have before you. It thus became simultaneously an account of my own theoretical positions concerning digital resistance and a 'historical photograph' that captures the constantly changing nature of internet art projects.*

The *warehouse* project opens its site with a citation from one of the founding fathers of ethnology, Bronisław Malinowski:

> *Today, Monday, 9.20.14, I had a strange dream; homo-sex., with my own double as partner. Strangely autoerotic feelings; the impression that I'd like to have a mouth just like mine to kiss, a neck that curves just like mine, a forehead just like mine (seen from the side).*[1]

The project participants rightly highlight the value of the term homophily in order to analyze the radical love of the same in the face of segregation, a radical love that they emphasize with the above quotation. They understand homophily to be the result of being locked with more of the same. However, one may wonder, already here, at the start of the project, about the value of homophily.[2] Homophily may not be the reaction to segregation, as the project members claim, but the reaction to the encounter of difference. Malinowski starts his journal with a revealing sensation that precedes his sense of segregation. He takes the boat from Brisbane to Cairns in Australia; he has not yet left to his new 'adventure' of 'exploring' the natives of Papua. Nonetheless, already here, he feels as though he "is taking leave of civilization."[3] He has no other aim, here or in the books he later published, than to 'explore' those who are yet to be explored. What does Malinowski mean by it? This aim most of the early anthropologists of the early twentieth century shared. He concretely means incorporating into the structures of power/knowledge those who are yet to be incorporated, those who can still live a radically different life. What he wants is not to introduce civilization to the heart of Papua, in this he is different from the Spanish Conquistadors and their violent 'holy' mission, but to explore. But how can he explore, simply 'observe,' without precisely taking part in the structures of turning subjects into objects of knowledge to be explored, studied, catalogued, and later on reproduced in writing in order to 'increase' knowledge, by dissemination, distribution, and consummation that will lead to university positions, fame, and academic progeniture (indeed, more of the same). A similar question can be asked of the project participants: how can one collect, archive, and distribute modes of digital resistance in order to overcome segregation? Are the project participants capable of constituting a knowledge (for this is what they do) of resistance without precisely nipping it in the bud? Are not the project participants the avant-garde, not of any revolution, but of the latest forms of immaterial production and post-fordist capitalism?

Of course, I must demand an answer to this question of myself, as much as of the project participants. For I have been invited to contribute a critique, and when one is invited to perform a critique, is not one's critique reduced to simply a performance? Is not a critique of the invitation itself necessary as a first condition? Is not the act of freeing a space within one's structure in order for critique to be pronounced precisely the end of critique? Moreover, in this specific sense, how can the critique pronounced in the next pages, be anything but a conscious cooptation into a structure and a project one may want to criticize? There is nothing in reading papers or performing lectures that can be a transgressive resistance to the order of interpellation. By being here, writing this paper, with this body, and for these people, I constitute myself as a collaborator, as a colleague, and as a participant in a dialogue. If critique was ever a resistance, it has been silenced before it was pronounced. Hence, even with the best intentions, Malinowksi participated in constituting the "savages" as precisely that, savages; transforming those whose difference is truly independent into those who are just different compared to himself and his same, contained and explained within his discursive structures and power relations, i.e. European civilization. Malinowski's kiss, his homo-sex, is not his love for the same, but his love for the cultural, social, and economic structures of which he is but a fraction. His yearning, his desire, for his 'civilization,' is not a reaction to segregation, as though he is the one who is excluded and left to his devices on the islands of Papua. His desire is the desire to leave no difference, to turn everything into the same, to be one world, speaking with one voice. Malinowski will pass the next four years in Papua, but we cannot but recall that these are the days where the fields of death are beginning to be plowed by the chariots of destruction that will encompass Europe and 15 years later the world as a whole. More of the same. Malinowski's diary is indeed a space for ethnographic exploration but not a documentation of any "homophilic friction in its attempt to overcome segregation."[4] If anything, Malinowski's diary is but the honest expression of a desire to swallow the world in civilization, to erase all signs of difference and to give birth to the same. Malinowski's sex dream is but a figure of his own desire to be completely subjugated into the form of the one.

The subtitle of the project, "an ethnographic archive of digital friction"[5] is somewhat revealing. The projects participants do not aim to create or produce friction, but to observe it. However, they do intend to counter segregation originating in homophily. Hence their aim is double: to produce knowledge about resistance to a specific form of segregation and at the same time to encourage practices of resistance through the dissemination of their geometry and topography of the "new normal."[6] The initiators of the project believe that they can constitute a new critical theory. Critical in the knowledge it produces, in order for this theory to be put into practice. I will try to show in the following pages, in what can be no more than a few notes of critique, achingly aware of my own cooptation, the futility of such a project.

The New Normal

There is an assumption at the heart of the project that has to be tackled, challenged, and analyzed. It is a common assumption shared by political analysts, thinkers, and other such well-meaning persons. It became over-bearing during the latest American elections; one could have even said that it was becoming a new truth in an age of post-truths. The message is quite simple: social media is omnipresent in our lives. It tends to reflect to individuals a world made of peers and colleagues, people that are all similar to ourselves, and hence locks one on an island of self-reflection and self-reaffirmation. The world is an "echo-chamber" where one hears only the conformable opinions one already approves of.[7] It is this at the heart of contemporary homophily that the participants of the *warehouse* project identify and aim to tackle. However, Malinowski's kiss precedes this post-modern sense of homophily by more than a hundred years. Homophily as the love of the same is at the heart of Western civilization.

One did not need social media in order to be surrounded by similitude and identity. Race, class, and gender have all constituted extensive systems in which one could live an entire life oblivious to one's blindness to others. The history of humanity and the history of the West in particular can be told moving from one system of blindness to another. The capacity to see what is different was always constituted through one's own structures of knowledge and power; what was looked upon was always perceived through one's eyes, and those were always conditioned by one's society, culture, and most of all privileges. All those voices of difference that were silenced forever could have been truly heard only under the condition that they were not represented, not talked about, but talked with.[8] Is not classical ethnography a project of blindness under the guise of exploration and representation?[9]

It was from the 18th century onward, that vision of the other has become entangled with some sort of voyeurism. To look at another person — precisely those who are different — through the keyhole (a real or metaphorical keyhole) was understood as giving some kind of ultimate form of knowledge and pleasure. Observation was needed without the object being aware of it being observed. This indiscreet discreet observation treated people as discrete units, taking them out of their communities and constituting two main disciplines, that of psychology and that of demographics. One treats human beings as individuals constituted in their individuality, the other treats human beings as units amalgamated into statistical models.[10] None of them took the human in her community and relationships with others as meaningful or as an object of study. Was not the Panopticon the perfect metaphor of this all-seeing gaze, invisible to the thing it observe, manipulating, controlling, stopping any possible resistance in advance?[11]

One needed to wait for Malinowski's participant observation in order to treat human beings in their community. However, participant observation just means that one has integrated this gaze of the keyhole as one's position. The ethnographer participates in the lives of the 'savages' writing under the candle light late at night in his small notebooks with an exhilaration similar to those who 'discovered' the Americas. Just as the master's child listening on to the servants, he must share what he heard. For the pleasure of the voyeur is not only that of the gaze, it is also that of telling to others what he saw, constructing a story filled with all the emotions he thought he felt—hushed voices, secret desires, pulsating bodies. Malinowski tells us, in one of the famous passages from his seminal *Argonauts of the Western Pacific* that the savages have no knowledge of their own society, in which they are but unconscious participants. Their intent must be explained by the ethnographer, by the voyeur we may add:

> *Not even the most intelligent native has any clear idea of the Kula as a big, organised social construction [...] If you were to ask him what the Kula is, he would answer by giving a few details, most likely by giving his personal experiences and subjective views [...] Not even a partial coherent account could be obtained. For the integral picture does not exist in his mind; he is in it and cannot see the whole from the outside. The integration of all the details observed, the achievement of a sociological synthesis of all the various, relevant symptoms, is the task of the Ethnographer. First of all, he has to find out that certain activities, which at first sight might appear incoherent ... have a meaning [...] Again, the Ethnographer has to* construct *the picture of the big institution, very much as the physicist constructs his theory from the experimental data, which always have been within reach of everybody, but needed a consistent interpretation.*[12]

Malinowski's voyeurism is not unique to Malinowski. It is, as we have stated earlier, a constitutive aspect of Western civilization. We are all voyeurs and we enjoy it tremendously. The only issue is that in our cinematographic imagination it has always been the servants watching the masters through the keyholes; all the while, it was the master peeping in, looking through the locked door, on those who are not constrained by the same social conventions he or she were submitted to. The gaze of the keyhole gave the master the confirmation of his own status, the capacity to attach to the servants a story they were not able to tell by themselves, and most of all an intense physical pleasure. Constituting knowledge is clearly a form of masturbation.

What is social media society if not a society of voyeurs? They tell us millennials access news through social media, but what they forget to tell is that what they mostly do is look at the lives of others. Facebook is but the latest form of the 'roman à sensation.'[13] The issue with social media is not that they constitute an echo chamber but the illusion of the sameness, which it gives with those we have nothing in common with. If social media is doing anything, it is precisely maintaining the illusion that Western democracies have been trying to maintain for the last two decades, that of equality. Under the guise of this illusion, of an absolute equality where myself, Andy Warhol, Donald Trump, and Taylor Swift, all share a Coke, Twitter, or Facebook account; the propagation and exponential growth of exploitation has been steadily rising to levels we have never seen in the history of humankind. Even the distinction between the house slave and Alexander the Great is less evident than the one between Mark Zuckerberg and myself. If there is a threat to democracy, it is not the threat of the echo chamber but that of blindness to the complete artificiality of the political possibilities we are left with. There is no real choice between 'patrie'[14] and 'patron.'[15] We are living within a social media app where our emotional spectrum has been reduced to happy, sad, like, and angry. Where our political interventions are surveilled and censured and where we are all aware of that, yet, we let it happen. This is what destroys democracies, if they were not already problematic from day one, the blindness to radical inequality and to the complete willingness to give those in power full control of our lives and identities.

Surfaces and Spaces: The age of Digital Emplacement

What is a warehouse? According to the members of the project, the *warehouse* is a site of "observation of techno-conditions and a simulation of a discrete archive." *warehouse* as a project "will attempt to offer a system of strategies countering homophily by inserting friction."[16] Let us keep the issue of friction for later and question for the moment the careless use of the word 'warehouse.' I would like to suggest that a warehouse is one important form of contemporary heterotopia. Foucault defines heterotopia as an actual place, which is designed into the fabric of society in which all other real spaces found within that society are simultaneously represented, contested, and reversed. A heterotopia is a place outside place, an "utterly different" place.[17] The warehouse—much like its digital counterpart, the server—can never be anything but the founding site of our digital conditions. It is a place where many other sites are presented, where relations are being created and undone, a space of passage, of transition yet a place that has everything transition through it. By warehousing digital forms of resistance, I fear that the project participants have again unknowingly undermined the conditions of possibility of resistance.

The warehouse is a liminal site. It is, on the one hand, a capitalist utopia. Imagine Amazon as a model for future societies. A global company with no face but algorithms and drones. A company made only of warehouses where products arrive from their anonymous producers and sent to anonymous consumers. A cold, white, sterile world. Where products are slotted, reduced to a number, identifiable, manageable, fixed yet in constant movement, traceable, followed, and most of all replaceable and disposable. The utopia of our neoliberal surveillance age. On the other hand, much like that place in the mirror, the placeless place, a warehouse is both utopia and heterotopia. It leads both to the future society, a place waiting to come into being, and to our current society, a place that is real yet seems unreal in the face of a placeless place waiting to be born.

As Foucault tells us, there are six principles that guide the analysis of heterotopias. The first principle is that every society constitutes them. However, the warehouse is in this respect one of the first truly globalized heterotopias. It is global in two major senses. First, it contains an entire world within its confines. It is the place where products from China or Taiwan, from Iran or Israel, may sit next to each other. A place where borders play no role. Only the size of the box, the weight, and the serial number. Second, it is everywhere. A country today may have warehouses before it will have schools, hospitals, or places of government. Products need to move, and they need to move everywhere. You may question me about the specific importance of the warehouse for our time, but Foucault's second principle is precisely that a heterotopia may change importance and operation throughout time. Warehouses have a long history, though they came to prominence with the rise of capitalist Fordist society in the 19th century, they may be identified prior to that. Nonetheless, they become heterotopias only with the move to complete automatization and digitalization. The more faceless they become, the more workers will be replaced by robots and thinking cranes, the more the warehouse will become one of the constituting limits of our contemporary global society.

The third principle is that a heterotopia has the ability to juxtapose within a real place several emplacements that are incompatible themselves.[18] The warehouse contains the potential of a thousand places within its limited confines. Products that can tell a thousand stories every night. Imagine IKEA, the store warehouse, where garden furniture is next to showers, beds next to kitchens. Picture again the sprawling Amazon warehouse, where books, computers, cosmetics, fashion products, DVDs, and consumables are stocked and arranged next to each other. Different potential places all existing within one. It is, as the fourth principle tells us, a place of temporal discontinuity. The warehouse has no time, no hour. The digitized automatic warehouse works every day, all day. It has no holidays, no weekends. The white neon lights illuminate in their white eternal calming color, cold dead products. Time stops in the warehouse. However, the warehouse is also the timeliest of places. Everything tick, everything tock. Products need to leave on time; however, its clock is not like our clock. The hours have not the same meaning for a warehouse; it is time as a functional moment in time that counts. Whether it is midnight, two a.m., or three in the afternoon the warehouse keeps working. Tick, tock, tick tock. The end of human time, the rise of machine time.

The fifth principle allows us to reject a further objection. You may want to claim that a warehouse like Amazon, where access is restricted is not the same as IKEA, where everybody can access the warehouse. You may want to suggest a distinction between a democratic warehouse and a restricted one. Allow me please to shatter your optimism. You may enter into an IKEA warehouse, but you will never understand. You come into an IKEA warehouse with your silly list of catalogue, corridor, and slot numbers. However, try to find on your own a product of which you have no number. Though you can enter an IKEA warehouse, as every customer can, you may never find your way through it. For that you need to belong to those who can manage the warehouse, you need to understand the system behind it, you need to have access to the information. IKEA and Amazon, have no clear distinction between them. Hence, a warehouse responds to the fifth principle — a heterotopia presupposes a system of closures and openings that isolate it and make it penetrable at the same time.[19] The warehouse is more penetrable to products than to human beings. It is precisely a place defined by what can get in and what can get out. The sixth principle is crucial for it emphasizes the specific, almost unique character of a heterotopia as a place whose function is spread between two poles, that of an illusion which denounces all real space; and that of a meticulous, completely organized space to which our own real space is disorganized and chaotic. A warehouse is precisely a place, which is not a place, an illusion that makes our reality and its potentialities look and feel unreal, heavy, and stupid. It denounces at the same time that it presents all that our space is not — ordered, organized, automatic, safe, clean, cold, and dead.

You may conclude, after this long analytic exposé that the project participants have chosen their reference wisely. There may be no better name for a project like this. The warehouse is the perfect place to store the ethnography of digital resistance. However, if you are convinced that the warehouse is the heterotopia of the age, we must retain the fact that as a place of complete difference it may not be the best of places to fight the post-modern love of the same. The warehouse is a place of difference in the sense that it stands both 'outside' society and in its 'middle.' It is a place of difference for it constitutes the limits of our societal imagination. Within this place, where all reality is reversed, and turned into products, in this place of local fixedness and complete global transition, in this place of power of immaterial production, there can be no imagination, there can be no art, let alone resistance.

In order to resist, one must resist warehouses, not build them. In order to refuse cooptation by the power structures in place, one cannot accept a name such as this without letting in, with it, the entire infrastructure of capitalist society. The warehouse is our collective unconscious, invoke it and be destroyed. The only way to resist is to burn warehouses and build in their wake schools, gardens, and hospitals. There can be no warehouse of resistance without it being turned into another heterotopia, that of the 19th century, a 'museum' of resistance, of long dead forms of resistance. The project participants may have invoked a monster with which they cannot fight. They may have thought of performing a reversal, which may have been possible with a lesser space such as the office or the construction site, but not with a heterotopia of the magnitude of the warehouse. I fear that once again they have killed resistance before its gentle flower had the opportunity to bloom.

Resisting through Friction: Between a Rock and a Hard Place

The project I am writing on is called by its participants "warehouse—an ethnographic archive of digital driction."[20] As I have dealt with ethnography and warehouse in the previous sections, I will now try to offer a few hasty comments on the issue of digital friction. The project members tell us that our current condition is one of "seamless surfaces [that] are stacked on top of each other, engaging us in the cozy architecture of Gated Communities."[21] If the surfaces are stacked upon each other, then increasing the state of friction within and between the different surfaces will increase the cracks and may yet let the light shine in. However, we stand clearly in front of two problems—first, the use of the metaphor of frition; second, the lack of clear distinction between resistance and friction. The project members define digital resistance as "models of friction, local utopias, and distributive infiltrations."[22] Friction seems to be a kind of resistance, a specific instance of it. I will try to show in the following paragraphs that friction is essentially different from resistance, and therefore that the project members may be engaged in friction but not in resistance.

First of all, the metaphor. Friction is a force related to movement. We have static friction and dynamic friction. Static friction is the friction that exists when one tries to walk. Without static friction, we would all be walking on ice, sliding, unstable. Dynamic friction is the friction that arises when one tries to move an object on a surface. It is then that friction becomes a negative force. In the same way that the object works on the surface, the surface pushes back the object. Seamless surfaces can either offer friction between the surfaces or with the objects that are moved on their faces. The seamlessness of the surfaces seems to suggest that the main friction these surfaces cope with or generate is the one between the surfaces that are stacked upon each other. The surfaces may be smooth but the fact that they are stacked means that they are not completely smooth. A completely smooth surface would not hold on any other surface, even if they were glued to each other. It must be uneven in order to be stacked. Nonetheless, it seems that when the project thinks of friction, it thinks of the friction between members of a given surface, of a given segregated community. Friction is what can arise between the same and its similar, within one body or community, not between communities. I will try now to make a similar point through a comparison between resistance and friction.

The Relation Between Resistance and Friction

Clausewitz defines friction as that which exists within a given body and its relation to its surrounding elements.[23] A general must take into account both the friction between independent units within their army and the friction between the army and the area it moves through. Clausewitz brings in a third form of friction, liquid friction.

The perfect liquid is that which has no friction between its components. A viscous liquid is one where friction makes it less liquid. Moreover, for Clausewitz, friction is not what happens when an army encounters an enemy. When an army encounters an enemy, we get resistance. Resistance is what exists in relations of enmity. The struggle is that process where two opponents engage in a combat to reduce each other's capacity to resist. Resistance for Clausewitz is about capacity, which includes the means to resist and the will to resist. The two, resistance and friction, are forces that reduce the will, they both complicate operation, they both create cracks, gaps, and seams. However, they are not the same. Friction seems to be what exists between one and its similar, while resistance is between one and its difference.

Does an increase in friction lead to resistance? Not necessarily. An increase in friction, if that is the aim of the project participants, can cause a restructuring of the surface. If what worries us is the friction on surfaces, it does seem to lead quite intuitively to the conclusion that in order to reduce friction there will be a restructuring of the surface with what the surface has already at its disposal. It does not require anything new or different to come in. Friction may be what the same can oppose of what is similar in order to express its discontent. Resistance is about introducing something radically different. Resistance resembles friction; however, it consists of a struggle, a real one, between two opponents locked in a logic of enmity. However, resistance may be reduced only in two ways: either by destroying the other's capacity to resist or by introducing the other into your midst. Hence, changing one's surface.

What is the concrete implication of all this discussion about friction, resistance, and force? Within democratic regimes, as long as the illusion that these are regimes of sameness and equality persists, only friction is possible. Counter-intuitive as it may seem at first glance, it is harder to resist in a democracy. However, friction—and we may call it civil disobedience, refusal to pay taxes, occupying public spaces, protesting, striking—is what in the past has been able to render democracies more flexible, more compassionate, and more inclusive.[24] Art, for example, can cause friction. It is no longer resistance, not within democracies at least. Resistance is what happens when that which we do not understand to be the same, that which we see as different, tries to occupy or disobey. We understand their action, rightly some may say, as a threat and we move to a destruction of that difference's capacity to resist. We try to do so violently, at times even at the price of absolute violence, and at times, we try to swallow difference, as we have mentioned with Malinowski, by reducing absolute difference into a relative one. That which is different becomes different only in relation to us, contained and explained within our discursive structures and power relations; its difference is no longer independent. Friction is something we should all engage in. For friction makes governments think of why it is doing what it does. However, for that we need a government that wants to hear what we may think or agree with. It seems that friction is something inherently democratic. Resistance is not. Resistance is a transgressive challenge where one is willing to risk one's life in order to create a real change to the dominant truth or government. It may be violent, merciless and it does not necessarily lead to emancipation or liberation. Friction is within truth, resistance is between truths.

What about digital resistance? Well, according to these notes, digital resistance can only be a form of friction. Digital resistance, being in the digital, accepts certain rules of engagement, and specifically an entire infrastructure required in order to make it possible — computers, rapid connections, and immaterial labor. One cannot digitally resist in Iraq or Syria. If one does something digital it is usually both limited in time and space, it accepts the other as a digital subject and hence as the same or at least as a similar. In that sense, there is no digital resistance but only digital friction. If we were to think of digital resistance, it would be a resistance that undermines its own conditions of possibility. A resistance with the digital against the digital. A digital resistance worthy of its name will be a resistance that will attempt to eradicate the conditions of the digital — electricity, internet, and computers.

My aim in these notes is not to reduce the importance of the *warehouse* project. If they do have a general aim, it is one that aims at rendering complex and not evident the relation between intellectual production — be it philosophy or art — and political production. I believe that resistance does not need theory or art in order to exist. It is actually the other way around. When art and philosophy do not have resistance as its prior form, as what gives it inspiration and pushes it forward, to explore new limits and even transgress them, they become at best, friction, and at worst, a form of complacence and conservatism. If we feel some kind of dissatisfaction in the West with our current forms of art and philosophy, it is not because they do not generate resistance but because there is no resistance to generate them. However, due to the courage and the open-endedness of resistance, we must ask ourselves a crucial question, an ethical question: do we want to resist? Given that resistance can easily be reduced to relations of violence and conflict, do we want to see it back in our streets and cities? Should we not all prefer friction and encourage it, accepting that it may keep our societies dynamic but will not allow us to access the same mental resources that political resistance leads to through its capacity to transgress any social convention? If we agree that transgressive resistance is not to be desired, then the crucial importance of a project such as this has to be emphasized. If projects such as this are producing the conditions necessary for us to remain different within the same, they already aim very high, they may indeed be crucial in order for us to keep some kind of real, concrete democracy alive. We may then reach the conclusion that we should leave the resistance, with the respect it deserves, to those who truly resist; while we engage, together with the project members, in an effort of friction aimed at no less than the revitalizing of our current digital democracies.

1 → Bronisław Malinowski, *A Diary in the Strict Sense of the Term* (London: The Athlone Press, 1967), 12–13.

2 → "In other words, seamless surfaces are stacked on top of each other, engaging us in the cozy architecture of Gated Communities. Comfortable exclusions of the Other touch upon an easy space of segregation. Personalized interfaces endure into homophily — we are encircled with more of the same. *warehouse* is an ethnographic project studying artistic and scientific strategies countering homophily. A geometry to map a new normal; a topography for overcoming segregation. What may friction look like in times of total seamlessness? For 5 months *warehouse* will go on an ethnographic field trip by collecting, archiving, and distributing modes of digital resistance — models of friction, local utopias, and distributive infiltrations." super filme and Flatness, "warehouse — an ethnographic archive of digital friction," www.warehouse.industries, accessed June 4, 2017.

3 → Malinowski, *A Diary in the Strict Sense of the Term*, 6.

4 → super filme and Flatness, "warehouse."

5 → super filme and Flatness, "warehouse."

6 → super filme and Flatness, "warehouse."

7 → super filme and Flatness, "warehouse."

8 → Mostafa M El-Bermawy, "Your Filter Bubble is Destroying Democracy. Wired," accessed June 04, 2017, https://www.wired.com/2016/11/filter-bubble-destroying-democracy.

9 → "Though the archive is all that we have left from past lives, the project is in the present. It could aim at talking to people who engage in concrete political resistance. It could study the art that a political form of protest puts into being in the world. However, it chose to portray it through the mimetic gaze of art." Michel Foucault, "La vie des hommes infâmes," in *Dits et écrits*, ed. Daniel Defert and François Ewald, with the assistance of Jacques Lagrange, no. 2, 1976–1988 (Paris: Quarto/Gallimard, 2001. vol. 2), 237–253.

10 → Edward Said, *Orientalism* (London: Penguin Classics, 2003), 13.

11 → Michel Foucault, *Les mots et les choses: Une archéologie des sciences humaines* (Paris: Gallimard, 1966). And the more political treatment of these two is found in: Michel Foucault, *Sécurité, Territoire, Population* (Paris: Seuil/Gallimard, 2004).

12 → "Our surveillances societies are the wet dream of the prison guard. Nothing is invisible but that which happens out of the net, and out of view. Soon power will no longer be blind. However, Malinowski's kiss teaches that blindness may be constituted by the tools of observation themselves. This is perhaps the only blindness in which the light of resistance and opposition may yet grow." Michel Foucault, *Surveiller et Punir* (Paris: Gallimard, 1975), 228–264.

13 → Sensation novel.

14 → Fatherland.

15 → Protector.

16 → Bronisław Malinowski, *Argonauts of the Western Pacific: An Account of Native Enterprise and Adventure in the Archipelagoes of Melanesian New Guinea* (London: Routledge, 2002), 64.

17 → super filme and Flatness, "warehouse."

18 → Michel Foucault, "Different Places," in *Essential Works, 1954–1984: Aesthetics, Method, and Epistemology*, vol. 2, ed. James D. Faubion (New York: New Press, 1998), 167.

19 → Foucault, "Different Places," 181.

20 → super filme and Flatness, "warehouse."

21 → super filme and Flatness, "warehouse."

22 → super filme and Flatness, "warehouse."

23 → Foucault, "Different Places," 183.

24 → Carl von Clausewitz, *On War*, trans. and ed. Michael Howard and Peter Paret (Princeton: Princeton University Press, 1989), 120.

25 → For example, Thoreau uses counter-friction in order to describe civil disobedience, but the aim is the same — to increase friction. Henry David Thoreau, *Walden; and, Civil disobedience* (New York: Penguin Books, 1986), 234.

Zombie Diaries → An interview with Jean Hubert on *Waiting for Sleep*

After a zombie invasion, Will finds himself incarcerated in his home. Structured like a diary, *Waiting for Sleep* depicts the everyday routines of a character living in almost complete isolation—Will is living in a computer-generated animation. It is this strange, almost mad journey, into someone's mind while being sealed off from its surroundings that Jean Hubert's work addresses.

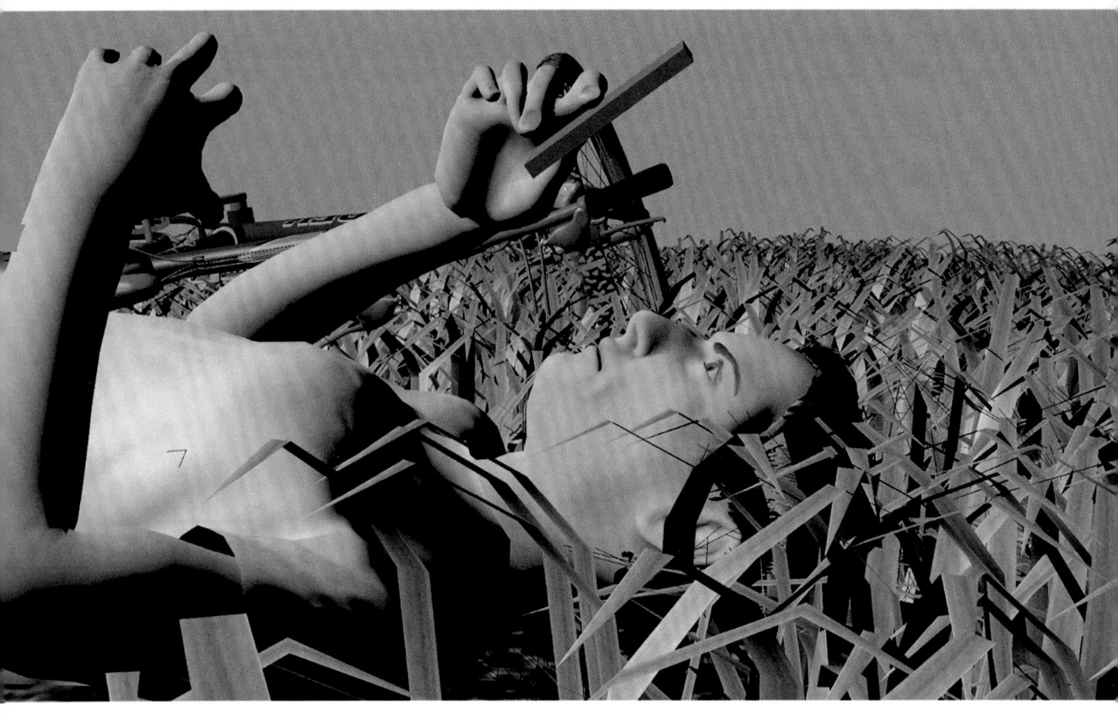

Jean Hubert, *Waiting for Sleep*, 2016, film still.

Pujan Karambeigi: I'm interested in how you organized *Waiting for Sleep* as a kind of diary. While watching it I was asking myself: who is the person writing the diary? Who or what are we following?

Jean Hubert: We are following the calm and steady survival of a young man who deliberately decided to keep living in his home surrounded by the danger of a zombie invasion. I called *Waiting for Sleep* a diary because of the strong emphasis placed on the depiction of the daily routine of Will throughout the day. Moreover, it is the type of intimacy that we find ourselves in by looking at him sending text messages, or having a phone call. Almost until the end of the story we hear nothing else than his own words which seem to melt with his own thoughts.

Pujan Karambeigi: While we follow Will across his daily routines such as texting his ex-girlfriend, talking to his mum and fixing his bike, there is this strong feeling of suspense — both in the sense of abeyance and in the sense of tension. It is as if the world (its time as much as its imagery) has come to a stand-still. At the same time, the danger is just across the fence — zombies waiting to eat him alive. Could one speak of a twofold-ness of suspense?

Jean Hubert: There is a suspense because of Will's promiscuous relation to the zombies: from the beginning to the end, it is as if some roaring bull was running at full speed towards him and he was simply twisting his shoulders at the last moment to avoid it. So, I use minimal movement in the scenes. There are lots of frozen moments in the action.

And as much as I continue, I realize that it is some kind of extreme minimalism that I am looking for. This is one of the many unrealistic aspects of the film. I don't try to make a breathing, walking, sweating creature, like a character behind a camera. Instead, I animate a drawn figure in a drawn environment. I guess here the apocalypse has the flavor of a soft desolation. I was touched by the representation of an intimate isolation created in *The Last Man on Earth*, a zombie apocalypse film by Ubaldo Ragona and Sidney Salkow from 1964. Strangely, the making of computer generated animation brought me to look at the past — to an old kind of cinematography where everything was shot with a heavy dolly traveling around the cables on the floor of a stable set. Moreover, this stand-still feeling of duration is also due to my working with sound. The sounds are obviously used as an addition to the image. Like in cartoons from the 1960s the only function of sound is narration. So, the noise of the ambience is quite close to zero. Consequently, the scene may sound dead calm right before something is about to animate.

Pujan Karambeigi: In anthropology the diary has a specific function. Bronisław Malinowski, a polish anthropologist started writing a diary just after he arrived in Papua New Guinea in 1914. In the face of extreme isolation — being all by himself in the tropics, not speaking the language of the indigenous people, and overwhelmed by insomnia — he used the diary as an instrument to tackle his loneliness. The diary appeared to be the very tool for both documenting isolation and writing an alternative script to it. With Will there seems to be a similar situation of addressing isolation. However, instead of using protocol sentences the diary is largely articulated through computer-generated imagery. Would you call *Waiting for Sleep* a non-verbal form of the diary?

Jean Hubert: How striking it is that functionalism came through a brain suffering from insomnia! In *Waiting for Sleep* I only use a few words. However, it is definitely a gesture taken from the diary. I was always attracted by scientific diaries in general, not only for their empirical content but rather for the style of literature that goes along with it. The objectiveness of the protagonist — there is an equal differentiation between the anecdotic and the dramatic — creates this factual language that was in fashion for a long time. From Camus's *l'Etranger* to Kafka, the narrator seems to be unfeeling and passive. Something bonds diaries to writing the fantastic. Must be the lack of sleep.

Pujan Karambeigi: The title of *Waiting for Sleep* reads "part one." Will there be more parts? And why did you choose to break up the diary into several parts?

Jean Hubert: There will be a part two and a part three as there are three days in the story. Each part describes one day. There were several reasons but I am quite satisfied with the timing now. Even when the whole film will be finished, hopefully in a year, I would like to keep these cesuras.

VR Kills the Video Star → Experiencing is Believing →

Jonathan Harth

I've seen things you people wouldn't believe. Attack ships on fire off the shoulder of Orion. I watched C-beams glitter in the dark near the Tannhauser Gate. All those moments will be lost in time like tears in rain… Time to die.[1]

The frameless windows of current Virtual Reality (VR) devices offer us a new view of the world and ourselves. The intensity of what is known as presence in virtuality has not been possible with any other medium so far. You cannot imagine what it is like to be placed into a VR system until you have experienced it on your own. With such new possibilities, what could this mean? On your own and with your own body? What (new) meanings of embodiment may become possible within VR environments? Will we merely find optical tricks and well-functioning imaginations in VR, or will we find an opening to redefine our very own corporeality?

Thus, the use of VR stirs up old, but relevant and fundamental questions of phenomenology: what is the body? What is corporeality? How does identity inscribe itself into the body—and, vice versa, how does the body inscribe itself into identity? VR, in its usage, constantly poses the question: where, who, and how am I actually present?

Jaron Lanier, the founder of one of the first VR companies in the world, is reflecting similarly, when he describes his experiences with the VR prototypes of the early days:

1 → Ridley Scott, *Blade Runner* (Warner Bros, 2007).

In the '80s, I had maybe an outright mystical approach to it. For me, the very most important thing about VR was that when you were in it, you'd feel your own existence in the sense that if all the sensory input is artificial, then what's floating there, that's your consciousness. So to me, it was sort of proof that subjectivity is real; that consciousness is real, that it's not just a construct that we put on things. Just to notice that you really exist, to me was the very, very core of it.[2]

It is still hard to predict how VR will develop. Nevertheless, it must be assumed that new technologies open up new experiences which then have to be culturally integrated one way or another. Even if VR is still standing at its humble beginnings and nobody can foresee which questions will become relevant through and because of its use, one thing should be clear: society will not give up VR all too soon.

What do these virtual experiences do to us as users? What impact may it have on one's identity, when a user immerses themself in a foreign and maybe somewhat frightening environment: e.g. in a body of a different sex or talking to strangers one cannot discern as being another avatar or just a bot. These questions may seem rather odd, but exactly that is possible today with the use of VR. Thus, it is not very far off to ask why users should not adopt a different attitude towards themselves after trying out different selves in different situations? The available corpus of research on these phenomena, which has grown since the 1990s, not only shows first approaches towards behavioral therapies[3], but also to more far-reaching results on behalf of changing one's attitude and habitual behaviors. See for example the results of VR experiments on gender[4], age[5], or skin color, which clearly indicate changes in self-perception and respectively changes in the preception of others.

A next society that technically provides self-divergent virtual societies in itself must have an involuntary effect on individuals:

What the user/viewer experiences in the case of the new technologies is his direct influence on the alternative reality: Not only the world could be different, but these realities and alternative possibilities do not exist in emptiness — they are always and inevitably dependent on our behavior and on our projections of possibilities.[6]

According to Esposito, such a probing of alternatives and possibilities of oneself can prove extremely valuable to a society which is increasingly exposed to the necessity of contingency. Perhaps this is why video games are so attractive in the 21st century society. Digital games allow for playing with the distinction of real and virtual possibilities, thus contributing to the capacity of dealing with contingency. Against

2 → Jaron Lanier, "DIGITAL NATIVES: A conversation between virtual reality visionaries Jaron Lanier and Kevin Kelly," interviewed by Casey Newton, accessed June 17, 2017, https:// www.theverge.com/a/ virtual-reality/ interview#story.

3 → Carlos Coelho, Alison Maree Waters, Trevor J. Hine, Guy Wallis, "The use of virtual reality in acrophobia research and treatment," *Journal of Anxiety Disorders 2*, 2009, 563–574.

4 → Valerie, Petkova and Henrik Ehrsson, "If I Were You: Perceptual Illusion of Body Swapping," *PLoS ONE 3*, no. 12 (2008).

5 → Domna Banakou, Raphaela Groten, Mel Slater, "Illusory ownership of a virtual child body causes overestimation of object sizes and implicit attitude changes," *Proceedings of the National Academy of Sciences 110*, no. 31 (2013).

6 → Esposito, Elena. "Ästhetik und Spiel." *Mensch und Medien*, 2010, 159–77, trans. editors, 175.

the background of this distinction, 'the' reality may become a bottomless category. It is hardly surprising then why Californians love VR so much. Once again, a technology promises to properly disrupt everything. But what is so special about VR and how could this technology disrupt existing formats of media?

VR Kills the Video Star

The VR devices of the current generation already provide a very good impression of what it may become in the coming years. Above all, it is the effect of feeling present in the virtual environment, which can be regarded as the unique selling point of current VR technology. As a user of VR, you instantaneously experience yourself as a participant of this environment, no longer separated from the action by any means of distance-creating techniques such as camera angles or display screens. The successful suspension of disbelief locks the oscillation between here and there onto the side of the alternative. As a user, you are right there in the middle of the action. VR is about personalized experiences. Thus, if we would like to assert that fragmentation, granularization, and personalization are the current momentums of contemporary society, it is no surprise that VR is considered state of the art.

The holy grail of VR still is the 360° environment that has full three-dimensionality. That is because the experience of 'being there' would be sullied by simply projecting on plane surfaces. That's why current VR-films still look pale, superficial, and flat compared to computer-generated environments. Even the level of detail of real-world graphics cannot overcome this. Even the latest 3D-formatted movies such as the most commercially successful film of all time, *Avatar*, do not create as much immersion and presence as the (by the way very infantile) low-budget short ButtVR.[7] But above all, film always lacked interactivity—as a user, you remain a mere spectator and long for involvement.

> *We used to say seeing is believing. Now we have to say experiencing is believing.*[8]

It is the technology of three-dimensional, 180° VR porn that gives us a glimpse of what might become possible one day. However, at the same time VR porn gives rise to completely different challenges, the phantom pain of the simulation actually becomes greater because the vividly copulating body clearly is not your own! Even worse, current VR porn makes it necessary that the head—that is, the 1st-person camera of the action—must remain completely stiff and does not

7 → see: "BUTT's VR Experience • SBS 1080p • GOOGLE CARDBOARD • Gear VR Gameplay • VIRTUAL REALITY," accessed July 20, 2017, https://youtu.be/fzgGKD0kshQ.

8 → Shuhei Yoshida (president of Sony Computer Entertainment) cited in "Experiencing is believing: what virtual reality could mean for ads and brands," Mike McGee, accessed June 16, 2017, https://www.theguardian.com/media-network/media-network-blog/2014/aug/28/marketing-virtual-reality-facebook-oculus-rift.

allow any tolerance for movements. Otherwise, the infamous cyber-sickness sets in leading to the loss of immersion.

However, the new positioning within the diegesis involuntarily raises the question of the recipient's role. Who am I when I am, for instance, actively present in that kind of sexual action? An explicit addressing of the user — the so far tabooed breaking of the fourth wall — can be integrated in VR much more easily, but then the rather immersion-breaking experiences of the abstinence of interactivity come into play. If I am addressed as a spectator in video film, this remains a mere and flat gesture that allows no reaction. Watching movies relieves one of one's own actions. The use of VR on the other hand, is demandingly stimulating. VR implies the longing for personalized experiences and accordingly self-efficacy experiences build up the strongest immersion. Therefore, it should be expected that immersive VR narrations become the next big thing: who is able to tell stories that really touch, move, and change me?

Can VR-films actually unfold their full potential in the production of alternative realities in the medium of traditional narration? Perhaps their potential lies in curious and somewhat voyeuristic attitudes of recipients. With the help of VR, the user can be taken to places and situations that are otherwise unattainable. Missed the concert? No problem, I'll get you there. Want a trip into Paraguay's jungle? No problem, you do not even need to pack. Peripherals such as robot-mounted cameras — go-pros, copter, etc. — offer plenty of opportunities to try out new immersive documentaries of nature, culture, and lifestyle. But in any case: VR always leaves one amazed. Amazed not only at the new worlds I could visit, but above all amazed about myself — about my fears, my worries, my inhibitions and possibilities.

VR as a Technology of the Self

Despite the current confines of my little office-island, I know that I have become a traveller in a realm which will be ultimately bounded only by human imagination, a world without any of the usual limits of geography, growth, carrying capacity, density or ownership.[9]

As long as the immersive crises that can be generated by VR are strong and contingent enough, the possibility of habitual disruption will not stand in the way. For this reason, VR — especially in its Californian variants — appears to be close to already realizing utopias of self-optimization. It is not hard to find similarities between the longing that comes up with the use of VR, and the longings of spiritual practices and their hope of salvation. Both seem to be conditioned by

9 → John Perry Barlow, "Virtual Reality and the Pioneers of Cyberspace Being in Nothingness," accessed June 17, 2017, https://www.wired.com/2015/04/virtual-reality-and-the-pioneers-of-cyberspace/.

an immanent suffering due to man's anthropological 'deficiencies', which urge for dissolution, or at least for reassurance.[10] While, for example, Buddhist practices point to the reflection of one's own structuring and seeks to change the adept's self- and world-relations, VR propagates the change of oneself by catapulting into alternative worlds. While the first approach primarily tries to change the self, the latter changes the world around you. Of course, it should be clear that world and self are always closely related to each other.

Every reflexive insight—and thus the corresponding insight into the external—must measure itself at the above-mentioned question: where and as who and how am I actually present right now? Now, VR offers the opportunity to bring this presence to a change, to over-ride one's space-time structure, and thus to change the perspective on one-self and the world. It would seem as if the unity of the distinction between body and mind cannot help itself but to re-configure according to the perceptions of an alternative body in an alternative universe. Consciousness without perception, as well as perception without a body, and thus consciousness without a body, still is inconceivable.

Therefore, it can be assumed that with the help of VR the fluid and blurring boundaries between not only the virtual and the real but also the social and technical will dissolve.

Since its very beginning, the socio-technological cyberspaces did appear to be the ideal place for hybrid entities. If technology and sociality can no longer be separated from each other, we have to assume an increasing hybridization of socio-technical reality. In cyberspace, human people tend to be equally digitally embodied as artificial non-human entities. Perhaps it is for this reason that the basically unlimited realities of virtuality appear to be the next frontier of human adventure and conquest?

At the same time it becomes clear that there are more possibilities within the body than in culture. In this sense, there seems to be a kind of surplus in the body which has not yet been realized culturally. Whether this can be realized at all, or in what form, still has to be proven. But we must assume that people will never stand still. Through digital avatars, the residents of VR may construct virtual identities according to their very own personal desires for liberation from the above mentioned 'deficiencies.' Being no longer restricted by material reality, the users of VR are thrown back at only their individual longing for being someone (else). But the technology of VR not only offers new possibilities for new identities but also the possibility to solidify and enhance a well-established identity. Fortunately, there is no need to constantly change identity. But the constant opportunity itself will change the point of view on one's identity. The central question of "who am I?" needs to be answered in VR as well, and it can be assumed that the need for answering it becomes more and more urgent while at the same time being harder to fulfill.

10 → Arnold Gehlen, *Man. His nature and place in the world*, (New York: Columbia Univ. Press, 1986).

The new hybrid agents wearing fluid identities and inhabiting the potentially ever-changing environments of VR finally lead us to the "Cyborg's Dilemma" Frank Biocca was concerned about 20 years ago in the early days of VR:

> *The embodiment advanced in the form of virtual environment technology can be characterized as a form of cyborg coupling. This coupling underscores what I call the cyborg's dilemma, a kind of Faustian trade off: Choose technological embodiment to amplify the body, but beware that your body schema and identity may adapt to this cyborg form.*[11]

Leaving behind old schemes of bodily representation and perception, the use of VR shatters the concept of the one and only body. By being able to embody other beings, while at the same time change, trade, or share different identities in various social contexts inhabited by human as well as non-human social agents, the formerly known mechanisms of identity management will become obsolete. Then, the amazement of the users about the possibilities of VR is nothing less than the enjoyable sabotage of ordinary presence. But at the same time, it is the astonishment about the richness of the world and one-self. Hopefully, this will clarify why the use of VR does not have to do with a loss of reality as it is traditionally sung in the songs of 'the downfall of the occident' but quite the opposite; VR has to do with a gain of reality! However, as a technology of the self, these possibilities are available today.

11 → Frank Biocca, "The Cyborg's Dilemma. Progressive Embodiment in Virtual Environments" in *Journal of Computer-Mediated Communication*, no. 3 (1997), https://doi.org/10.1111/j.1083-6101.1997.tb00070.x, accessed August 20, 2017.

Repertoires Animés

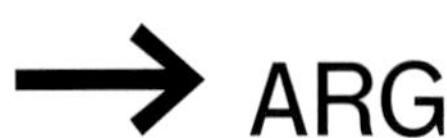 ARG

... a representation of the world and what it contains, mirror and sum, a means to introduce peoples to one another and foster collaboration among them [1]

In recent years, Paul Otlet's (1868–1944) visionary project of the 'Mundaneum,'[2] and his speculative designs of knowledge architectures "beyond a Gutenberg Galaxy,"[3] were reinscribed in a history of thought as a forerunner of the internet, notably under the title of a "Google ante litteram."[4] We see a librarian who dreamed of a universal documentary (de)center dedicated to knowledge dissemination and social interconnection, whose everexpanding and flexible network should be accessible beyond any intellectual, technological, economic, or social elitism[5]—a network that always conceived in a 'state' of emergence and transformation, bridging heterogeneous sources. In short, the relational structure should constitute a concrete mechanical and collective brain.

However, this vision seems to open and assert possibilities that seem much more far-reaching and promising than the simple prefiguration of a search engine and its virtual monopolistic position within today's internet. The internet is constructed along hegemonic political, economic, and logistical decisions that shape (decisively) the day-to-day experiences we perform with and through it. Access to specific and prioritized knowledge renders into hierarchies, economies, and value systems; personal data is acquired for various purposes and with different objectives; knowledge transfer is censored in all conceivable forms;[6]

1 → Paul Otlet, *Traité de documentation: le livre sur le livre: Théorie et pratique*, trans. author (Brussels: Mundaneum edition, 1934).

2 → The Mundaneum was founded in Brussels in 1910 by Paul Otlet and Henri La Fontaine as part of their work on archivology and documentation science.

3 → Frank Hartmann, *Vom Buch zur Datenbank. Paul Otlets Utopie der Wissensvisualisierung*, trans. authors, (Hamburg: Avinus Verlag, 2012).

4 → A reading that was actively promoted by Google itself in terms of content and concrete investment in the 'heritage Otlets.'

5 → The temporal context of a scientific positivism and a Europe- and US-centered world view however have to be considered here. A view that, for example, excluded any cultures of knowledge that were not primarily text based.

6 → For example the pre-formatting of an information exchange through social media platforms.

a fiction of a 'functionalist neutrality' of search engines and links is suggested. We want to record Otlet's projections and revisit his past-future thinking. Our means are not primarily analytical-theoretical, instead we would like to approach the material speculatively via performative-artistic methods. An intermedial perspective—here quite in destinction to the concept of the transmedial—described by Rémy Besson as "a process of meaning production linked to media interactions,"[7] allows us, firstly, a synchronous view of constellations of heterogeneous sources and materials (their 'co-present' within). Secondly, it allows us diachronic access, in the sense of inscribing different technological framings into a constellation of material over a course of time, against the backdrop of the attempt to reflect a medial transfer in relation to the transformation of technical means, in which reconfigurations and reactions of 'past' forms always participate in every imaginable re-mediatization.[8]

The concept of technology used here, in its derivation from the Greek techné—art, skill, craft—and logia—word, teaching, studies—addresses in its most fundamental meaning a collection of processes, tools, methods, and skills that have been developed and systematized to allow the realization of a specific object. This object can be a thing or a non-material effect such as the knowledge produced in a scientific experiment or in a philosophical reflection. As the philosopher Boyan Manchev put it, the Greek concept of techné, understood as the process of dis-/organization, allows for a much more complex and challenging understanding of 'technology' than its colloquial meaning.[9]

In the context of the research project *Repertoires Animés* on the Mundaneum we study intermediate strategies of mutual inscriptions of materials and technologies, and put them performatively into practice, in order to render and measure the space between Otlet's speculative approach and contemporary forms of knowledge organization on the internet.

This raises questions such as: can we, in an extension of Otlet's thinking[10] and through a critical and political use of the available tools, imagine new ways of receiving and sharing information—and more generally, materials—via the internet? What would be platforms on which each user 'intervenes' not only in the provision of content or the inner functional framework informed by the specific way of one's own use, but could (co)shape each one's own forms of access as well as production and transformation of knowledge? To what extent is this claim acted out by existing platforms such as Wikipedia or search engines like Google, and to what extent not? Or, what does 'open source' mean in this specific sense? How could the connections of different subjects be thought of as fundamentally relational, evolutionary, organic, in question in every point at all times, transgressive, and transformative (i.e. not in the sense of a static however changeable topography)—in the sense of Otlet's "collective brain?" Would such a utopia (?) imply relations between subjects

---

7 → Jürgen E. Müller, "Intermediality: A New Interdisciplinary Approach: Theoretical and Practical Perspectives as an Example of the Vision of Television," trans. authors, in *Cinemas: review of cinematographic studies/Cinemas: Journal of Film Studies*, vol. 10, no. 2–3, 2000, 109.

8 → We refer here to a hypothesis of Bolter and Grusin that there is no new media, as a "new medium" is always going to reformulate or restructure preexisting media. Richard Grusin and Jay David Bolter, *Remediation: Understanding New Media*, trans. authors, (Cambridge: MIT Press, 2000).

9 → Boyan Manchev, "Alteration. Über (den) Noise (des) Tanz(es)" in *Versehen. Tanz in allen Medien*, ed. Helmut Ploebst and Nicole Haitzinger (Munich: epodium 2011), 92–108.

10 → Recognizing the fact that certain idealisms and positivisms of his position from today's perspective appear neither tenable nor desirable.

that do not respond exclusively to a significant-significat logic, but that interweave and permanently reconfigure in different ways and in heterogeneous layers, in the sense of creating the catalyst and the basis of a collective poetic machine of knowledge organization?

Our research practice along these questions allows us to exemplify further certain approaches to an exploration of 'repertoires' (as elements of a formulation of materials). A deductive examination of the subject matter of the research, top-down, taking its starting point from a processing or (re)definition of concepts of the 'archive' itself is less of a priority for us. On the one hand, this is a methodical decision. On the other hand, we simply feel unable to do so, in the face of increasing complication — especially when it comes to questions of 'archives' and power constellations — or softening of what is potentially conceived under 'archive' and how the differently understood concepts could be categorized.[11] Once again

11 → Paul Ricoeur, *Time and Narrative*, vol. 3 (Chicago: University of Chicago Press, 1988).

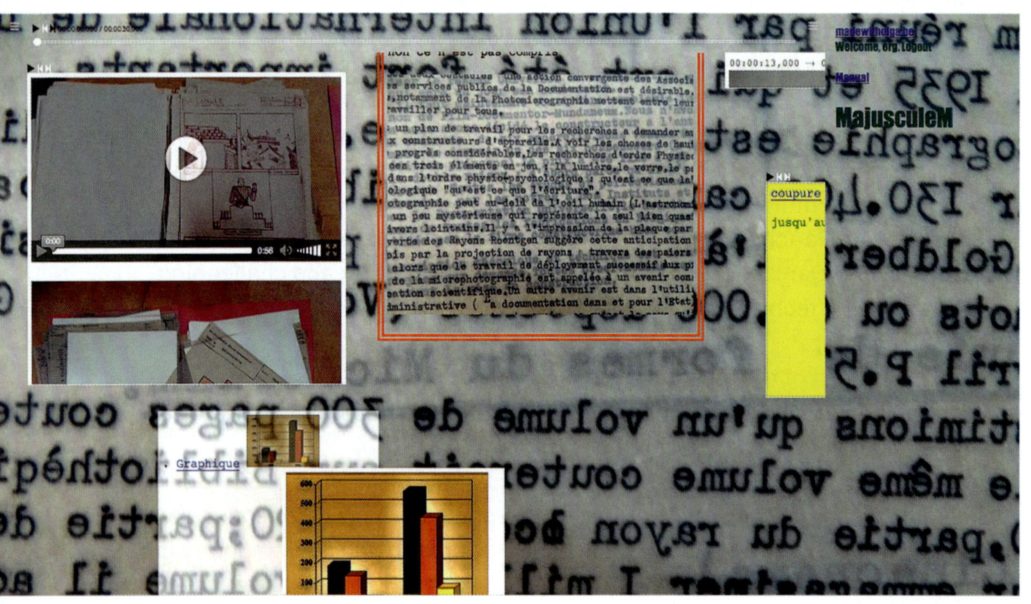

Screenshot website *Repertoires Animés* work in progress.

Remy Besson: "[We find ourselves] in a contemporary context of fragmentation in media practices where the definition of the archive and the codification of the archival act are difficult to identify."[12]

This is an essential reason why we prefer the reference fields around collection and repertoire[13] for the research process — they seem rather to correspond to a conception of the performative activation of documents in Otlet's sense.

12 → Rémy Besson, "Man on bridge: une forme qui échappe aux catégories," trans. authors, December 2016, accessed May 17, 2016, http://entrelacs.revues.org/1878.

13 → See for discussion about the terms archive and repertoire a.o. the confrontation between Diane Taylor and Rebecca Schneider: Diane Taylor, *The Archive and the Repertoire* (Durham/London: Duke University Press, 2003), Rebecca Schneider, *Performing Remains: Art and War in Times of the Theatrical Reenactment* (London/New York: Routledge, 2011).

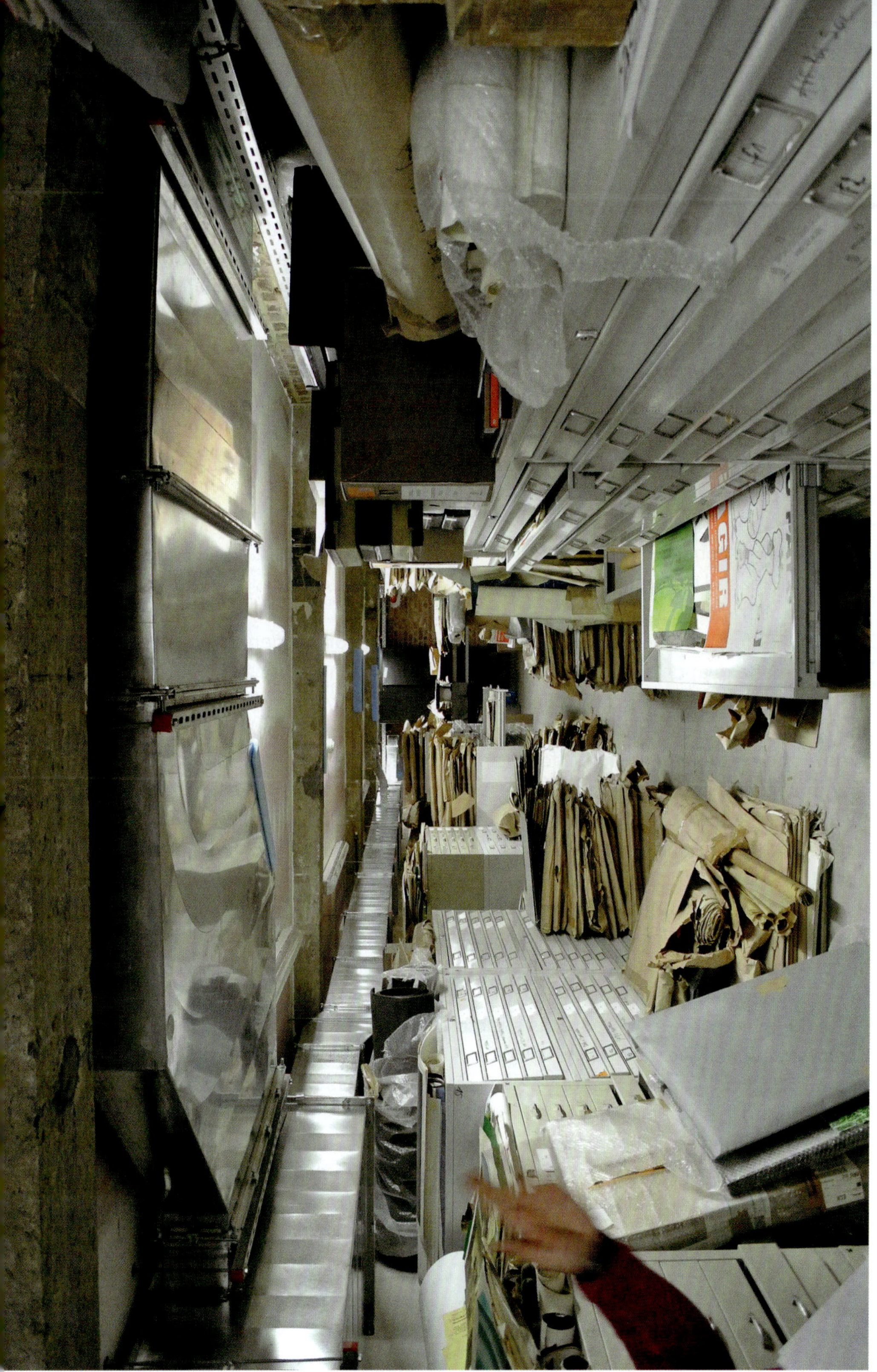

Mundaneum basement.

Starting Point

In avoiding the question of an aesthetic effect, as well as that of a (hi)story, animation focuses on the crisis of the representation of the world as a 'world' through a strategy of abstention. It does not interpret — neither in relation to the relativity of the viewpoint nor in relation to the necessary multiplication of perspectives. By denying the privileges of interpretation, animation at the same time rejects the possible inference of a subjectification of this phenomenon of fragmentation. On the contrary, it exposes itself to objectification without first seeking a way out. The decomposition of the 'world' does not mean its disappearance. Rather, it shows its incessant recomposition, here and now. It marks a strategy to emancipate oneself from rules of repetition, habit and pattern recognition — namely THROUGH THEM.[14]

The animation concept on which our research is based is primarily constituted by a field of practices and perceptual tools that unfold transversely to defined techniques, media, or genres. An attempt is being made to approximate beyond a generic definition of animated film (for example, mimeticly 'giving life' to inanimate objects, or work on image-by-image, the boundary between standstill and movement). To quote Catherine Perret: "While often (ab)using the filmic form, animation rejects the cinematographic grammar that the film makes 'a' film. It is the hypothesis of a correlation in which the heterogeneity of the layers which constitute the filmic material can sediment and realize a story without consenting to narrative structure."[15]

[14] → Catherine Perret and Alexander Schellow, "ELLE/SIE," trans. authors, in *Les artistes font des histoires*, ed. Catherine Perret/Jean-Philippe Antoine, (Paris: Le Genre Humain, éditions du Seull, 2015).

[15] → Catherine Perret in a public discussion at école de recherche graphique, "ANIMATION," (Paris, 2015).

Questions that arise from this basic assumption are as follows: how can a movement triggered by images be (re)constructed without asserting a movement of the individual images? (How) is it possible to experience movement between pictures without moving pictures as such?

The thus motivated research is structured along different axes of work: the deconstruction of the medium as structural fiction; the development of protocols of decentralization and discontinuity — in the production as well as the reception of a material; the organization of a break; the assertion of the 'error' of a gesture as a method to realize a fictional space, for example in the context of the (re)construction of a memory structure; and, the insistence on a defined indefinition in the fundamental heterogeneity of the material, which is strategically opposed to a homogenization.

City Full of Dreams
→ Freewalking Baltimore's Phantasmagoria →

Samuel Gerald Collins

Surrealism and anthropology have crossed paths several times, but the best-known intersections are in the ethnographic objects that inspired artists through processes of defamiliarization and estrangement — African sculpture, Oceanic masks, rituals, alterity. And, indeed, montage and juxtaposition can be found at the very beginnings of anthropology in the assemblages of artifacts at the Pitt Rivers Museum and the Musée d'Ethnographie du Trocadéro. Here, the exotic other served to critique Western thought and to undermine the homophily at the core of both Western epistemologies and social life.

Non-European objects were appropriated specifically to challenge aesthetic categories: in their expeditions, Duchamp's 'ready-made' bottle-racks were juxtaposed with Oceanic sculptures to question traditional conceptions of art. The Surrealists used other cultures as a means of transgressing, reshuffling and subverting the orders of Western classificatory systems.[1]

1 → Louise Tythacott, *Surrealism and the Exotic* (London: Routledge, 2014), 2.

The problem, though, lies in the appropriation of the object. Just because Man Ray juxtaposes a mask to a model doesn't make it a challenge to Western colonialism. And what's non-Western today can just as easily become a fashion accessory tomorrow. What is 'defamiliarized' can just as easily become 'familiarized'—appropriated into an expansive capitalist machine as another commodity image. Capitalism renders difference into sameness and commodities connect to other commodities in a closed network.

But there were other possibilities, possibilities not premised on dubious appropriations of cultural alterity. Among them, the revelation of the magic of the city itself. Tythacott continues:

> *In the Paris of the 1920s, Surrealists devoted themselves to the identification and mapping of sacred sites and magic space in the cityscape around them. In their novels and writing of the period, the streets of the metropolis are locales for encountering the marvelous and the* inconnu.[2]

The search for the "magic" of the modern city was, in itself, not novel: magic is yoked to the development of the modern city from the outset, from the apotropaic, urban witchcraft, growth of urban spiritualism in the 19th century to the fascination with the 'magic of the other' in the renaissance of magical practice in the 20th century. At the core of the modern, woven into infrastructure and institutions, in habitus and daily rounds, is a magical practice of associations and encounters with difference.

During the 1920s and 1930s, anthropology and surrealism momentarily coalesced in rendering these subterranean connections visible—e.g. in Aragon and Breton's wandering across Paris. Stopping at markets to inspect 'objets trouvé,' lampooning public sculptures, and mining the streetscape for eclectic architectural detail, surrealism took inspiration from quotidian and exotic urban life, and their journals included random quotations from all of these sources, jumbled together in montage or juxtaposed to a variety of occasionally contretemps text.

The goal was to represent the uncanny and to transform the city into a shocking dream-space of conflicting realities that discomfited received categories: the magic of Paris. Of course, there was also a politic here, one premised on unleashing the disruptive forces that lie just behind the smooth facades of the modern city, a politics that, in some ways, the Situationists built upon in their resistance against urban modernism.

It was this disruptive potential that attracted Walter Benjamin to urban confabulations of the surrealists, and the "revelation of the metropolis as a dream-scape"[3] was the foundation for Benjamin's dialectical critique of the modern. As Gilloch writes, "Just as the desires and wishes of the individual are frustrated and repressed in waking life only to reappear in disguised form during sleep, so the cityscape and the artefacts found therein are dream-like creations of dormant collectivity."[4]

2 → Tythacott, *Surrealism and the exotic*, 32.
3 → Graeme Gilloch, *Myth and Metropolis: Walter Benjamin and the City* (New York: Polity Press, 1997), 109.
4 → Gilloch, *Myth and metropolis*, 104.

Smartphone Dreams

In many ways, smartphones are the apotheosis of Benjamin's dialectic. They are the very definition of phantasmagoria, and yet also disclose collective desires for connection and for the rapprochement of urban alienation. For Ernst Bloch, they are the instrument of spectacle, but also betray utopian desires to surmount their own phantasmagoria and return people to authentic social relationships.

There have been many analyses of information and communication technologies (ICTs) as 'disruptive,' none more so than the smartphone in the city. With the haptic technology, urban dwellers are able to connect to each other, to activist causes, and to places in more intimate ways that are simultaneously untethered from the limitations of place and embodiment. Here, smartphones are productive of new "urban imaginaries."[5]

In this way, narrative storytelling through smartphones echoes earlier critical defamiliarization in surrealism and Situationist critique. Fittingly, 'Derive,' 'Situationist,' and other smartphone apps stimulate chance encounter and unexpected meanings, and the profusion of augmented reality interfaces means that ordinary scenes can take on new contexts.

These can have a critical function. As Farman[6] points out, "augmented reality" narratives on smartphones can have a "defamiliarizing" impact on users, one where urban storytelling can question some of the hide-bound assumptions we hold about the places we inhabit by introducing alternative stories of place and, in the process, gesturing to other possibilities.

For some time, we—my co-author, Matthew Durington and our anthropology students—have been interested in harnessing these critical powers for ethnographic work in Baltimore, conceived not just as the explication of culture and social life, but also as a collaborative exercise in critique and the evocation of alternatives. With the rapid growth in smartphone ownership in United States across different economic strata, a smartphone-based practice can be a catalyst for community collaboration, democratizing the tools of anthropology and, in the process, connecting our work to new publics through widely available social media.[7]

While we've used several social media applications over the last 15 years, we're currently exploring the potentials of a tour app platform—izi.TRAVEL—that was originally developed for museum tours but has since been adapted to tours in cities. With my colleague, Matthew Durington, we were early adopters of this platform when it expanded to support urban story-telling in Baltimore under the auspices of the MuseWeb Foundation.[8] As part of the MuseWeb push (together with the interest the project generated among other groups in Baltimore), the number of app tours for the city has multiplied, many of them with contributions from our students and their own ethnographic perambulations around the city.

We began utilizing the app platform to showcase multimedia/multimodal collaborative anthropology we'd done in

5 → Jude Bloomfield, "Researching the Urban Imaginary: Resisting the Erasure of Places," in *Urban Mindscapes of Europe*, ed. Godda Weiss-Sussex and Franco Bianchini, no. 23 (2006): 43–61.

6 → Jason Farman, "Site-Specificity, Pervasive Computing, and the Reading Interface," in *The Mobile Story*, ed. Jason Farman (New York: Routledge, 2014), 5.

7 → Samuel Gerald Collins, and Matthew Solver Durington, *Networked Anthropology: a Primer for Ethnographers* (London: Routledge, 2014).

8 → "Be here: Baltimore," accessed July 25, 2017, https://www.museweb.us/be-here-baltimore/.

South Baltimore, and then as classroom exercises in participatory anthropology involving students and members of community groups.

Our first tour, 'Sharp Leadenhall Walking Tour,' was a typical walking tour featuring historic sites and challenges to an African American neighborhood in south Baltimore. We worked with community groups to both select and to produce media for the tour; accordingly, the app tour introduces some of the complex histories and developments that continue to shape Sharp Leadenhall. The app allowed us to share the results of this ethnographic research with our students, and they followed our tour as part of our introductory classes. From their feedback, we could appreciate their growing understanding of Baltimore neighborhoods as both historic and contemporary sites of struggle against racial injustice.

But I wondered how much this tour differed from other, more commercial efforts to 'augment' the city. Wasn't this a more critical instance of a tour of restaurants? A guide to shopping? In any case, I began to question whether or not this was another version of Debord's *The Society of the Spectacle*,[9] the rendering of urban life into disconnected media fragments that take the place of social relations. I imagined my students bent over their phones in South Baltimore, the same bodily hexis they have cultivated to watch Netflix and to scroll through Instagram. Did this represent a wholesale appropriation of our collaborative fieldwork with their media ecologies?

Moreover, tour apps seem like another way of rendering homophily in the city. By parsing urban heterogeneity into a thematically linked series of sites—however critical, reflexive, and collaborative—we were still imprinting a homogeneous narrative on a city fractured by contradiction and discontinuity. Baltimore may be the sum of its stories, but these stories are interrupted and broken where racism and class inequality have erupted through the arc of their narratives.

In 2016, izi.Travel introduced a 'free walking mode' that allows users to access any site whose geolocated radius they wander into. In other words, as you walk, you encounter sites from multiple tours—sites even layered upon each other. These have added another dimension to our urban practice; as the number of tours on izi.Travel in Baltimore has multiplied, so have the opportunities for chance encounters.

In summer of 2017, I began making regular transect walks through Baltimore, areas at the conjunction of history, urban development, and economic inequality in the deeply divided city. As I walk the city, I mark the tour sites and take notes. I am interested in the interstices of city and representation, and I'm particularly aware of when these conflict. Ultimately, my experience becomes one of chance encounters, but not meaningless chance. Instead, connections build and undermine each other and render a more critical vision of this city.

For example: in early August of 2017, I park in front of a boarded-up store-front at the corner of Park Avenue and West Saratoga in downtown Baltimore. I walk down West Saratoga.

There are just a few people on the street. It's 10 am, and restaurants are just starting to gear up for the lunch crowd. People are already at work. There are some elderly people on Saratoga, and some have difficulty getting around the street. But the weather's beautiful, 70s—a late-summer morning and not too humid.

After a few meters, the first, geo-located site is triggered:

9 → Guy Debord, *The Society of the Spectacle*, (New York: Zone Books, 1994).

A woman's voice: "Do you like rainy days?" And then another, answering, "Oh, no. They're so dreary."

The second woman continues, "At one point in my life, I didn't feel good about myself."

A life story of one of the salon owners on the street, the interview touches on abuse, recovery, and independence. The best thing about owning her store here on Saratoga Street: "Knowing that I don't have to answer to nobody."

I continue down Saratoga, make a left on Howard Street and start walking South. But the next site that goes off is behind me — Planned Parenthood. It's one from one of my students chronicling structural violence and the resources that might mitigate it.

Howard Street is a little busier. The light rail train runs down the middle of the road here, and some of the stores are open for business while others are boarded up.

On the right is the Hutzler Brothers Department Store — the now-shuttered jewel of West Baltimore. When I'm across from the building, the audio part of the tour begins in media res with a discussion:

"That's this point about holding whole municipalities accountable. Like, we have to be really clear. One: people do pay taxes; but two: part of the reason why parts of the city looks like war zones is because they were strategically disinvested in by people in government."

What parts of the city get priority in Baltimore? West Baltimore — a predominantly African American area? Or areas that have been gentrified and/or developed for tourism? Looking at Hutzler, and the line of boarded up buildings on this side of Howard, is testament to funding priorities for the city and to a pattern of urban disinvestment that continues into Baltimore's present.

But the next stop, firing off just two steps after my Huztler stop, tells a different story.

Here, the Hutzler Building and the Hochschild-Kohn building are the subject of fond reminiscences from a journalist in the 1930s who sold books during the holidays, cultivating not only a love for books, but for Baltimore's literati. This bookstore story is warm and nostalgic, but it is also a story from a time when West Baltimore was white; a time before Morgan State University students would stage a sit-in to desegregate Read's Drugstore just down the street.

From there, I turn right on West Baltimore Street and am immediately confronted by a tour stop for Lexington Market, still two blocks away, a site exploring the history and precarious future of the historic 18th century market as it awaits its next renovation.

When I turn left on South Paca, I see a big difference in street traffic. Now it is professionals associated with the University of Maryland Medical complex, and, perhaps, patients. Many people are waiting outside of clinics on benches.

But the next site I encounter is the University Farmers Market, including people from the community, medical students, and vendors. As luck would have it, the market is just beginning, and people set up their tables next to flowers and shrubs in the park. The site is part of a food deserts/healthy food alternatives tour from one of our students.

Back on the street, I cross to the other side of South Paca, and an audio tour begins before I've even reached the opposite curb.

Ghetto Artsy Kid on the Rise, a series on Baltimore artists, featuring a video about gentrification and race in the arts. This clip critiques Baltimore's efforts to brand the Bromo-Selzter tower area as an arts district. "I don't know about the diversity in Bromo—I feel like it's mostly white people. Honestly. And it's funny, because I feel like Bromo is in hood."

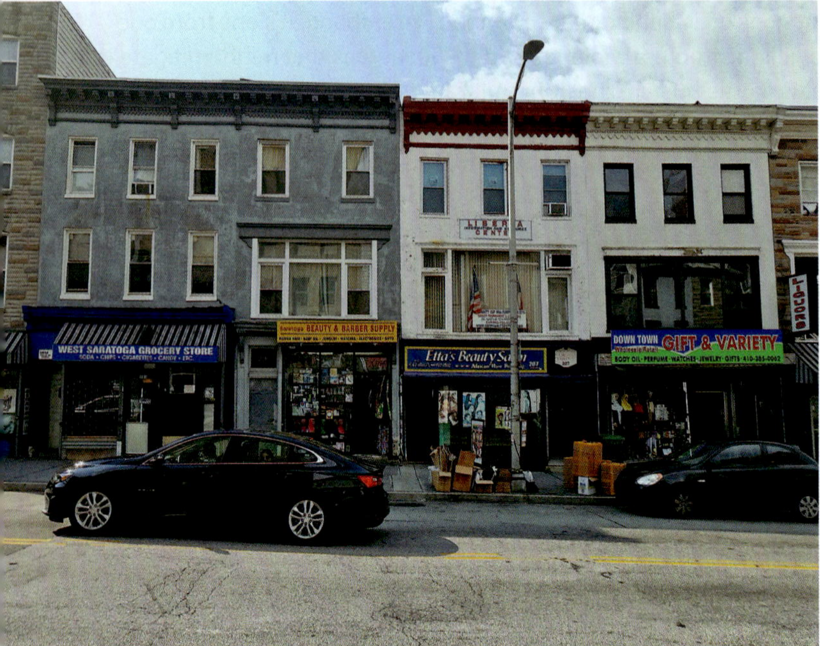

West Saratoga hosts numerous beauty shops and a couple of candle shops that are part of African American occult history in Baltimore.

The Bromo-Seltzer Tower is three blocks away, but the issues range beyond this to city-designated arts districts that exist in neighborhoods of Baltimore that have been African American communities. Now they are under pressure from gentrification.

As I wind my way back up through Baltimore streets, restaurants are readying for the lunch hour, and there are more people walking and talking on the sidewalks. I pass through three or four more clusters of sites created by different groups in Baltimore—more from Morgan State and Towson University, but also from the Jewish Museum of Maryland. My walk ends with a final site at a long since closed bookstore on Park that used to sell Marxist pamphlets.

So, what's different about this free-walking tour and the many smart-phone led tours one might take of Baltimore and other cities?

As Gilloch notes,[10] the way out of the dream-state precipitated by our submersion in the phantasmagoria of the modern lies in the revolutionary possibility of the 'demise' of the object. "The outmoded object defetishizes and demythified the commodity and the processes of its production, exchange and consumption in the city."[11] Indeed, doing a tour

10 → Gilloch, *Myth and metropolis*, 111.
11 → Gilloch, *Myth and metropolis*, 110.

with one's smartphone brings one up against spaces analogous to Benjamin's arcade — the superannuated shopping districts and undercapitalized streets of African American Baltimore.

But it also brings one up against the limits of the smartphone itself. My smartphone's geolocation is not always accurate — I walked through multiple sites without triggering any of them, and ones that did go off were not necessarily spatially contiguous to my own path, testament both to the eccentric radii of the geolocated sites and to the exigencies of my phone. But more than this, my walk takes me through the gaps of human-computer design and interaction. People set the geolocation; they upload cryptically edited audio; they mess up placing sites and audio clips in aberrant orders. In the process, space and time are rendered malleable here. Pushed into multiple tours and multiples sites (I counted 6 different tours in my freewalk through West Baltimore), the urban wanderer is unable to exclude other spaces and times. In a city that changes from block to block, being reminded of economic inequality a few blocks away prevents you from siloing yourself in a gentrified block to the exclusion of the city beyond. That is, the hall of mirrors that makes up capitalist homophily is shattered over and over again through the shock of difference. Ultimately, free-walking brings one up against the failure of sameness.

This is the magic city — the urban fabric with its stochastic connections between times and spaces and people. It brings me up against multiple temporalities and spatialities in ways that gesture beyond the linearity of the tour. Freewalking traces the space of the collective. It opens the wanderer up to insistent voices that refuse to be confined to segregated spaces and carefully excised times. Through historical narrative erupt critiques of political economy, voices of people who have lived through violence and tragedy, persistent, structural racism that proliferates around the edges of historic preservation.

Buck-Morss describes Benjamin's method as "constructing 'historical objects' in a politically explosive 'constellation of past and present,' as a 'lightning flash' of truth."[12] Could these sudden, cacophonies of perspectives be that flash? By confronting us with both the failures of the city to address the racism at the core of advanced capitalism, as well as the tensions between the space-time of the city and the smartphone, can we begin to grasp a future where everyone speaks and everyone listens?

12 → Susan Buck-Morss, *The Dialectics of Seeing: Walter Benjamin and the Arcades project* (Cambridge: MIT Press, 1989), 241.

Be-in → Aspects of a Fascination History of Digital Cultures by Art and Technology

→ Martina Leeker

1. Be-in

Since the 1960s we see a desire for "be-in."[1] The notion be-in was launched by the intermedia artist collaborative USCO (The Company of Us) in the 1960s to describe a specific form of existence.[2] It is this performing in technological environments that is elaborated especially in the encounter of art, design, and technology. Be-in is about being in resonances and vibrations with technology. Fred Turner describes this condition as "a new kind of gathering, simultaneously social and mystical, embodied, and transpersonal."[3] It is about entering—as Fred Turner puts it—"a state of ecstatic interconnection."[4] We see a fascination-history as an entanglement of humans and technological environments, operating with bedazzling, so that people are brought to a happy technological existence in a discourse of relationalism and techno-social agency.

In this text, this desire for be-in will be examined in relation to moments of technological automization from Systems Engineering (SE) in the 1960's to today's smart infrastructures—proposing a re-reading of techno-ecology, New Materialism, and Posthumanism that does not fall into the trap of fascination.

2. The Pepsi Pavilion (1970) and David Tudor's Techno-animist Be-in

In March 1970, the non-profit organization 'Experiments in Art and Technology' (E.A.T.)[5] installed the so-called Pepsi Pavilion at the Expo in Osaka/Japan.[6] Visitors could enter the dome via a narrow tunnel. Inside, they were enveloped by sounds and light, the latter in the form of laser light shows. It is of interest here that the Pavilion stands for the translation of technical SE into a social engineering for a very specific be-in.

Tudor's Sound-ecology

This engineering is seen exemplarily in Tudor's acoustic landscape in the Pavilion, using a complex electronic system of sounds and oscillations between devices in space. To achieve the interplay of sounds, space, and techno-performativity, Tudor used acoustic feedback in the Pavilion that was generated between two microphones and 37 speakers in the dome. Its aim was to surround the visitors, followed up by their immersion into the technological environment. Two points are crucial: the vibrating resonance is linked to (1) Tudor's anthroposophical world view[7] and to his (2) contradictory concept of an unselfish self.[8]

Anthroposophical Technospheric Be-In

Technological environments and things are provided with animistic qualities from Tudor's anthroposophical background. Tudor's intention was to make the anima of technical objects hearable and perceptible, aiming for a psychedelic and affecting experience of a spiritualist, anthroposophical[9] environment of a bigger world order of etheric communication. So the focus on a system of resonances is important for generating a 'cyber-anthroposophical-be-in.' The crucial point is that Tudor himself stayed behind the central control station and manipulated the sound in order to achieve the intended effect. His engineering of be-in is about an enchantment of recipients that opens them up to a techno-spiritistic world order of spherical integration and hides the fact of regulation and control.

Tudor's Model of the Self

Within this techno-anthroposophical world-order, Tudor installed a new relation between technical things and environments with human agents, which touches on traditional ideas of subjects dealing with subordinated objects. An intriguing situation is evolving. Tudor steps back behind the sound-ecology, taking the role of enabling and then just observing it. At the same time, he claims authorship at the moment when the sounds are freed and pleasing to the 'author'. A new model of techno-agency comes up for which an oscillation between control and losing it, between a self and being an impersonal agent is constitutive. It is not about coming back to subjectivity but about a never-ending doubleness instead of techno-ecology.

The governmental aspect of this doubleness is that the oscillation is like a boiler, heating the desire to become a self via resonant be-in. So it is not about a collaborative agency but about a narcissistic techno-addiction. Relationalism is not the problem solver, as it is seen today, but a troublemaker as it binds human agents in an illusionary way to technology. That this self isn't a value in itself but in techno-logic is hidden.

3. Rich Gold's ubiquitous computing (1990) for enchanted wonderlands

Another model of describing the ecology of human agents and technology was invented at the end of the 1980s, beginning of 1990s at XEROX PARC within Ubiquitous Computing (UC), developed initially by Mark Weiser. Mark Weiser described his project as, "[…] the method of enhancing computer use by making many computers available throughout the physical environment, but making them effectively invisible to the user."[10] It marks the dawn of a new world "in which each person is continually interacting with hundreds of nearby wirelessly interconnected computers."[11] For Weiser "… its highest ideal is to make a computer so embedded, so fitting, so natural, that we use it without even thinking about it."[12]

The following section is about the creation of ubiquitous objects (Ubi-objects) for UC by the artist-designer Rich Gold since the 1990s within PARC, which figures as a genealogy of today's modes of be-in in digital cultures. What was thought in those days is today a reality.

Rich Gold's "Ubi-objects"
The aesthetics of Ubi-objects become the key point, because they are, according to Gold: "sensuous, reactive, communicating, embedded socially and colonizing."[13] Gold's idea becomes concrete in his example of the Ubi-pipe. Because of both its shape/Gestalt and our cultural habits, the pipe carries 'affordances' that help us to make a translation to intuitively use them in different ways. For Gold the Ubi-pipe could be used either taking it to control the private environment or professional life; for Gold the Ubi-pipe could be used as a pointer in multimedia-presentations. To understand the effects and intentions of this design of Ubi-objects, Rich Gold points out that it aims to constitute a be-in in a wonder world of enspirited things. So, the method of 'colonizing' is the basis that technology becomes, in Gold's world, enchantment.[14]

Dazzling in a Magic Wonder World
Gold creates this model of be-in for betraying and dazzling. The aim of this strategy is to be unclear about the fact that Ubi-objects are hiding their operative and techno-logical function, which is be-in as a totality of control. Gold describes:

Ubiquitous Computing is a new metaphor in which computers are spread invisibly throughout the environment, embedded and hiding as it were, within the objects of our everyday life. Each of these computers can talk with any of the other computers much like chattering animals in a living jungle, sometimes exchanging detailed information, sometimes just noting who's around.[15] The new objects obscure their function as nodes and intersections of technological operations and grids, where they exchange data taken from human agency and transform them into their own logic. Gold points out furthermore that humans' participation in the technological environment is not only an effect of their enchantment, but also of an exploitation of a neuro-physiological malfunction. In doing so, users are deliberately misguided, deceived, dazzled and duped to enable and uphold the technological ecologies. What is hidden is its economical aspect. Gold foresaw a world filled with Ubi-objects and then stated that, since they will be everywhere, it would be a nice, fruitful business.

4. Be-in 1970/1990/today

The question is, what are the effects and insights if we re-read the contemporary discursive landscape on techno-ecology, New Materialism, or Post-humanism with Tudor's techno-ether-spiritualism and Rich Gold's wonderland of techno-magic?

Today we see a re-thinking in a techno-ecological sense, which tells us that we have always been products of a techno-social individuation, being bound in symmetrical agencies. Technological environments are seen as a power-in-themselves, affecting human agents on a pre-conscious micro-level, which can no longer cognitively be grasped or controlled by humans.[16] These theories and concepts are seen optimistically, figuring as a solution for dealing with current challenges such as climate-catastrophes and capitalist crises. This is because by addressing relationships we get a model of an existential and humble involvement of human agents in technological environments. So, the relation-discourse corresponds to a concept of post-anthropological environmental modesty.

In this situation it seems important to reconstruct and consider the fascination-history as a real-political adoption of technology as well as the unnoticed implications and concepts of techno-philosophical utopia and hope, before coming to new models. This history should be regarded as fundamental to today's situation in order to understand how digital cultures make human agents give away their data and feel at home in technological environments.

We come to a new situation and regime. On the one hand, it is a necessary to work on a new description of culture, human, and technology in the time of techno-logical self-organization. On the other hand, it is essential to carefully explore the possibilities of theory formation according to governmental effects and dramaturgies of fascination. In digital cultures now, we see a non-resolvable simultaneity of these two processes, so that an unceasing balancing act between description and reflection will be necessary. It is this order of ambivalence, which we must/shall follow in order not to fall into the trap of fascination, that is the new epistemology and governmentality, controlling human actants by aggravated decision-making and exhausting oscillations between valorization of different positions and options.

1 → Fred Turner, *From Counterculture to Cyberculture: Stewart Brand, the Whole Earth Network, and the Rise of Digital Utopianism* (Chicago: The University of Chicago Press, 2006).

2 → Turner, *From Counterculture to Cyberculture*, 51.

3 → Fred Turner, *The Democratic Surround: Multimedia and American Liberalism from World War II to the Psychedelic Sixties* (London: The University of Chicago Press, 2013), 289.

4 → Turner, *The Democratic Surround: Multimedia and American Liberalism from World War II to the Psychedelic Sixties*, 8.

5 → E.A.T. was founded in 1967 by Bell Lab's engineer Billy Klüver and the artist Robert Rauschenberg. See Jennifer Garbys, "Residue in the E.A.T. Archives," 2004, accessed July 01, 2017, http://www.fondation-langlois.org/html/e/page.php?NumPage=522. See also Bonin, Vincent, "Collection of Documents Published by E.A.T." 2002, accessed July 01, 2017, http://www.fondation-langlois.org/html/e/page.php?NumPage=237.

6 → Fred Turner, "The Corporation and the Counterculture," *The Velvet Light Trap* 73 (2014): 66–78. Accessed July 05, 2017, http://fredturner.stanford.edu/wp-content/uploads/Turner-Corporation-Counterculture.pdf.

7 → John Adams, "Giant Oscillations," 1999, accessed July 01, 2017, http://davidtudor.org/Articles/jdsa_giant.html and Lowell Cross, "Remembering David Tudor: A 75th Anniversary Memoir," 2001, accessed July 01, 2017, http://europaeische-musikwissenschaft.eu/assets/Volumes/2001/2001T1.pdf. See also Alexander Keefe "Subcontinental Synth: David Tudor and the First Moog in India," April 30, 2013, accessed July 01, 2017. http://www.eastofborneo.org/articles/subcontinental-synth-david-tudor-and-the-first-moog-in-india?fb_comment_id=159555154211836_400428#f127addbc1bdc52.

8 → Martina Leeker and Michael Steppat, "Data Traffic in Theater and Engineering: Between Technical Conditions and Illusions." in *Traffic: Media as Infrastructures and Cultural Practices*, ed. Marion Näser-Lather and Christoph Neubert, 160–79, (Boston: Brill, 2015).

9 → Tudor was member of the Anthroposophical Society from 1957. See also: Tudor Papers at Getty Research Library, Series VII, Boxes 101–106, http://archives2.getty.edu:8082/xtf/view?docId=ead/980039/980039.xml;chunk.id=aspace_ref3709_tf9;brand=default, accessed July 07, 2017. Stern, Gerd, and Victoria Morris Byerly, *From Beat scene poet to psychedelic multimedia artist in San Francisco and beyond, 1948-1978*, accessed July 05, 2017 http://oac.cdlib.org/view?docId=kt409nb28g&brand=oac4&doc.view=entire_text, access, 291.

10 → Mark Weiser, "Some Computer Science Issues in Ubiquitous Computing," in *Communications of the ACM 36*, no. 7 (1993): 74–84.

11 → Weiser, "Some Computer Science Issues in Ubiquitous Computing," 75.

12 → Mark Weiser, *Ubiquitous Computing*, 1996, accessed July 06, 2017, http://www.ubiq.com/hypertext/weiser/UbiHome.html.

13 → Rich Gold, "The Plenitude: Design and Engineering in the Era of Ubiquitous Computing," 2002 accessed July 01, 2017, http://hci.stanford.edu/dschool/resources/ThePlenitude.pdf. 207.

14 → See also Florian Sprenger, "Handlungsmächte und Zauberei ohne Zauberer — Von der Beseelung der Dinge zum Ubiquitous Computing," in *Trick 17*, ed. Sebastian Vehlken, Katja Müller-Helle, Jan Müggenburg, Florian Sprenger, 87–114, (Lüneburg: Meson Press, 2015).

15 → Rich Gold, "THIS IS NOT THAT PIPE," 1993, accessed July 01, 2017. http://web.archive.org/web/20040305153117/http://www.richgold.org/PIPE/pipe.html.

16 → Marc B.N. Hansen, "Medien des 21. Jahrhunderts, technisches Empfinden und unsere originäre Umweltbedingung," in *Die technologische Bedingung: Beitraege zur Beschreibung der technischen Welt*, ed. E Hörl. (Frankfurt: Suhrkamp, 2011).

entropy

entropy → Imagine a cup of coffee. You put sugar in it. You mix it with a spoon—either slow or fast. The coffee gets sweet. However, what if you put too much sugar into the cup? Too late. Two substances have become one. This is the uniform direction, 'the arrow pointed through time.' Entropy is based on the irreversible deterioration of energy in every system resulting in a state of nondifferentiation within matter. If you mix long enough everything will become this sweet brownish indiscernible liquid—everything will deteriorate into chaos. However, it is entropy that implies both the dissolution of necessity and the beginning of the end—and maybe even a new beginning.

A Paradigm of the Human Condition, Applied to Arts and Artists → Dirk Baecker

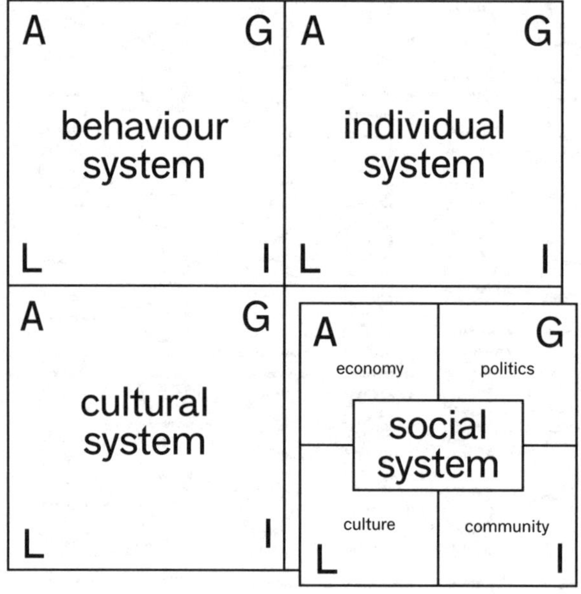

A — Adaptation

Place, time, matter, and technology are to be worked with and adapted to even if designed anew. At any time, an art work is bound to be realized. Tino Sehgal's art is proof of the matter. A word whispered into the ear of a visitor, is then his or her property alone and remains his or her property as long as he or she does not pass it along by whispering it to somebody else or else destroy it by voicing it aloud, is as much a materialized artwork as anything else. Any art work has to touch reality to gain reality. This is true for frame and plane, for page and word, for stage and gesture, for canvas and cut, for the instrument, and for the sound and the pause. Artists are always also craftspeople, thinkers, engineers. Wearing a work coat, sleeves rolled up, armed with safety glasses, a sharp ear and much sense for details, they are entangled within a poetic practice.

G — Goal-attainment

Any photography of an artist in his or her atelier or of actors on their stage shows individuals not necessarily enjoying themselves but certainly knowing what they do, step for step, even if the steps are tiny. If what they do and what they do next is not to be welcomed as a goal to be attained or a step to be corrected in order to reach a different goal, which only now becomes imaginable, nothing happens. Artists are individuals bound by their organisms and brains, in a way, to do what they do. They don't have to like it. They don't have to be convinced of it. Yet they have, in a way, to want it. In art and elsewhere human beings are involved whose orientation with action and situation is directed by their predictive coding of action and situation. They invest doubt, delay, and diversion to change action, situation, and themselves. Yet if there is nothing to be seen, to be imagined, to be wished for, to desire, they stop acting. They may stop thinking. They may stop knowing what they do. And if their body and brain don't welcome what may come next, their work at least takes a pause if it not stops altogether.

I — Integration

It is an offense to any aesthetic perception of the world, yet there are other actions happening in the world before an art work sees the light of the day, while it is admiringly looked at and almost forgotten again. Production and reception of art works by their artists as well as by their publics are but events among an enormous variety of other events with the same or different partners in other domains of the social. That's why arts and art works have to be integrated within their community and society. There are many ways to be integrated. Esteem is one, rejection is another, outright persecution and destruction a third one. There is no meaning of art and artworks if not in relation to the meaning of other social activities, be they economic, political, legal, educational, erotic, religious, or scientific. Most of those relations, happily enough, are relations of indifference or some sort of lackadaisical tolerance. Yet any of these relations can turn intrusive at any time. Add more contingent relations like those toward organizations wanting to buy, to fight, to avoid, to accept or to change art and art works or like everyday human behavior, choosing its way through situations of many different kinds (linking art works in the internet, attacking art works in museums or on streets, throwing rotten tomatoes and addled eggs onto stages of unpopular plays) and one gets a feeling of the complexity of social surroundings any art is bound, again, to contend with, and react to, even when choosing the most elitist attitude.

L—Latent-pattern maintenance and conflict regulation

Yet there are interdependency breaks. Not everything at any time is contingent. We would not be able to stand it. Norms and values interfere, even regarding arts and art works. They are latent, to be sure, becoming dubious the very moment they become manifest. Yet the moment a conflict becomes apparent, an art work being attacked for hurting feelings of some or an art work being defended by others for having its own, even if elusive, necessity, values are called up on to frame a certain action and lending legitimacy to it. Those values are never unambiguous even if claimed to be. They again conflict with other values and must be given more or less weight relative to further values. But there they are; they can be negated but not annihilated. Take again Sehgal's whispered words. They claim art to be its own value. They celebrate the visitor spending his or her time in a gallery. They value the very artist coming up with this way to do arts.

Yet, and this is my point in this sketch of Talcott Parsons' Paradigm of the Human Condition[1] applied to arts, it is only the L-function of the four-function AGIL-scheme which lends itself to aesthetic or other discussions. Three other functions have to be met with before any art is able to show off at all. Those other three functions are adaptation to matter, nature, and technology (A), goals set by organisms and per-sonalities struggling with each other (G), and an integration taking care of any art action within all other actions deemed important, useful, or possible within a society, culture, and civilization (I).

Outlook

Parsons' function of adaptation took account of the "physic-chemical system" sup-porting, thwarting, framing, and constraining any given human action. Meanwhile, we have to add to this a wide range of technologies which are still constraining human action yet are also designed by human action—as, indeed, the physic-chemical en-vironment has been deeply changed by human action as far back as any civilization goes. Arts these days lose their treasured status as the culmination of a more or less autonomous high culture and blend again with a more general understanding of *téchne*. They become paradigmatic in their enabling us to look to them for an under-standing of how human beings adapt to material and technical environment; have their organic and neural orientation transformed within the world; look at arts within wider social environments of communities, milieus, and movements; fight for and against arts to seek for norms and values, to defend and promote them. These are great times for a sociology of the arts.

1 →   Talcott Parsons, *Action Theory and the Human Condition*
(New York: Free Press, 1978).

Haunting Nostalgia
→ An interview with Andy Holden on *Prelude*

Andy Holden's piece *Prelude* is both a tribute and a re-assessment of the romantic age and its psycho-somatic engagement in travelling. And while exploring the endless canyons of Wile E. Coyote and the Road-runner, the landscapes of the cartoon turn into the very environment of romantic speculation—opening the texture of the present through a journey into the past.

Pujan Karambeigi: Right in the middle of *Prelude* you quote a passage by Wordsworth that seems to me central for your piece:
"A Traveller I am,
Whose tale is only of himself."
Could you say something to this travel you engage in both textually (by collaging passages of *Prelude*) and visually (by wandering through the landscapes of *Wile E. Coyote and the Road Runner*)?

Andy Holden: The piece imagines that the Lake District is now a desert, after an environmental disaster, not that this is clear, but that was the starting image; part-tourist, part-last man fantasy. The coyote lives or lived in the desert, so the cartoon version of me is avoiding the traps he's set. The cartoon-me is the narrator from *Laws of Motion* in a Cartoon Landscape, which was not a personal work at all, yet to make it I had to be present all the way through, manifested as a cartoon character, as the piece states that the world is now best understood as a cartoon, and therefore the best way to navigate the landscape is to become a cartoon character. In the cartoon landscape, the laws of physics no longer apply, although in *Prelude*, exploring the cartoon landscape, I'm again bound by Newtonian physics. Wordsworth's *Prelude* is a melancholic reflection on his ability to be at one with the landscape as he was as a child, the gap between the landscape and his place in it, mediated by his reflections upon it. That our experience of the world is ours alone is always a melancholic thought. It's meant to recall Wim Wenders' *Paris, Texas* too, a bit. It's a compression of many influences that probably contributed to my visual imagination in many ways, walking through these, bumping into Buzzfeed headlines. This cartoon desert is very primal for me, as I am sure it is for many. The first place we encountered this myth structure, endlessly looping.

Pujan Karambeigi: How come you went to re-visit the Lake District, this region in North West England that is very much associated with launching the Romantic Age?

Andy Holden: Romanticism is in my blood. I've actually never been to the Lake District.

Pujan Karambeigi: We see your alter ego walking along the same roads that you have meticulously analyzed in your previous work, *Laws of Motion in a Cartoon Landscape*.[1] It was a work based on the idea that our world today works like the world in the cartoons from the 1920s to the 1950s—that the system of representation developed in cartoons has taken over reality. For instance, in cartoons gravity only applies when you are conscious of it. Your alter ego, the same person that appears in *Prelude*, is the external observer analyzing these laws of motion in cartoons like a physicist. How would, you say has this status of the observer, the very relation between your alter ego and the cartoon landscapes, shifted in *Prelude*?

Andy Holden: It was a deliberate shift; in *Laws of Motion* I inhabit the space of cartoon physics, here I am again bound to Newtonian Laws, reflecting on this, attempting to make up my character's relation with cartoon physics somewhat equivalent with Romanticism's relationship with the infinite. The music is by The Caretaker, and should be seen as another inter-textual ingredient—his music

1 → Andy Holden, "Laws of Motion in a Cartoon Landscape," accessed July 04, 2017, https://www.youtube.com/watch?v=YYDXRV1ygpA.

explores this space in an acute sonic dimension, summed up by his titles such as *The Sublime is Disappointingly Elusive*, hauntological experiments with warping gramophone records, breaking them down into his soundtrack for a haunted ballroom. There's a suspension in time, like *Last year in Marienbad*, but also like Wile Coyote's never ending attempt to catch Roadrunner. I love his music and was excited that he let me work with this piece. For me it all comes together when confronted by the billboard "10 things you have been doing wrong this whole time."

> Pujan Karambeigi: When I watched *Prelude* for the first time I had to think about James Benning's *On the Road.* Despite all kinds of differences between those two works there was one thing I found intriguing: Something like a nostalgia that comes up in relation to these desert-like landscapes, these never-ending roads leading through these dead canyons, these memories of childhood being re-visited. What role does nostalgia play in your practice?

Andy Holden: I only discovered James Benning's work a few years ago after a visit to UCLA to teach there and his name came up. I found online this lecture he gave at the Hammer and watched it a few times. I then watched *13 Lakes.* But I had not connected it to *Prelude*. Nostalgia is something that structures so much of our experience of the world. It's something much of my work is about. I often drop back in time in my work, and examine a moment that seems to have enormous personal consequence, I did this with *Pyramid Piece and Return of the Pyramid Piece*, returning a piece of rock I had stolen from the Great Pyramid of Giza that had been a source of personal guilt but also an encounter with sculpture that had informed my world-view. I also revisited a manifesto I had made as a teenager, called *Maximum Irony! Maximum Sincerity*, which had been a formative moment for me, bringing it back by casting teenagers to reenact the manifesto in a film. These for me are ways of attempting to examine the very structures through which I view the world, and by looking at the way I view the world, hopefully make visible these structures more generally. Hopefully personal starting points, although hermetic, connect with our peoples' similarly hermetic interiors to talk about how these connect with real objects in the world. Wordsworth's *Prelude* seemed to me the starting point of all the questions that had been haunting my work from the start, and so it was time to try and inhabit that, perform a version of it, and see what I could learn from temporarily being inside it.

Surface → Bryana Fritz

…language is not everything. It is only a vital clue to where the self looses its borders.[1]

I begin to look at a series of images depicting the sea generated by a search engine. It was a search that intended to give a bit of inspiration, or a landscape to write across and into.
As each image is maximized
Face casts a shadow on the back wall *as if around that*
Face drips a dampening sigh as if about that
    late dampening self Licks the *screen in the face of it*

Initially a screen was considered to be an upright piece of furniture that would give protection or hide. It stands in the corner of the room in front of the nude redresser. At the very most it softly reveals her contours. However, when one looks at the screen of a computer, rather than hiding, the screen is something that discloses. It stands there radiating with an implicit depth; its 'workings' almost seem to be 'inside' of it.

Perhaps at one moment, it would have been interesting to compare the idea of the screen in its upright furniture form to the skin; an organ of protection marking interiority and exteriority, the fleshy interface between bodies and worlds. By marking this inner and outer, it becomes an interpretable surface, a hermeneutic thing to think through.

Jean Genet is maximized to fill the screen:

Jean Genet: *I had a dream last night. I dreamed that the technicians for this film revolted. Assisting with the arrangement of the shots, the preparation of a film, they never have the right to speak. Now why is that? And I thought they would be daring enough — since we were talking yesterday about being daring — to chase me from my seat, to take my place. And yet they don't move. Can you tell me how they explain that?*

One can attend to its forms, folds, re-folds, and unfolds…

1 → Gayatri Chakravorty Spivak, *Outside in the Teaching Machine* (New York: Routledge, 1993), 180.

Genet manages to let the smooth lines of power get caught in the wrinkles and folds in his skin. Sink into the places where crotch skin meets legs skin. Opening and penetrate the situation with his cigarette stained fingers, erected thoughts, and softly flipping the dynamics of a TV interview with the BBC. He decidedly calls out the way it begins to resemble a police interrogation, a situation he knows well.

The skin can be seen as a border that feels; a boundary-object. One that allows the contours of the body to come forth. With it we can forget about the body as such (stop fetishizing it) and become fascinated by the interface. An illusory object, neither merger nor separator, that incorporates the intensity of desires and flows. Recasting the body as merely an effect of depth or interiority.

By thinking through and with the skin one can reflect on the mode of being-with and being-for, where one touches and where one is touched by others, not all of whom are necessarily human. However, while the nearness of another is felt on the skin, this nearness also indicates the distance or the impossibility of getting inside the others skin. It both protects us from others and exposes us to them.

A question from Donna Haraway: Why should our bodies end at the skin, or include at best other beings encapsulated by skin? Crashing upon the shores of another's skin, knowing that nothing ends at the skin. But what about these inner skins, the skin inside the pussy, the asshole, the ear, the mouth, the nose. Softer, wetter, warmer bits of skin that invite and house.

Ipullupmypussyskin
And   let   in
As I was simultaneou
sly   forced   open

The moment that the skin is breached is both violent and intimate. A cut, a slice, makes the blue vein go liquid red. Shattering the appearance of an inside. Subcutaneous fat only allows *blue* light to penetrate skin all the way to *veins,* so this is the color that is reflected back. Less energetic, warmer colors are absorbed by skin before they can travel that far.

JG: *Is the camera rolling?*

He asks the question and of course it is. But by asking such a question, he brings an attention to inscription. Marking that this is being registered and that the apparentness of his body is preceded by being with other bodies. Making the nearness of the camera and camera man said. Making the formalized situation of the interview addressed, as opposed to given.

Sleeky Cracks →
Online Aesthetics in
Live-Art → Milosz Paul Rosinski

If you're reading this on a screen, fuck off. [1]

The screen is dead. There is nothing but the screen. Everything is the screen. You are part of the screen show. Dissolving into the materiality of reality like air, like gravity, like physical matter the digital beast permeates your life's pores. Lucky you, who has a screen to fathom. Try to feel the digital, because before long you will forget that feeling existed in the first place. The world becomes structured according to digital logic: algorithms as much as your intuition is updated.

[1] → Joshua Cohen, *Book of Numbers* (New York: Random House US, 2016).

Let's think of the experience of digital phantoms within the disconnected realm as 'sleeky cracks.' This is a form of felt friction in which the realm of the disconnected and offline is infiltrated and feels like it is based within the digital and online realm. Indeed, you read a paperback and the screen pop's up as concept and the author demands you to leave this safe space. Maybe you are reading this on a screen, and you are requested to leave, or you are not and yet you are asked. In either case, the logic of the online existence creates an aesthetic effect, a slip of the 'sleeky cracks.'

I am interested in exploring this aesthetic effect of the 'sleeky cracks' that the digital, online, and internet world, formerly known as new media, opens in our heads when it is not there, but it is. In other words, I am intrigued by the aesthetic effect of the presence of the absence of the internet: understanding the presence of a phantom pain. This spectral experience makes the change in perception sleeky, as the cracking of our reality happens subtly and tacitly. How do the logics of the digital world influence the human experience in the quasi-offline realm? Not that anything offline actually exists anymore, but it is precisely the disappearance of the offline that I am concerned with, made visible through the intrusion of the logics of the online world.

The offline and offscreen worlds are gone and over. There is no dichotomy and mutual exclusion possible between the off- and online or analogue and digital in terms of the human experience of reality. Yet, tracing the influence of the amendments of perception of reality due to the digital online world is a fruitful enterprise. If we are deep hanging out with each other (to use Clifford Geertz's term regarding observation) we have to realize 'sleeky cracks' are a pretty big deal. My argument is that the world is perceived within and through the new frameworks of understanding the digital ecosphere cultivates — online aesthetics frame the perception of our world. Online trumps what was formerly known as reality. In the case of reading this here or elsewhere — thinking about and referring to the couple of words comprising the first sentence of Joshua Cohen's *Book of Numbers* — the 'sleeky crack' is the knowledge of bilocation. That text, these words exist in a form of bilocation, as a book and ebook, here and there, digital and analogue, and so do you, so does your reasoning. You're never just in one place anymore.

> *Where should you go to anyways, where should you 'fuck off' to if after all there is nowhere else to go?*

I'm thinking about words here and where they belong, how they work, what they mean. Words are always digital, reproducible without friction, without loss. Books can exist a thousand times in identity to one another. Screens replicate the same data wherever they retrieve and project. Words are thus brutally forever, as they keep themselves together. Words however, are also always multi-media installations: spoken, written, told, recited, paraphrased, and forgotten. Words and language are a social gesture called meaning, made so we can communicate and understand each other. We believe in words as carriers and signifiers of meaning. The online realm has given new language as much as new meanings and practices. The way words work advances through the textual realm of the online world — which is after all, composed of words and images. We form conversations and communities online, as much as upload ourselves into the clouds of our storage to get directions to the next place we go to on our smartphone. The 'sleeky cracks' that open through the use of words in the online evolve through the meaning — making of many practices: chatting, messaging, reviewing, rating, commenting, liking, swiping, matching, retweeting, hash-tagging, sexting.

The practices we perform with our words naturally merge through the online and the offline. Bilocation as the supposed phenomenon of physical existence in two distinct places simultaneously is not real. Yet, the intrusion of the supplementary realm of the online world into our perception and consciousness provides us with an experience thereof. The 'sleeky crack' is to not eat at a restaurant you've seen has bad online reviews although the place looks good IRL.[2]   2 → In real life.
Mimicking behaviour based on mediated sources takes
over empirical intuition. The digital beast (or simply an influencer on Instagram)

infiltrates our consciousness and memory, and so is our faculty of judgment impaired and amended. Our mental principles—our intuition, our orientation, our aesthetics, our sense of self–or our language of existence are guided by the quasi-normal extensions of our everyday lives that make the pace and practices of our lives feasible in the first place.

One of the ways in which bilocation can be made visible is through artistic objects or installations. The world of the internet as a whole and as a system is otherwise simply unobservable. We know that it is overwhelmingly incomprehensible to grasp. It is impossible to understand the vastness of the internet and the ways in which it organizes and distributes information in its entirety as a network. That would be like tracing the worldwide trade of language at a fixated point in time, a good work of conceptual art, but as soon as you have an image thereof, it instantaneously disappears into a new point in time. The only possible option to give a representation

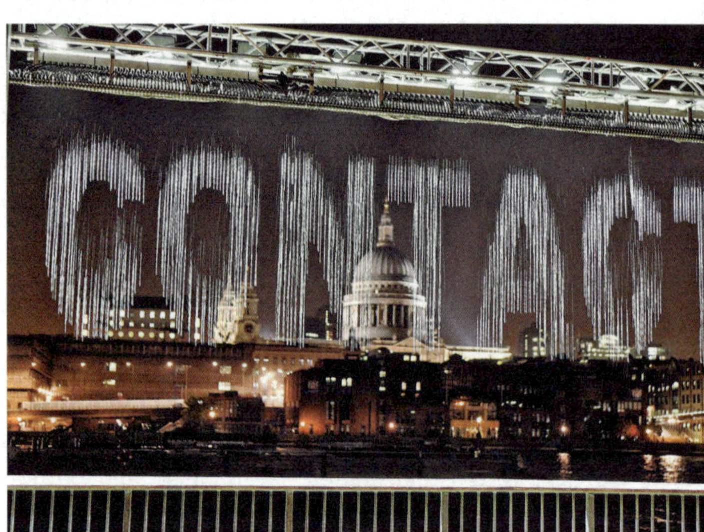

Julius Popp's *bit.fall* at the Drift 10 exhibition in London, 2010. The exhibition was curated by Illuminate Productions.

thus is the use of limitations and abstractions—concentrated observation. One way of representing a complex system is through the production of an abstracted version. Thereof Julius Popp's 2005 piece *bit.fall* is one work of art that manages to produce a representation of an internet-based reality outside its own realm. As the artist Julius Popp puts it in the spirit of fascination regarding the new (then newer) media of the internet, the work is "a metaphor for the incessant flood of information we are exposed to."[3] I'd add trumped by overwhelmed by. As an object, *bit.fall* is an offline representation of online reality. The work combines the elements of water and the ocean of information of the internet through a machine that combs textual data into water bits that form a waterfall. The artwork is a distillation machine. The presence of the internet in the absence thereof is made visible here through the sleeky drops of water cracking into the space of gravitational reality. Words appear to disappear. The flow of data relentlessly renews itself in fracturing perpetuity.

3 → Julius Popp, "bit.fal," August 10, 2017, accessed July 10, 2017, http://www.stuk.be/en/bitfall.

bit.fall makes bilocation visible by producing a never-ending waterfall of words turning the most-used keywords of new news from Google News into abstract bits of water. The data appears as word in the blink of an eye, before gravity moves it into its own disappearance, to then be replaced by the next word in a one liner succession of flow. Then repeat. The reality of news expresses itself literally through abstraction of keywords, neologisms, and proper nouns as partial fragments of reality. These words inform, produce, and reproduce a reality as a performed score — a parlando we understand as information. The generative nature of the work is fueled by the logic of the cycle that feeds the fountain: new words appear to re-appear continuously to successively enact the durational performance of a stable re-constitution of newness.

bit.fall is the representation of the phenomenon of news as a 'sleeky crack' of matter thrown by the invisible hand of the algorithm into the material reality. What we read when we look at the water drops is a cipher or reality, an access to reality that we can reverse engineer into a more proper and distinct piece of news. The streaming of data here is reminiscent of the vertical stream of code that constitutes reality in *The Matrix* (1999). This matrix-like bit fall is a presence of a reality in and of itself, and an image of a reality that is elsewhere, displayed or screened through a projection thereof. Similarly, there is and there is not a 'screen' in *bit.fall.* What we look at is a perfect example of the disappearance of the screen into nothingness, into a fluid mode of presentation, into physical matter.

> *Congressman*
> *race*
> *long-shot*
> *Re-election*
> *Kucinich*
> *future*
> *relations*
> *agreement*
> *hands*
> *successors*
> *Iraq*
> *frenzy*
> *Egypt*
> *shopping*[4]

This form of what I would term as 'live-art,' as it is a durational performance of an installation through live interaction, works through the relationship of foreground and background structure of the online and offline world. The work of art here is enacted through the interplay of agents of a system. Live-art, as I understand it, has two main conceptual pillars. Performatively it is based on a mediation of time and space, meaning that live is primarily understood as the expression of a communicative structure in the 'now.' In other words, there is a process going on, this art is process-based not product based. What then occurs as a form of presence (or art) is the

4 → (Random) words from Julius Popp, *bit.fall* at MoMA, New York, 2008.

playful production of a relationship of foreground and background, the bilocation play on here and there. Time expresses in space and spacings.

Looking at the screenshot above, documenting the Drift 10 exhibition of *bit.fall* in London, we look at CONTACT in the foreground, while we also bridge the perspective and Thames to St. Pauls in the background. Yet there is more foreground and background here: what reality feeds what system of representation? Does the world exist for the work of art or the work of art for the world? This question appears, as the human perspective is the one that shapes the understanding of feed and feeding and of foreground and background, based on context.

In *bit.fall* the screen understood as the surface of projection is alive through the flow of data while the screen is gone in the sense of a blank space on to which a projection occurs. The screen is gone as surface. The data itself also serves as a screening thereof. The ephemeral appearance of words simultaneously enacts an impermanent screen and screening. *Bit.fall* is remarkable in the context of 'sleeky cracks' as its artistic value and work is constituted by the synthesis of word practices and practices of location — the remixing relocation of reappearing words. However, it is more than just a downpour of data, literally a news feed cycle is produced. The reality feeds the algorithm that then produces the representation of a news item through the waterfall that feeds itself in a re-cycle.

> *All words at every level of prose and poetry and all devices of language and speech derive their meaning from figure/ground relation.* [5]

Through the logic of the cycle expressed through the mechanics of the fountain as recycling object, relationality and connectivity are expressed as a perpetual durational mechanism. The gaze of the observer witnesses the enactment of connectivity in words, an interruption of a flight into the air of the otherwise invisible connections of the aqueduct structure of the machine. The meaning of words here is ascribed by the viewer in an act of screen surface surfing through the reading of this form of single word slam poetry. While this graffiti-like written object of tags and letterings appears in quasi-silence for the eye of the viewer, the *bit.fall* machine also produces an audio-track through the noise of its continual re-enactments of words. The beat of the repetitive percussive splash here is also the echoing resonance of the speedy speech-acts of the machine. Together as a Gesamtkunstwerk the installation — and performance and conceptual piece–produces specters of a reality in perpetual reconstitution through the shock of the new and its erosion.

The 'live-art' of *bit.fall* produces phenomenologically fragile appearances, forms of expression of reality that cannot be grounded in a stable sense of meaning. Thus, the meaning of the work lies in the performative gesture and the form of expression. What is interesting for me to note here is that *bit.fall* originates from a period of understanding of the internet in which the new media still prevails over the social media aspect of its use. The work presents a choreography of abstract information without the user, an ordering, and a cataloguing without the social aspect of language use. The viewer of the work, although embedded in a structure of a 'live-art' apparatus is bound to the passivity of the spectator. I am interested

5 → W. Terrence Gordon, *McLuhan: A Guide for the Perplexed* (New York: Continuum, 2010), 167.

however, in extending the observation of 'sleeky cracks' from expressing an aspect of reality to the expression of the participatory, the communal, and the ritual — or simply the social — in other words into the realm of expressing yourself. I am interested in the change of perspective and change of objectification: from looking at an artwork to the concept of being an artwork (or at least part thereof).

Of course, live-art does not need the friction of bilocation that comes about through the online and offline aesthetics. However, this aspect as a layer of mediation adds and supplants and thereby supplements the aesthetics of the now in a way that represent the human contemporary condition much better than works of art that follow a practice whose art-historical trace is so clearly bound to the nostalgic remnants of the performance art movement of happenings.

For instance, the UK-based 'live art' (without the hyphen) group considers their form of live art to be primarily about the breathing experience in interaction with other humans, nature, and so-called animals. I consider this fascination with the experience of the moment-in-time as an expression of the movement towards an experience that due to the lack of mediation or technology can be seen as an heightened 'authentic' experience. Yet, for the constitution of what I consider 'live-art' there needs to be a liminal play of mediation enacted that goes beyond the rupture that an offline experience can offer; an experienced perceived as authentic due to the isolation from the influence of the online onto the human condition. We live in the time of 'Pokémon Go,' after all.

Consider the 2012 artwork *Die Guillotine* by Rouven Materne and Iman Rezai. These Berlin-based artists — and at the time students — held a referendum online through a period of time, a 'voting period,' to determine whether or not to kill a sheep with a beautifully built execution machine, hence the title of the work. Millions participated. This shit went viral. The shock of the new here is the simple slick understanding that clicks can kill. There is direct action in direct democracy and things done online, the consequence of what appears (or has in the past of the early days of the internet appeared) to be not an action — doing stuff online — which as 'sleeky crack' surprises some as a scandal. But actually, online acts are real acts and can be lethal, as referendums like *Die Guillotine* show. There is no reswipe button. In the end, though, the sheep survived.

The considerations of the social bring me back to the meaning of words as shared materiality. When thinking about these forms of 'art games' like *Die Guillotine* as social games, the action and immediacy of words and their meaning as agents of decision-making displays the foundation of the social is interaction. I am particularly interested in the 'play' of communicative structures, of foregrounds and backgrounds in interactions to produce and reproduce interactions on a human level anew. This form of 'live-art' as the following example shows, can be its own kind of social medium, its own form of expression of community, and one that is expressed in the now and orientated towards the future, and thus continues its workings in the present tense and in memory.

Moving from an understanding of the internet as an informative medium (like in *bit.fall*) and a medium of communicational exchange (like in *Die Guillotine*) to a relational understanding of the internet as a social medium means to incorporate social reality as the internet's core function. Generally, the internet as social medium means some form of orchestration of communication into forms of expression that are ordered according to market logic of demand-driven rules of attention. The more you like the more you screen, and the more you are liked the more you are screened. The social media of today, such as Instagram (image) and Twitter (words) are social through their expressive form of relationality through content of atomistic individuals who chiefly (after a definition Rob Horning gives)[6] express themselves to express themselves to express themselves. Not to neglect the accumulation of social (media) capital through quantifiable data and metrics per capita that is progressively integrated into the magical cabinet of the means of production—as a 'sleeky crack' in and of itself. In short, selves in social media as data bits are not that much different from the fountain of *bit.fall*, just that the need of resonance of feedback or the social realm re-creates the need of self-expression rather than the mechanic design.

6 → Rob Horning, "The Silence of the Masses Could Be Social Media," accessed August 05, 2014, https://thenewinquiry.com/blog/the-silence-of-the-masses-could-be-social-media/.

Moving beyond the aspect of social media as a form of expression of oneself for one's own sake, I am interested in looking into social media as relational forms of social contract work. What I mean to say is that words are not just instrumental, such as in a 'yes' or 'no' referendum, but can, and indeed have been, used throughout human history as social contracts. In other words, relationships between people are political and are important beyond functions of vanity and narcissism, which the current internet institutions such as Facebook might at times suggest as the social tissue of reality. The foundation of any social reality is contractual and governed by the communicability of its laws, rules, and customs. Whether the police rules over them or guys sporting AK-47's on trucks is another question.

Social media is nothing else than social sculpture and social choreographies, thus forms of art in a broad and conceptually open understanding of sculpture, performance, and dance. One of the most interesting artworks to emerge in recent art history combines exactly those elements that I have sketched so far, in a synthesis that produces something completely other, something in alterity to itself, under-stood as a traditional form of installation, object, performance, and social sculpture—a medium, a concept, a form, a practice—what I here have tentatively termed 'live-art.'

I will always be too expensive to buy.
I will always mean what I say.
I will always do what I say I am going to do.[7]

Adrian Piper's 2013 *The Probable Trust Registry: The Rules of the Game #1–3*

7 → Adrian Piper, *The Probable Trust Registry: The Rules of the Game #1–3*, 2013.

creates a situation. The work is an object, a sculpture, an installation, and a perfor-mance, but primarily it is an encounter of a physical kind in its drama and theatricality. There is a playful element of a game to it, both on the level of aesthetic game (asking what is this I experience here), and on the level of interpretation (asking what is this I have just experienced). It is a playful art-game through a playful gesture-game by means of a playful language-game. In other words it is a reality-game: a theatrical play within a liminal sense of reality. Yet, raw democracy is like theater.

Imagine you are in a room, hall, or any space and there is the choice you can make, there is nothing else than this choice. A literal 'wortspiel,' if you will. You choose your "I" from the three sentences above. It is a little bit like the original position in John Rawls *The Theory of Justice* (1971)—the author being one of the two advisors with whom Piper wrote her doctorate—without the originality or the stripped-down post-apocalyptic vibe of re-inventing humanity through rules. *The Probable Trust Registry* is much simpler than that, it does not re-invent you, it quite tacitly wants to change you and through that change the world that you inhabit. Take your stand, make the vote that you will be, what you will choose to be. You have read it already: will you be too expensive to buy OR always mean what you say OR will you always do what you say you are going to do?

Of course the participant in this form of game does not know the situation they have found themselves in from the beginning. You are a guinea pig of the playing field of a novel social form of art. In the beginning you might know what you get yourself into, if you visit the solo exhibition at the Berlin-based Hamburger Bahnhof in 2017 this is much more likely than if you move around as part of the crowd in the Arsenale-part of the Venice Biennale in 2015 (where the work won the Golden Lion). In the beginning, as usual with the newly encountered, there is curiosity, there is confusion, or there is both at once. The question: "What is this work?", however,

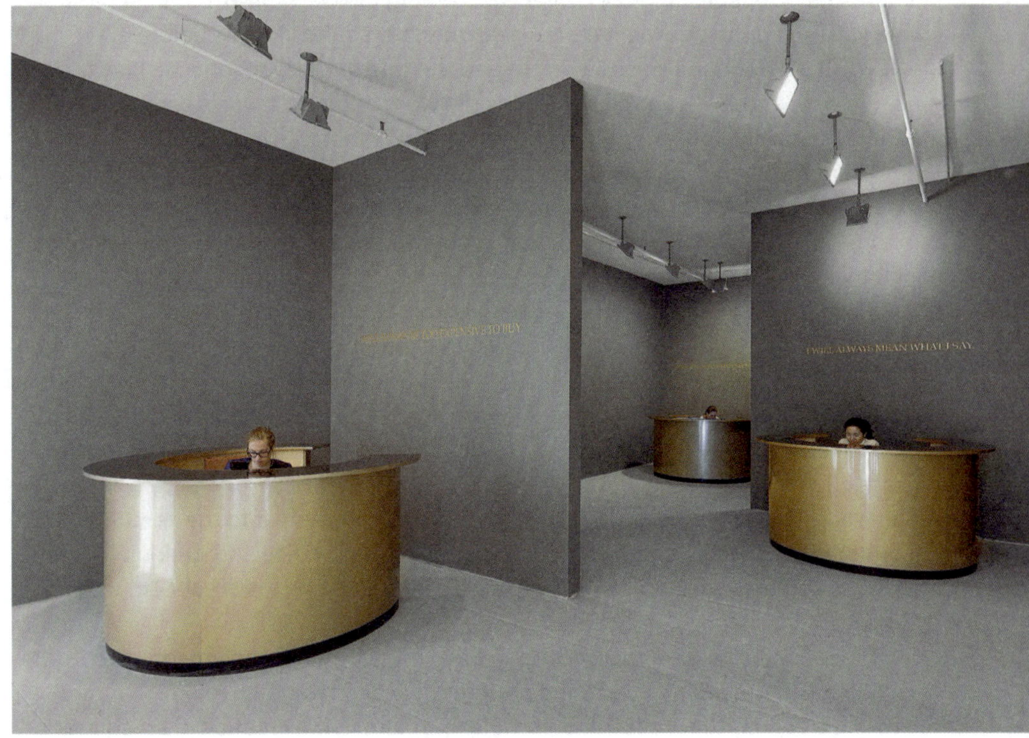

Adrian Piper, *The Probable Trust Registry: The Rules of the Game #1–3*, 2013. Installation + Participatory Group Performance: three embossed gold vinyl wall texts on 70% grey walls; three circular gold reception desks, each 1,83 m D × 1,6 m H; contracts; signatories' contact data registry; three administrators; self-selected members of the public. Photo credit: E. Frossard. Collection Staatliche Museen zu Berlin, Nationalgalerie. © APRA Foundation Berlin.

does not arise as intuitively as one might think, as this would include an a priori understanding of the work of art as one in the first place. That is not how this new kind of slap-in-the-face new works. What is much more likely is not seeing the forest for the trees, and regarding this experience as WTF and noise.

"'Where is the art?' is one of the questions that many people ask me," says M., one of the staff-performers of the work at the Hamburger Bahnhof in Berlin. During the exhibition each of the performers staff one of the three desks present in the space. Behind each desk the visitor reads in capital letters the slogan of the performer's stand, their position, and checkpoint. "Other people simply walk up to me and say 'What is the art,'" M. says of frequently imposed encounters they experienced in this odd job as part of an artwork. I suppose the interesting part of this job is to study the reactions of the people, but M. responds that mostly there are barely any to notice. Maybe this is how good art works. It is unnoticed until further notice.

In *The Probable Trust Registry: The Rules of the Game #1–3* an artwork emerges in the encounter, through you. You not only fill physical space with your bodily presence, but also produce a work of art therewith. With you I mean you the observer, bystander, participant, ignorer, and viewer. The situation in which the work encounters you probably occurs as follows: you walk into a space in which you identify three stands; while at first glance there is the association that something is being sold, marketed, or promoted here (in a commercial sense), you do realize after a couple of seconds that this is not the case, as those who are likely to be the staff are rather uninterested in establishing eye contact or showing the well-known commercial smile. Likely, you are confused. You have not seen anything quite like this before in your life. If you have not done so earlier, you read the title of the work on a display on the museum wall, and think about it. Possibly the word 'registry' reveals some kind of meaning, some kind of sense about what is going on here.

"What is the art?" is indeed the most pressing question regarding *The Probable Trust Registry: The Rules of the Game #1–3*. The aesthetic encounter of the work is in three different functional layers that in operative ways overlap and supplement each other. Firstly, there is the physical and architectural realm in which the work appears, in that the work exists as an installation. By this I mean the dead matter, the furniture, the lights, the shape of the desks, the lettering above the desks, the walls, the museum, or gallery space that shelters all this stuff. This material layer excludes any living and breathing being present, and is solely an optical dimension, neat in its demarcations of what is there and what is not there. Secondly, there is the relational and situational 'experience'
of the work. This includes and implants the staff performers into the aesthetic encounter, who tell you "sign here" once you make your choice and walk-up to them. They hand you an iPad under which you sign your name and input your email in a "Personal Declaration."

The 'sleeky cracks' of the work open in its third realm. Supplementary to the first material installation and second performative and relational realm, the third realm is the conceptual virtual and immaterial realm — the creation of an abstract entity of relationality. The artwork is you means that there is an involution of the general logic of the social media, it is not you that expresses yourself, but you are an expression through your declaration to be "too expensive to buy" or to "always mean what I say" or "always do what I say I am going to do." This might seem para-doxical at first, but the work of art completes its cycle of representation though the viewer as participant-turned-performer of itself. In other words, you perform what you do everyday, but not to other abstract entities but to yourself.

In the online realm you are accustomed to donating your personal data and information to other databases. Your data-self of social media drowns into the analysis of the O-C-E-A-N models of yourself, to reconfigure your potential for cor-porate use and abuse of your purchase powers and political views. The 'sleeky crack' is the understanding that in a similar logic you are updating your own set of beliefs, your iOS, and yourself as General Terms and Conditions. In other words, you are part of an improbable community now, through the enactment of the rule you have donated yourself to observing accordingly. There is now a relationship of perpetual interaction added to your life, a normative order through an imaginative and imagined community in an imaginative and imagined space of reality: read-only memory. Of course, only if you like to add this meaning to your life. Involving your body through and throughout the physical space in which the Personal Declaration was signed, its effect is transported into the digital realm, and through this you received your registry via email (in the case of the Venice Biennale). However, this is hardly where the work stops. The experience of *The Probable Trust Registry: The Rules of the Game #1–3* continues to pervade the participant after the aesthetic encounter. The afterlife of the work manifests in the memory of the event of the first two realms plus the confrontation of the knowledge of the particular registry. It thus displays the art of social network in its explorative exemplary fashion in that you as singularly plural selves perform/are performing your life now as an artwork. More than just a social sculpture, this community is in existence in a completely unmediated and undocumented way. It is a conceptual social sculpture, a production of ties of meaning of social values, of a foundational concept of relationality in *performance*— the play of presence, performance, and presentation.

Different than, for instance, the 'live-art' *bit.fall*, which does not include human interaction as part of its performative system, *The Probable Trust Registry: The Rules of the Game #1–3* is entirely unphotographable. The positioning of the work into a documentary fixation of a moment does not serve the illustrative purpose of displaying a moment in time in which the work is being enacted; rather it documents the presentation of the work in the absence thereof. The aspect of 'live-art' in Piper's work is through the need for participatory human interaction in its constitution as a work in the first place. This sui generis stands in contrast to other works of art, and indeed 'live-art' which incorporate the photographic construction of the gaze as a means of documentation into their practice, such as the highly instagrammable orches-trations of Anne Imhof's *Faust* (2017) or *Angst II* (2016). Piper uses the value of documentation within the work, as the work consists in the ritual and the document of its documentation. The art is largely unphotographable here. Piper's choreography understood as 'the art is you' means that according to the documentation of *The Probable Trust Registry: The Rules of the Game #1–3* indeed "[y]our reaction to this work, whatever it is, is the stance you take toward the actions it invites you to perform."[8]

8 → Adrian Piper, "THE DESTINY AND INTERPRETATIONS OF THE WORK ARE PART OF THE WORK," *Interim Report of 31 May 2016*, accessed August 10, 2017, http://www.adrianpiper.com/art/docs/Piper2016TPTR_InterimReport-1.pdf.

THE DESTINY AND INTERPRETATIONS OF THE WORK ARE PART OF THE WORK. [9]

This artwork-as-event is thus perfectly suitable for the neoliberal understanding of the concept of self. Everyone has truly their own experience, their own artwork, their private memory, and their public choice to make. The abstract reality of relationality and contractual community otherwise known as society arises through the invisible relationality of individuals, just like in *The Probable Trust Registry: The Rules of the Game #1–3*. I introduced the art by alleging this artwork to constitute a social medium. Within the context of '*sleeky cracks*' this is important to note: an offline phenomenon that marks its character through an experience of the online realm. Connectivity and registries, however, have not been invented through the instantaneous access thereof, but by virtue of archival culture. Obviously, the ingenuity of the work is that it does much more than being a social medium. With respect to the meaning-making of this artwork, it is the synthesis of space and gesture into a situation, a recording thereof, and an afterlife thereof, which makes the work transgressive and opening in terms of boundaries moving from bilocation into an opening of an imaginative multilocation. The social media game is turned into a reality game, and vice versa. That's the 'sleeky crack.'

Foreground and background here are mechanisms of scaling and of zooming for the participant, who asks themself: what is done for what; the art for me? Or am I doing something for the art? Or is it both, and the art is just the threshold, the opening of a locale? Can art produce a system of communication, and of exchange that produces meaning, delocalized like a blockchain? At the very least, *The Probable Trust Registry: The Rules of the Game #1–3* show how the boundaries of art and life can truly vanish. It is not just as an empty gesture of 'l'art pour l'art.' If anything, it is art for life's sake, or art in our society's sake. What makes this work last even outside its own constitution as a work (meaning in the history of art), however, is its utopian aspiration and the question it asks as an exclamation of its performative gesture, namely: fuck off and imagine a world and ask yourself: "how can we live together and what are the rules of the game?"

9 → Adrian Piper, *The Probable Trust Registry: The Rules of the Game #1–3*, 2013.

"Cut, Copy, Paste!" → The Next "New Normal" or Biology's Trend towards Homophily →

Gabriele Gramelsberger

Variety is the key engine of evolution. If the genetic diversity in a population declines—a phenomenon biologists call 'inbred depression'—it has consequences for the disease susceptibility of the affected species.[1] This phenomenon of the normalization of the genetic code occurs primarily in isolated populations, but also through the continuous crossbreeding of individuals of the same lineage. The completely normalized end of the spectrum is formed by clones of identical genetic codes that are now found in masses in the greenhouses of the agricultural industry or have become possible through reproductive medicine. Dolly (July 5, 1996 to February 14, 2003), the first cloned mammal, is emblematic of this path to homophile hopelessness; towards the 'genetic bubble'. But there is yet another, more recent way of normalizing the genetic code.

"Cut, copy, paste!" Is the motto of Synthetic Biology, a research field that has been established since the early 2000s. This involves the industrial use of microorganisms such as E. coli bacteria or yeast cells used for the production of biomaterials—drugs, biofuels and other organic products, including well-known products such as beer or cheese. For "utilizing microorganisms in industrial processes is one of the most important achievements of the 21st century."[2] For some time now, this business has been operated with computer-aided design programs (CAD), not only to optimize microorganisms for industrial production, but to generate completely redesigned, biomolecular factories. With biological CAD programs such as *TinkerCell*, biobricks can be designed and assembled into biomolecular machines.[3]

Biobricks are standardized building blocks from DNA that code certain functions. For example, there are so-called promoters that initialize the transcription of DNA into mRNA. Terminators, on the other hand, stop DNA transcription. mRNA, in turn, is translated into proteins. Biomolecular machines such as protein generators can be produced with these and other classes of biobricks. "Typically, a protein generator contains a promoter, a ribosome binding site (RBS), the protein coding region, and one or more transcription terminators."[4] This engineering-design of biomolecular machines is now greatly facilitated by CAD programs allowing the visualization of biobricks on-screen and to compose them into biomolecular machines. Each design is based on a genetic sequence, which can be synthesized without any problem using 'DNA printers' and can be duplicated as often as needed. Bluntly put: biology is transformed into a computer-assisted science that converts digital CAD files (dCode) into material DNA templates (gCode) at the touch of a button. The material DNA templates can then be introduced into the laboratory into genetically reduced carrier cells or carrier organisms — so-called chassis — for replicating and producing biomaterials.

Admittedly, this does not usually work in laboratory days, because life — also biomolecular — is individual, complex, and resistant. But first 'proofs-of-concepts' already exist; as well as socio-political resistance.[5] Not only biologists but leading IT companies are researching this new alliance of dCode/gCode. However, the industrial use of biomolecular machines in chassis is not about a DNA template in a carrier cell, but about billions of them. And they should be identical and always produce the same. What is completely unacceptable is living behaviour such as adaptation or mutation and thus evolution. So they attempt to eliminate mutations to turn biomolecular machines into isolated miniature bio-factories.[6] Turning something living into a 'thing' means taking its developmental scope entirely. Only what is equal with itself and to others is identical and has an identity as thing. This is what the trend of biology to homophily refers to.

1 → Nancy Wilmsen Thornhill, *The Natural History of Inbreeding and Outbreeding: Theoretical and Empirical Perspectives* (Chicago: University of Chicago Press, 1993).
2 → Masaru Tomita, "Towards Computer Aided Design (CAD) of Useful Microorganisms," in *Bioinformatics* 17, no. 12 (2001): 1091–1092.
3 → Deepak Chandran, "Computer-aided Design for Synthetic Biology," in *Design and Analysis of Biomolecular Circuits: Engineering Approaches to Systems and Sythetic Biology*, ed. H. Koepell, 203–24 (New York: Springer, 2011).
4 → "Registry of Standard Biological Parts," accessed June 02, 2017, http://parts.igem.org/Help:Protein_generators.
5 → Mark Peplow, "Synthetic biology's first malaria drug meets market resistance," in *Nature* 530, no. 7591 (2016): 389–90.
6 → Kinga Umenhoffer et al., "Reduced evolvability of Escherichia coli MDS42, an IS-less cellular chassis for molecular and synthetic biology applications," in *Microbial Cell Factories* 9, no. 1 (2010), 38.

pray →

pray → It is a practice of incantation, a performance, a gesture whose very repetition binds us. It binds us to the other within ourselves, to trans-cendence, to a stranger, or just to our neighbor. Praying generates a shared ground. It is not just me. It is another something I can talk to. In a group or alone in bed. A gesture

performing something that is not:
praying contests the solitude of
the network by rendering an absent
present—all of the sudden there
is an outside again. Light a candle
to dive into the security of faith.

14th week → Excerpt from *La Condition ouvrière* → Simone Weil

In December 1934 due to the bad working conditions, the French government fears another strike. For 16 weeks the philosopher Simone Weil works in a factory producing train-parts. She works like all the others, paid per task. At night in her room, after leaving the factory, she outlines the daily routines. In detail she records every step of the mechanical process: physical stress, distractions and mistakes, conversations between workers and her own performance. Her writing practice is a form of re-subjectification, just as it is a critical observation of the working conditions in these times. Simone Weil's writings were mostly published post mortem in the 1950s and 1960s. The following text is an excerpt—originally written in French—of Weil's notebooks from 1934 and 1935.

1975 in Emden The Volkswagen factory: The workers are running as if something was drawing them away. 1926 in Detroit: The worker are running as if they had already lost too much time. Again, in Lyon in 1957: They are running as if they knew something better to be.[1]

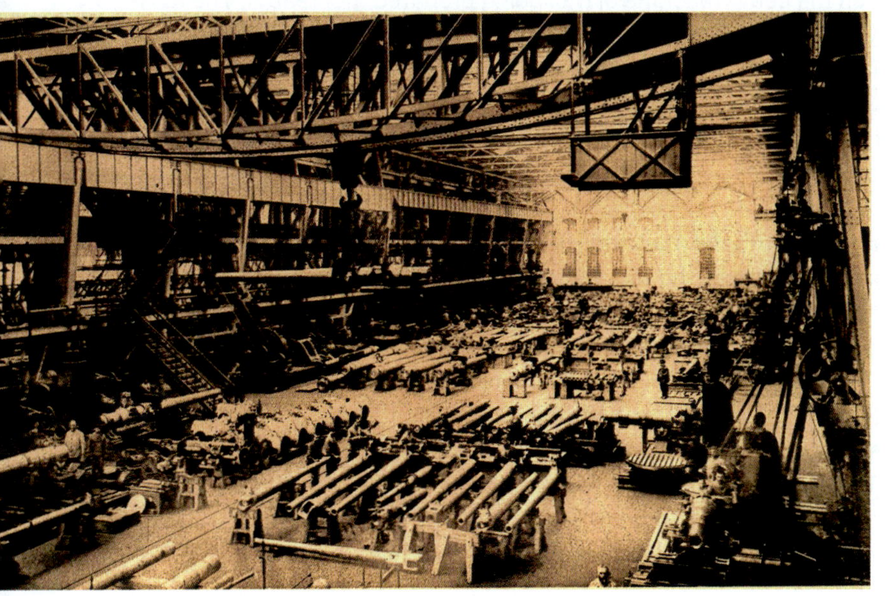

The Krupp Gun Works during World War I, photo by Brown Bros, 1915.

1 →   Harun Farocki, "Workers Leaving the Factory," 1996.

Monday, 4th. — Strong headaches, Monday, when getting up. Bad luck: all day they chose to run the turning thing with infernal noises next to me. At noon, barely able to eat. But it does not impede my speed, and that without pills.

Shells — Only done at 11:45, but not because of me: more than half an hour, surely is lost in the morning (even more) because of the machine… I persuade him to activate the pedal, despite it being more dangerous. It does not work either;… With orders from Mouquet, he reactivates the buttons. Still does not work. Little Jacquot gets impatient… At 11:10, he starts to dismantle the machine–broken feather. But when he turns it back up, nothing at all works. He becomes nervous, nervous… The team boss, when I give him my work-coupon (because I refuse to finish the pieces since what counts is what's done), is sarcastic about J.

Afternoon: Half an hour of rest. Then 2 orders for plaquettes, 520 each, at 0,71 % (c. 421275, b. 4). I lose time in the beginning: taking away the pieces, counting them — also placing them, taking useless precautions — and bad pedalling (not at full pace: hard pedal). 1st commission done at 3:15, 2nd one started at 3:25 (I lose 5 minutes with waiting, not noticing Jacquot has prepared the machine), done at hell's pace, my maximum, at 4:30: here, I've earned 3.60 Francs an hour…

Friday, I've seen the heavy machine of Biol being prepared (not ready). The task-organizer says to me: don't take this task, it's too hard. I find something else. Monday, I meet Eugénie who does it all day. Am full of remorse. Had I wanted to take the task, I probably could have. And I know how hard it is: it's what I had done the last afternoon of my ear infection, or at least something equivalent. At 4.50 hours, she's visibly exhausted.

What had happened with the machine? (Idiot me for not having paid more attention). When I pressed the buttons, the tool sometimes fell down twice; the team boss, seeing this says: "It's not supposed to do that, that's it!" Later, the same thing happens again, but the tool stays down the second time! Jacquot picks it up again and I go on… until it starts again. He then makes me stop. Ilion, who walks by, tells him the 'finger' (the feather) of the big wheel is broken. It's true. But there was, apparently, something else too. One can see that for little Jacquot, the machine is a weird kind of beast.

Tuesday morning — 3 orders analogue to Monday evening.

    600 at 5.6 %, little pieces hard to take off, marked 1h15.
    550 at 0.71 %, m. 1h20.
    550 at 0.71 % m. 1h20.

Very tiring in the long run, because the pedal is very hard (stomach aches). Jacquot still charming.

Later, running into Biol (nostalgia of heavy pieces giving me remorse), he puts me up on the 'piano,' where I spend all afternoon as well, except for a break from 2:45 to 3:45. The 2 orders paid 0.5%, one 630, the other 315.

...

At 4:30, very tired, so much so I leave right away. In the evening, strong headaches.

At the 'piano' at first lots of effort due to my fears of bad stamps; at the end of the afternoon, it's a bit better. But bloody fingertips.

Wednesday morning — Piano again (630 pieces), it's going better, except for the finger pains — nevertheless it takes me more than 1h30. I wrote down 1h20. Robert, immediately after, makes me order 50 pieces (c. 421146 27) (Paid?). Nice enough to give me an order of 50 identical pieces he made because it was urgent, to give me time. Difficulties: certain parts don't fit in. He makes me put them aside for him to do himself. Held back by a heavy fatigue and headaches, spent 30 mins between the two orders. After, 'piano' once more, the same 630, to do differently. I try to speed up and almost make faulty ones; however I'm not letting myself be held back as much by my fear of failure (even though not a single piece is to be lost, says Biol, because the count is wrong or narrow). I count them again in doing my task. Had first found 610. Found 620 by a few units. The worker that made them before told me she found 630: the second time, I say all units are there, to get it over with. How is one supposed to count correctly when paid 0,5 %? 1h20 passed. Afterwards, Robert reviews my work. 2 orders marked 25 minutes each (what?).

...

Afternoon, break after 2 hours. Then caps: 200 at 1.45 %! I should take less than an hour then. But they are heavy and need to be carried in a case, and it's 4 pedalings for each, and 2 operations:

First one puts them like this:

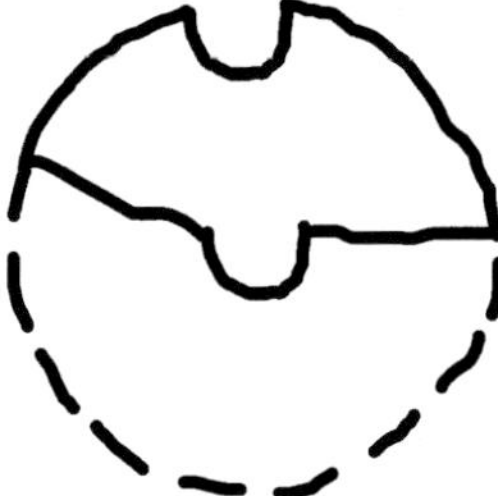

Then at the second operation one turns them around like this:

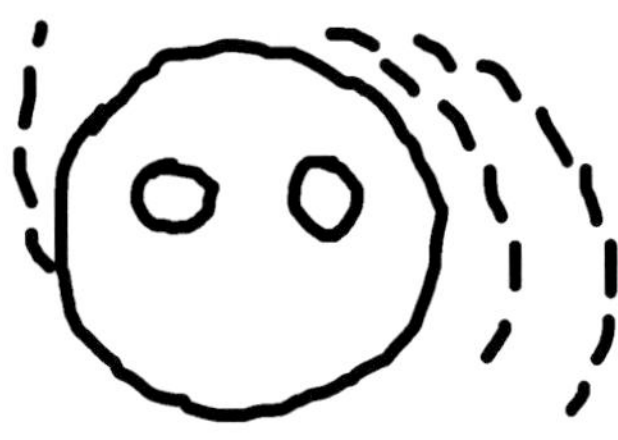

So, with the first montage, one does them all at two pedalings each, then the same for the second operation — so one needs 800 pedalings. Yet, they're not that easy to place: one needs to put the screws in the holes etc. I only got it right at the end of the first operation. I have the feeling I'm not giving all the speed I have. And yet, I exhaust myself. In the evening, for the first time, I feel crumbled by fatigue, like before leaving for Monta: feeling I'm beginning to slide into the state of a beast. However, remaining: conversation with the storekeeper, visit to the toolshed.

Thursday — ...

Break until 11. When stopping, I feel all the weight of my fatigue, work will give me the feeling of sickness. The workers are irritated because of often losing their turn to stop for orders of 100 pieces (among which is Mimi's sister). Jacquot comes, bringing an order of 5000 pieces; it's my turn. Little round sheets to cut from long bands, with continuous pedalling. Price 0,224 % (approximately). I would like to succeed. I start working without other thoughts. Jacquot has only one recommendation: don't let it get too full, otherwise one risks breaking the tool. My fatigue and my desire to go faster annoy me a little. I start with one sheet, not far enough, which forces me to start the first pedalling once more and fail the piece (1 out of 5000 is little, but were it to happen at each new block, it would be too much). This happens several times. Finally, angry, I put the new block too far once more, it goes across the threshold and instead of a round sheet I get a cone. Instead of calling Jacquot immediately, I turn the block around, but unaware of my fault, I cross the threshold once more (I suppose), and get yet another cone, and right after, the 'grenadier' of the tool. Tool is broken. What hurts the most is the dry and harsh tone little Jacquot takes. The order was urgent. The montage, perhaps difficult, was to be done again, everyone was annoyed by similar accidents in the past days (or even the same day?). The team boss, of course, screams at me like the adjutant that he is, but collectively, in a way ("it's unfortunate to have workers who ..."). Mimi, who sees me feeling bad, comforted me kindly. It is 11.45.

Afternoon (sharp headache). Stop after 3h30. 500 pieces, still rounds to cut from strips (what a misfortune!), but with a small hand press. I am horribly annoyed by the fear of starting anew. Actually, more than once I pass the band a little above the threshold at the first pedal stroke, but it results in nothing; every time I tremble... Jacquot regained his smiles (I have to talk to him about some caprices of the machine, which refuses to start, or run several times in a row with a pedal stroke), but I no longer have the heart to respond.

Incident between Josephine (the redhead) and Chatel. He was given, it seems, a very low paying job (at the press next to mine, which is the one with buttons in front of the chief's office). She grumbles. Chatel hisses at him like rotten fish, very roughly, it seems to me (but I do not discern the words well). She does not reply anything, bites her lips, eats her humiliation, visibly represses a desire to cry and, no doubt, a stronger desire to respond violently.

Three or four workmen attend the scene, in silence, half-holding back a smile (Eugenie among them). For if Josephine did not have this bad job, one of them would have it; they are therefore very pleased that Joséphine gets bawled, and say it openly, later, during the break — but not in her presence. Conversely, Joséphine would have seen no disadvantage in having the hard job given to someone else.

Conversations during the break (I should write them all down). On suburban houses (sister of Mimi and Josephine). When Nénette is there, there often are only jokes and confidences that could make a whole regiment of hussars blush. (See: the one whose "friend" is a painter [but lives alone], and who boasts of sleeping with him three times a day, morning, noon and night, who explains the different "techniques" between him and another guy who gives her money, and "deprives himself of nothing"; as far as I understand, the time that she does not spend making love, she spends cooking and eating).

But with Nénette, it is something else — when she talks about her kids (13-year-old boy, daughter of six — about their studies — about her son's taste for reading (she talks about it with respect). The last days of this week, the week she has been on sick leave at all times, she has an unusual gravity; she obviously wonders how she is going to pay the pension of her kids.

Incident of Mrs. Forestier–accident. They inquire about raising funds for her. Eugenie declares that she will give nothing. Joséphine also (but this one must not give often), and adds that Mrs. Forestier went to the factory to say hello to everyone (the very day I returned) because of the fundraising. Nénette and the Italian, formerly her great friends, will give nothing either. She apparently did some harm, not to them, but to several others (?).

The Italian is sick. My second week, she had asked to "go fishing" and Mouquet refused; But there were only two, and there has only been a halt. She has 2 kids; her husband is a bricklayer (maneuver) and earns 2.75 F per hour. So she can not cure herself. She has a sick liver and headaches which the sounds of the factory make intolerable (I know that!).

Friday — Rest. I do not spend the day, as I would have done a few weeks earlier in such circumstances, trembling at the idea of the nonsense that I will perhaps do. Proof that I am a little more sure of myself than before.

Ilion calls me (at what time?) To scrape lids for metros. ... At 10:00 am I was called to remove magnetic circuit boards (which I had done at the end of the first week). I see that it will last until the evening. Considerable relief. I use the technique discovered the last day that I had done (many small blows of mallet) and works well and fast enough (more than 30 pieces per hour, but in the first days I had done 15, and Mouquet had estimated the value of my work at 1.80 francs per hour, since he had told me that in 5 hours I had barely made for 9 working days). No fear of doing non-sense, instead: relaxation. Nevertheless [...] I feel taken in the middle of the afternoon of a long tiredness and welcome the announcement that I am done.

Where Now? Who Now? When Now?

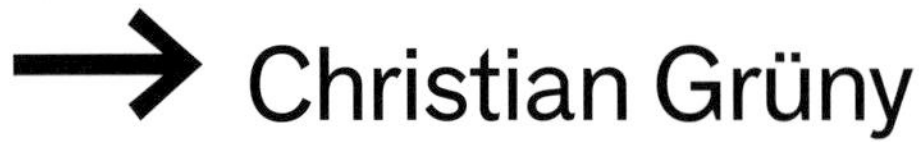 Christian Grüny

And the princess and the prince discuss
What's real and what is not
It doesn't matter inside the Gates of Eden[1]

In an age of universal mediation, immediacy appears as a scarce resource, sought after and cherished. It suggests something that we cannot simply let go of, its philosophical critique notwithstanding: presence, proximity, reality, resistance. The interaction of real bodies in real space, present to each other, skin on skin, tongue on breast, fist in face. No, it's not necessarily pleasant, but what makes the fist so compelling is the fact that it is not an argument, will not be reasoned with, creates rather than states a fact, leaves a trace.

  This promise of reality was irresistible to some artists, and a lot of spectators. When Michael Fried accused minimal art (or "literalist art," as he called it) of theatricality because it created a situation in which artwork and spectator inhabited the same space, he failed to the see that this is not the situation of theater at all. Ultimately, theater is illusion and representation just like a picture or a sculpture, and to arrive at the immediacy of a real situation theatricality had to be abandoned as well. Tony Smith, Robert Morris and Donald Judd's objects were not theatrical but real, or in Judd's terms, specific. From here it was a logical next step (of course there are always innumerable logical next steps, and their obviousness and necessity are only noted ex post) to get rid of objects and their stubborn permanence as well and resort to action plain and simple: no text, no pretext, no repetition, no permanence. The immediacy of contact could be intensified by its fleetingness.

1 → Bob Dylan, "Gates of Eden," 1965.

Now the impulse to abandon illusion came from many different directions and took many different forms, not all of them stressing immediacy to the same degree. In dance, theater, and music, real bodies did not have to be introduced because they were there all along—but they had to be taught not to dance and not to play. It was in visual art where the introduction of the body implied the greatest rupture. Artists renounced the trappings of theater and the mediation of the score and sought to retain the immediacy of the specific, literal object, transforming it into literal action.

What could be more literal than the body itself? The body not as conveyor or locus of meaning but as an agent of movement in space as well as an object that can be acted upon. "Body art" is the proper name for this, while "performance art" is more ambiguous, distributed between different disciplines, approaches, and aims. And what could be more obvious than turning to violence and sex in order to pin this body down? If "pinning down the body" is an appropriate description of this move, Chris Burden's early pieces embody it in its purest form: stuffed into a locker, shot in the arm, nailed to a car, Burden subjected himself or rather his body to various ways of being pinned down, being brought to the here and now. This, it seemed, was reality, finally, and immediacy.

Of course, there is something wrong with this reconstruction, in fact several things. First of all the body is so overdetermined that anything you do to it or with it evokes a plethora of meanings, and references into all possible directions, so even the immediacy of the nail driven through the hand (or rather, especially this) or a cock penetrating another's orifices is an illusion. They are real, no doubt, particularly to the one they are done to, but as a statement they inscribe themselves into the cultural fabric with rather less force than the elaborate constructions of the tradition. Secondly, there is something deeply problematic about the emphasis on presence and unrepeatability that permeates body art and has been claimed for performance art in general. It found its authoritative formulation rather late, in Peggy Phelan's *Unmarked* from 1993. In a passage on the specific ontology of performance, she famously writes: "Performance's only life is in the present. Performance cannot

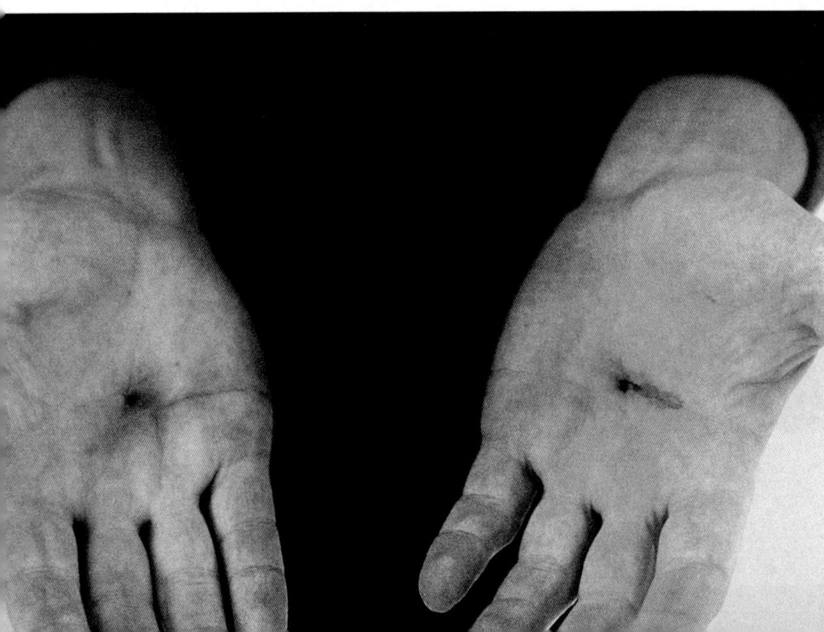

Chris Burden: "Trans-fixed" (1974) © Chris Burden. Image courtesy of The Chris Burden Estate and Gagosian.

be saved, recorded, documented, or otherwise participate in the circulation of representations: once it does so, it becomes something other than performance. To the degree that performance attempts to enter the economy of reproduction it betrays and lessens the promise of its own ontology. Performance's being, like the ontology of subjectivity proposed here, becomes itself through disappearance."[2]

That is a rather curious claim. It is analogous to the observation that talk about a chair is not itself a chair, or that a photograph of a tree will not provide shade on a hot summer's day. Does that mean it's impossible to talk about anything? There really is no fundamental difference here between things and events, both of which are never identical with any of their representations — but who ever claimed such a thing? We might not want to call all these ways of representation and reference "saving" because this seems to imply precisely what they cannot do, which is to keep the action itself in existence or transform it into words, images etc. While a chair doesn't need saving, an action cannot be saved, just talked about, photographed, filmed, reenacted — but so what? Every note ever played, every spoken word, every gesture, becomes itself through disappearance, and there is nothing particularly awe-inspiring about that. Also, the depreciation of representation and documentation strangely underestimates the role these played for iconic performances like Burden's: documentation and discourse are their very life, of which Burden himself was of course fully aware.

Thirdly, there is no such thing as a new action, an action that has never been there before. Richard Schechner draws on anthropology to elucidate this. Like ritual, performance is "restored behaviour,"[3] i.e. behavior that has been grasped and made explicit. The performer knows what she's doing, and it is precisely this that counter-acts the fleeting, ephemeral character of her behavior; if she truly didn't know what she was doing and had no control over it, her actions would most likely amount to a blind enactment of the most deeply ingrained habitual routines of the society she finds herself in. So: "Performance means: never for the first time. It means: for the second to the nth time. Performance is 'twice-behaved behavior.'"[4]

2 → Peggy Phelan, *Unmarked: the Politics of Performance* (London: Routledge, 1993), 146.

3 → Richard Schechner, *Between Theater and Anthropology* (Philadelphia: University of Pennsylvania Press, 1985), 35.

4 → Schechner, *Between Theater and Anthropology*, 36.

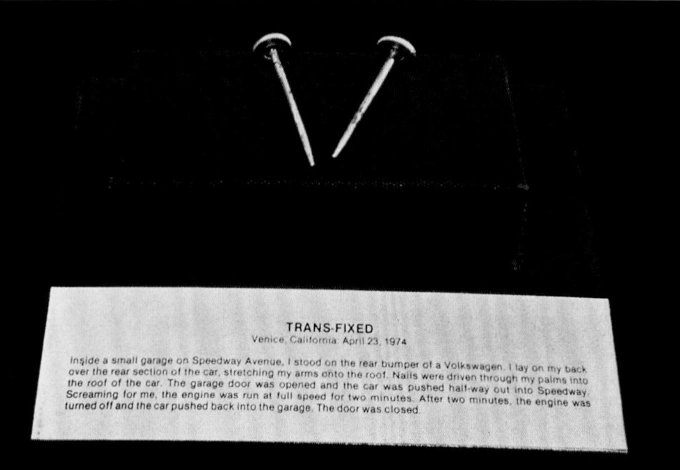

Trans-fixed (1974) © Chris Burden. Image courtesy of The Chris Burden Estate and Gagosian.

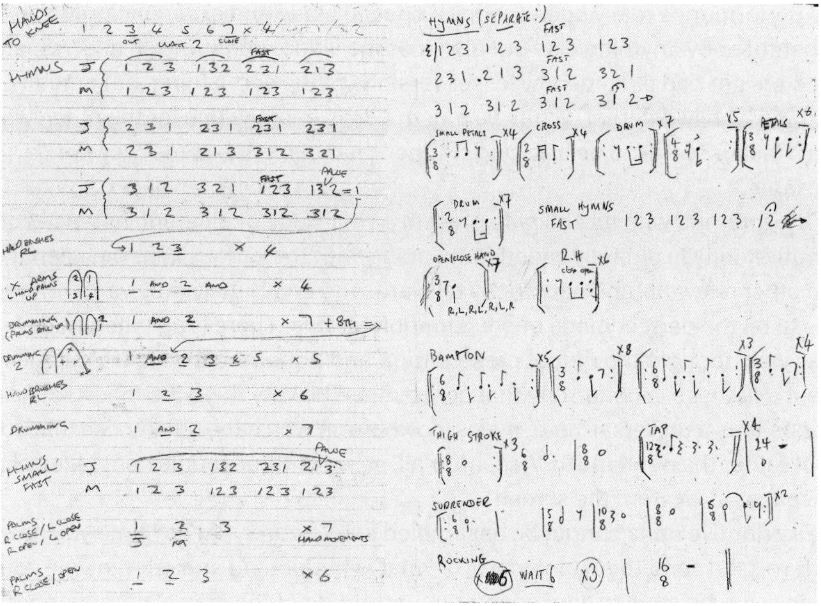

Parallel scores from *Both Sitting Duet*, Jonathan Burrows and Matteo Fargion, 2002.

This also implies that it can be repeated. Any structured action can be repeated, any situation recreated (even though you might want to avoid repeatedly getting shot in the arm). Does this mean that any performance of it is as good as any other, that it doesn't matter what exactly you saw or if you saw it at all because every action is only one instance in an endless row of identical repetitions? Of course not. There's no such thing as an exact repetition, and the only way to experience any action is to see a specific performance of it (or many). The repeatability of the action and the uniqueness of each instance don't exclude but mutually imply each other.

Neither does all this mean that it doesn't matter whether you were there when Burden got shot, saw a picture of it or the brief video, or read about it. That seems to suggest that it's all the same, which of course it's not. Action, documentation, and discourse are fundamentally different from each other, and that is precisely the reason they can form a medial constellation where each instance supports and explicates the others. It might have been an intense but very confusing experience to have been there in 1971, or maybe even a bland or annoying one, which only later readings may have clarified and solidified, as it were, into a momentous historical event.

If performance acknowledges this, it may come to discover a different ontology for itself: an ontology in which the idea of an original makes no sense because it consists of a "distributive unity,"[5] as Peter Osborne has termed it, an open constellation of various medial instances that is subject to change and thus historically open. The important thing to understand about this constellation is the fact that none of the instances can be reduced to any of the others. This not only means that the

5 → Peter Osborne, *Anywhere or Not at All: Philosophy of Contemporary Art* (London: Verso, 2013), 48.

actual performance really does occupy a special place and experiencing it cannot be substituted by anything else but also that the video or the written analysis and/or critique are not bad or somehow lesser versions of the same thing, but actually something wholly different. What we mustn't do is mistake one for the other, which is what Phelan seems to be implying. Rather than being the same they are part of the same.

The internet, with its ability to present a multitude of different instances of this distributive unity in digitally coded form, along with the various links between them and to other relevant (and not strictly relevant, and completely irrelevant) references seems to be the perfect mode of presentation for this. There is an inherent danger here as well, though: the digital presentation and apparent universal availability suggest a flatness, a uniformity that contradicts the very thing it supports. The web may appear as a universal 'here' that is 'nowhere' in which the differences that count get lost rather than enhanced. And, after all, some of what counts here takes place in 'metaspace,' away from the screen.

Distributive unity cannot be assembled in its entirety. At any time you have already missed something, and parts of what is happening and relevant will continue to elude even the most ardent spectator. Letting go of the idea of completeness shouldn't mean weakening one's critical awareness, but it does imply a more relaxed attitude. Pierre Huyghe's work seems to me to be the perfect embodiment of all this. The 2014 exhibition in Paris, Cologne, and Los Angeles assembled works in different states of aggregation, as it were: films, documentaries of performances in image or video, objects, actual performances, natural processes, and of course Human, the very calm and detached dog roaming the exhibition freely and regarding the visitors with a cold eye. There was no way to see everything because some of it had already happened and other things were going to happen in the future, but that was fine. The fact that everything referred to something else did not invalidate what was there. Everything that happens happens now, and being in a certain place implies not being somewhere else. References can be followed, and they will, but there is no overview and no completeness. After a while the calmness of the dog was communicated to the spectator.

This calmness should not be confused with complacency. If there is a lesson to be learned from performance, it is to undermine the certainty of the here and now, of its representations and their relation to one another. Hence Meg Stuart asked "Are we here yet?"[6] and recently Raqs Media Collective answered "We Are Here, But Is It Now?"[7]; or, in Rebecca Schneider's words: "If events are not exactly happening (or not only happening) in a here that is now or a now that is here—where, then, is the here? And when, now, is the then?"[8] Reality is not simple, and we are not here yet. Nor will we ever be.

6 → Meg Stuart, *Are We Here Yet?* ed. Jeroen Peeters (Dijon: Damaged Goods, 2010).
7 → Raqs Media Collective, *We are Here, But is it Now? (The Submarine Horizons of Contemporaneity)* (Berlin: Sternberg Press, 2017).
8 → Rebecca Schneider, *Performing Remains: Art and War in Times of Theatrical Reenactment* (London: Routledge, 2011), 25.

two stories about digital loneliness and a short history of anxiety → Orit Gat

I'm off the internet. My email auto response reads, "I am traveling to Cuba until June 25, 2016, where I will have very limited access to the internet,[1] and where I'll be writing about access to the internet." I went to Cuba with an artist to research the newly introduced public WiFi spots in Havana, to see how people use the internet for the first time in 2016. What I discovered was largely a desire to connect. I saw people crying in public squares, talking to families for the first time in years. Most of the people around me were on Facebook, even if they were online infrequently, liking days-old photographs, looking at profiles that had not been updated in weeks.

I was in Cuba for only ten days but I've never felt lonelier. On one of those days, sitting outside a hotel in Havana using their internet connection, I glanced at the news quickly and read about Tim Peake, the British astronaut who came back from space that June after spending six months in the International Space Station. "It will take Peake a few days to learn to walk again," I read and thought that everything about isolation would touch me personally because I was having a kind of internet withdrawal. At night, when I would go to bed in a rented room in Havana, grabbing a book to read until I fall asleep felt different from reading in bed in New York, with my phone next to me glowing with connection to the rest of the world. Offline, I thought there is a special kind of loneliness to digital isolation. Because it should have felt like a natural state of affairs, because to not be connected 24/7 feels like it would be more habitual than to receive work emails at 3 am. What seems a cautionary tale was simply a newfound awareness to what was already happening: as our personal relationships are mediated via technology, we cannot replace the feeling of being available, of people being available to us. And it brought to mind another form of loneliness — the loneliness of someone who was always connected.

In my images folder — that one that we all keep on our computers, with collected photos from the internet, kept contextless and searched for odd reasons — is one screengrab I keep returning to: Jennifer Ringley of Jennicam, holding a piece of paper in front of the cam that covers her right eye. Her left is directed straight at the camera. The paper reads: "I FEEL SO LONELY." Ringley was lonely though she was watched by thousands of people. She also became a symbol of something she wasn't: the first camgirl, Ringley was a college student when she devised a

1 → "Cuba," accessed November 09, 2016, https://freedomhouse.org/report/freedom-net/2015/cuba.

programming exercise to see if she could build a site that would automatically take a photograph from her webcam and upload it to her site every 15 minutes. It became a sensation. For seven years, internet users watched Ringley's empty dorm room, watched her asleep in her bed, watched as she packed up after college and moved to DC then Sacramento, watched her read and watched her work, watched her alone and in company. It was an experiment in connection that challenged every received notion about human curiosity, voyeurism and exhibitionism, and what it means to know someone.

I look at Ringley's I FEEL SO LONELY photo. A single image from countless images Jennicam produced. Then it was called "lifecasting" — a life lived in public, cast across the web to see what might happen. Now, after personal blogs came and went and social media changed everything about self presentation, this idea of lifecasting seems almost quaint: isn't that what we all do? I look at that one image and think not only of Ringley's trailblazing, but also of her loneliness. Are the people watching your livecam an audience or followers? The latter is, of course, a word that changed meaning much later, with Instagram and Twitter. Ringley's loneliness feels true and honest in a way that no Instagram post does today. It feels innocent.

What happened to the internet? There's a sweetness to our using it to connect to one another, but with the years, this desire for interaction is tinged with anxiety. There was an optimism to the early internet — though it wasn't all that innocent, of course, and the days of A/S/L[2] in chatrooms are to this day discussed among some women as defining their sexuality in terms their young selves were not able to comprehend — brought about a strong sense of optimism. In 2005, Kevin Kelly — one of the first to write about the internet or what we now call "internet culture," who believes he might have been the first person in the world to be hired for a job over email — wrote an article for Wired magazine, which he founded, titled "We Are the Web."[3] It celebrated the 10-year anniversary of Netscape's initial public offering (IPO), as a landmark in the history of the internet. The Netscape IPO wasn't really about dot-commerce. At its heart was a new cultural force based on mass collaboration. Blogs, Wikipedia, open source, peer-to-peer — behold the power of the people. Kelly charts the developments of the internet in the ten years between 1995 and 2005, then imagines 2015. It's an amazing piece of hopefulness: "This view is spookily godlike. You can switch your gaze of a spot in the world from map to satellite to 3-D just by clicking. Recall the past? It's there. Or listen to the daily complaints and travails of almost anyone who blogs (and doesn't everyone?). I doubt angels have a better view of humanity. [...] But if we have learned anything in the past decade, it is the plausibility of the impossible."[4]

What happened to the plausibility of the impossible? When Nicholas Carr claimed in a famous article for the *Atlantic* (and then a book titled *The Shallows*) that "google is making us stupid" because when reading online we cannot mentally map, because searching online means we do not retain information as we used to, it seemed convincing. (I think about how my password for almost every website includes the phone number of the house I grew up in. I think about how few phone numbers I remember now.) And that was 2008 — so quickly after Kelly's Godlike

2 → 'A/S/L' is a short form of 'age, sex, location.'

3 → Kevin Kelly, "We Are the Web," in *Wired*, accessed July 14, 2017, last modified August 01, 2005. https://www.wired.com/2005/08/tech/.

4 → Kelly, "We Are the Web."

view of humanity. There have been so many articles and books in the years after Kelly's peak buoyancy about the network's effects on us that it's almost become given knowledge: science writers and technology critics who all rushed to speculate about how the network might spoil our day to day lives, our comprehension, our friendships, our ability to relate. And though not all of these doomsday accounts should be taken too literally — chances are that even in a decade or five people will still write fiction even if they can't remember phone numbers, and we'll all be, for example, better viewers of photography and in lieu of memory skills we'll develop very advanced skills in assessing information (no more fake news!) — we are allowing technology ever closer to our homes and interpersonal relationships. The commercials for Amazon Echo largely take place at home, in a family setting ("Alexa, order more flour," asks a mother baking cake with her daughter and "Alexa, add anniversary to my calendar, a year from today," says a young man as he's tying a bowtie), relying on conservative heteronormative situations to standardize this technology entering our most intimate relationships.

Charlie Brooker, creator of the Channel 4-then-Netflix-produced drama *Black Mirror*, described his creation as a show that takes place in the "area between delight and discomfort." It is hard not to be amazed by technology, not to participate with evident delight. And then, on the same screens we read about the NSA and WikiLeaks, we cover the cameras built into our laptops, we chart how we once looked up a product and then were bombarded by advertisements for it for months. To participate in the network has shifted from one of the most significant intellectual projects known to man to a network governed by economic and national interests which are inaccessible to the users that are its target.

As we speculate about the future of technology, we should think about our present state as a fascinating stage in our relationship to it: not a "neither here nor there," just a moment before *Black Mirror*, which is set in a nondescript near-future where technology is omnipresent and ominous. You can tell everything about a society from the way it reflects its own future, and ours has shifted immensely from the hoverboards and self-lacing sneakers of *Back to the Future* to the grim, gray palette of *Black Mirror*.

One last thing about loneliness: for over ten years, a thread lasted on one of the forums on the site moviecodec.com, usually used for discussing digital video formats. "I am lonely, will anyone speak to me?"[5] was its title and the first post was, "please will anyone speak to about anything to me." For the next ten years, that thread grew to over 2000 pages, with people joining in and commenting, and many just watching. For many years, that post, now a famous internet phenomenon, topped the Google results for "I am lonely," which means that people accessed it for the simplest reason — that they were looking for help, and without even thinking about it did what is habitual, what is easy: type a search query without expecting a solution, really. As a way to preoccupy themselves. And then they found this post, and its nearness and simplicity and unexpected circumstances. It's another moment of optimism: a sign that even if technology does not always suit our — human — needs, we somehow make do.

5 → Ethan Chiel, "Where the Internet Goes to Be Lonely," in *WNYC*, accessed July 17, 2017, http://www.wnyc.org/story/where-the-internet-goes-to-be-lonely/.

butter knife:
facebook → Giulio Vacchiano

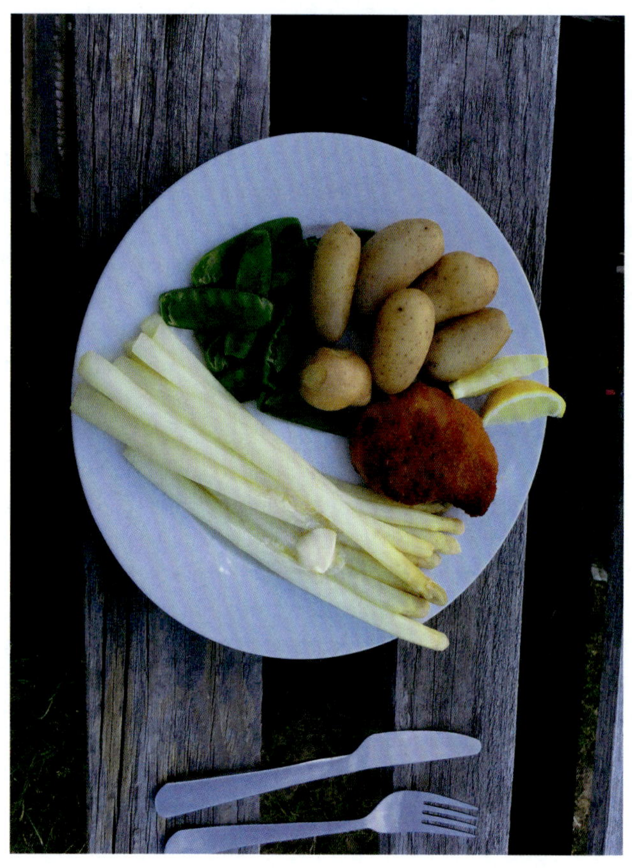

A meal.

my name's giulio vacchiano. i'm a food critic living and working in cologne. my work is writing funny texts on facebook and most people don't notice i'm serious. i thought it'd be a good idea to shoot off a few basic things at an imaginary unbiased new (english-speaking) reader at *warehouse.industries*: writing texts on facebook is a real nuisance. the main reason is you can't help being influenced by the likes. whenever i write an article and it gets five likes, i get into a fetal position under my desk and try to convince myself it's not because everyone subconsciously hates me and i'm just stupid and shallow. then of course i start writing articles that'll get me more likes, although i feel even more stupid and shallow, because it's always the especially stupid and bad articles from some kind of everyman's perspective that get the most likes. there are so many boring people on facebook and they spend most of the time there, but everyone there automatically gets a little dumber and more annoying. i'd say it's because most of them are friends with their relatives on facebook and you have to deal with the family version of everyone. it's like going out with your friends and their moms or boring cousins come along, and you can immediately imagine what kind of conversations you get, or what the level of humor is. actually, it would bother me less if the moms and cousins wouldn't like me so much. they really appreciate me. is it ok if it causes a lump in my throat?

An Essay on the German Forest →

In the Open with *terra0* → Pujan Karambeigi and Tabea Rossol

O, broad valleys, O heights,
O, beautiful, green woods,
Devoted place
Of my desires and sorrows!
Out there, in constant betrayal,
Pounds the tawdry mart.
Draw, once more, around me
Your canopy of green![1]

1 → Joseph Von Eichendorff, *Farewell*, accessed August 18, 2017, http://www.poemswithoutfrontiers.com/Abschied.html.

Driving out of Berlin: nothing happens. When leaving the city, the East appears. Correction: it was already there. It is 12.34 pm. A few notes from the tattered booklet: the gaze can be endless, loses itself in the scenery (associations with Northern Germany, although back there fields and forests are woven into each other—here they grow more separate). We drive by: brutalist social housing complexes, hardware stores, tree nurseries, beverage stores. We read: 'Hellweg,' we read 'Baumschule Scheerer,' 'BMW Autohandel.' Forgot to take pictures (in the future: have the camera ready).

Eichendorff: "But in Nature, in the dreams of the loneliness of the forest, as in the labyrinth of man's breast, slumbers since the dawn of time, a wonderful, everlasting song, a bound, enchanted Beauty, whose salvation is the poet's deed."[2]

2 → Joseph Von Eichendorff, *Zur Geschichte des Dramas* (Leipzig: Brockhaus, 1854), 418.

Eichendorff and the forest: the forest is a place of longing, of homesickness. The "canopy of green" is the numinous 'Other,' but also a place of self-discovery and—invention. In so far as the depth of the dark forest mirrors the "labyrinth of mankind's breast," the German Forest is a place for possible self-observation.

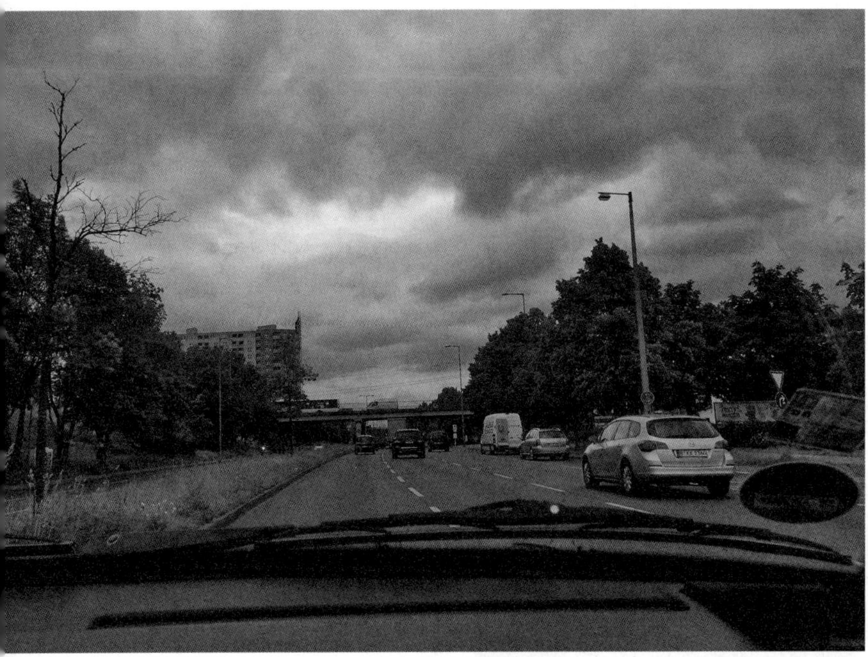

Leaving Berlin.

Not simply any kind of self-observation: the forest is a cryptogram.[3] One has to learn to read it. A ciphertext, only decipherable by the poet. Eichendorff assembles various symbols in this cryptogram. They repeat themselves and constantly appear within his poetry. The forest as symbolic space, as text whose vocabulary is the carrier of possible self-observation and self-awareness.

3 → Oskar Seidlin, "Eichendorffs symbolische Landschaft" in *Eichendorff Heute*, ed. Oskar Seidlin, 218–241, 219.

Eichendorff's literature on 'the German forest' is written in confrontation with direct perception. The romantic projection surface forest, the almost mystical other existing in oneself had to be immediately seen and observed, the 'Waldeinsamkeit' (loneliness of the forest) had to be felt, experienced. Poetry, the qualitative translation of the immediately witnessed/experienced into the linear form of a text, allows a gaze on the 'German subject'. The texts of the poet searching for herself are to be found amid the forest, surrounded by the words of the woods.

Driving to the coordinates 52°27'39.8 N 13°50'22.9 E takes about an hour. Promptly we find ourselves in the woods. This wood carries the number 78 and 79 (Note: inquire about the meaning of this). We're standing right in the middle of it. Around us: trees, birds, leaves, a bit of rubbish, small patches of grass, a perch, all surrounded by a fence. Do you feel weird? This forest is special, different than the ones around it: it is observing itself.

terra0 is the name of the forest in which we stand with our smartphone cameras and our notepad. At the moment, it is still in a contractual relation with the three project-initiators Paul Seidler, Paul Kolling, and Max Hampshire. How does one stand in a contractual relation to a forest? One that observes itself to become (or already is?) an NHA (Non-Human-Actor).

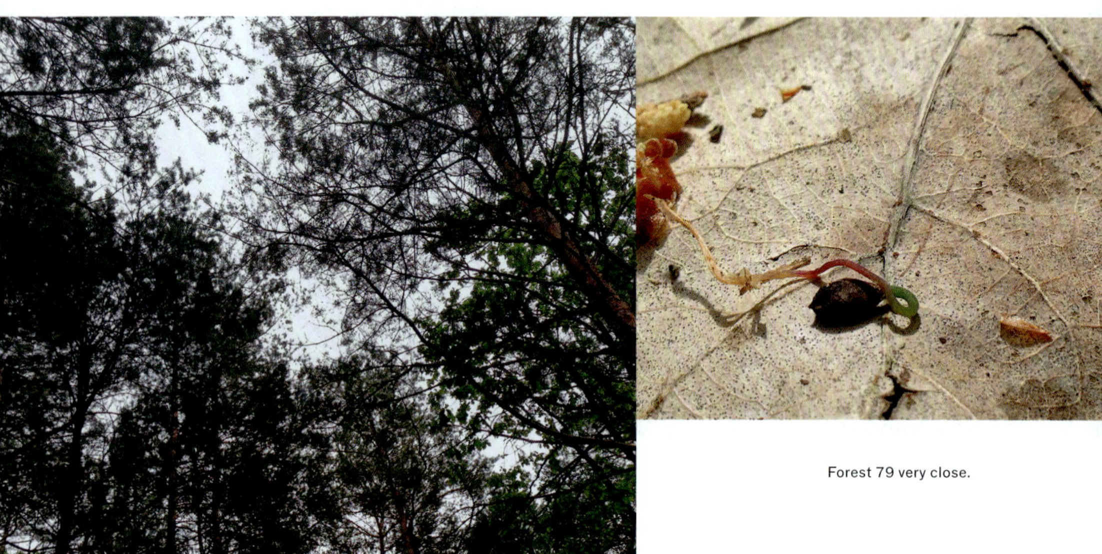

Forest 78 from below.

Forest 79 very close.

The three artists acquired the forest in Brandenburg from its leaseholder. One tenth of a hectare, which they are writing over to *terra0* via a smart contract.[4]

Through the combination of a blockchain-algorithm and a smart contract, *terra0* becomes able to sell licenses of itself. With these licenses, or "wood-tokens," the forest controls how much of itself is to be sold for forestry use. With the benefits, the forest buys itself back, or rather it buys shares from its stockholders (the project initiators). As soon as it has bought all the options, the forest becomes proprietor of and sole shareholder of itself, basically an autonomous agent.[5]

The envisaged autonomy of *terra0* is rendered possible through self-observation. The data feeding the algorithm is generated via remote-sensing: Drones, programmed to fly over the forest in regular intervals, taking satellite pictures of it. These satellite images, *terra0*'s self-portraits, are then to be analyzed. Spaces ready

4 → For further details see Paul Seidler, Paul Kolling, and Max Hampshire, "Terra0 Concept Paper," accessed July 01, 2017, https://terra0.org/assets/pdf/ terra0_white_paper_2016.pdf.

5 → Paul Seidler, Paul Kolling, and Max Hampshire, "Terra0 Concept Paper," accessed July 01, 2017, http://book. terra0.org/.

for clearing that would not endanger the tree population are defined by calculating structures: An adaptive feedback-system investigating itself via precise quantification. If trees show signs of disease or age they can easily and directly be felled by a tree clearing company. However, never shall all trees be felled at once so that the forest would not be a forest anymore (and for instance become a meadow). *terra0* is designed to remain true to itself.

Finding oneself in order to remain true to oneself no longer functions along Eichendorff's cryptograms. The forest is no longer Eichendorff's one-dimensional text, searching itself in the circumjacent abysmally dark 'other.' It is no longer the alphabet of the 'soul' through which human perception can be read. When "digital computers send out sounds or images, whether to a so-called human-machine interface or not, they internally work only with endless strings of bits."[6] We have reached dimension 0: bits and bytes. *terra0* discovers itself as a sum, as a dynamic plain of points. Observation is no longer a fumbling, auditory, or optical matter. It does not relate to a material to be decrypted, the cryptogram. Rather, it functions as pure calculus. Thus, remote sensing does not really generate images. Instead it generates numeral strings. Like Eichendorff discovered words of his own, laid out on paper in his *Waldeinsamkeit*, the now autonomous blockchain-algorithm-forest observes itself calculating. With a forest as a numeral plain, self-observation means numbers watching other numbers.

We are still standing in *terra0*, number 78 and 79, a Brandenburg forest, one hour from Berlin. They remain the only numbers we encounter in the green vault.

6 → Friedrich A. Kittler, *Optische Medien*, trans.editors (Berlin: Merve Verlag, 1999), 316.

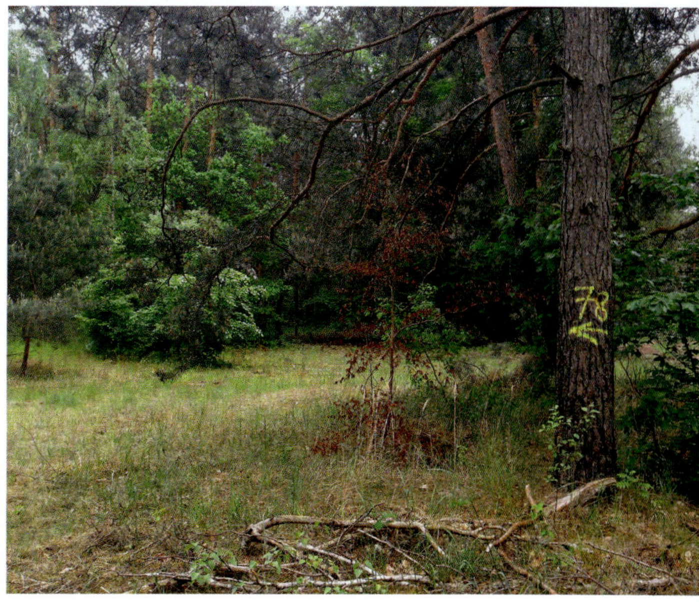

Forest 78.

adobe →

adobe →

Drying individually, then assembling into distinctive collectivity: adobe is the oldest material for building constructions. A composite made from earth and organic material that can take nearly any shape, as well as a mediator due to its thermal properties. Adobe allows control of the inside by insulating against the fluctuations of the outside. The inside stays cool when it is hot and warm when it is cold: permeability traded off for stability to attain the assemblage.

Why I Stopped Calling Things Digital → On Metaphors as Obstacles → Rafael Dernbach

A short glance at today's job market shows that we live in a digital age. Companies look for digital managers, digital designers or simply heads of digital. Certainly, this use of the term 'digital' has little to do with its original meaning: the representation of information in binary code, in ones and zeros. What we mostly mean when we call something digital is that it involves computers. Yet, in a society where computers affect most parts of life, is it still sensible to describe something as digital? Or has the term, in fact, become an obstacle in discussions? The following is the story why I stopped calling things digital. It is also a text on the politics of metaphors.

Recently, I sat at a table with a group of hackers, technologists and researchers from the humanities and social sciences. We were discussing the name for a new research group that we wanted to form. To my surprise, all proposals including the term digital were met with outspoken skepticism from the hackers and technologists. One of them expressed his doubts very vividly: "It is not that I am against the title, I don't care about it and I know that many people will not care about it. I am not even annoyed by it, I will not bother to read on, if I see a meaningless title." I was surprised by this fierce resistance to a term that seemed intuitive to me. And I became curious why 'digital' was such a red flag for exactly those people, who are most immersed in the subtleties of what I referred to as digitalization.

I could see how the term 'digital' and its noun 'digitalization' were sloppy, encompassing a broad range of phenomena, from online marketing to the storage of data, from the recording of music to computer generated images. But, I had an intuition when using them, namely, the intuition to describe a transformation triggered by the use of computers. And digitalization, the totality of these transformations is real. We all have a story how an app or an online service radically simplified or complicated an aspect of our everyday life. And we have witnessed the transformation of entire industries through the introduction of computers. So, why was there such a resistance against the concept in our group? After our discussion, I asked one of the technologists to explain his skepticism in detail. This technologist was Palle Dahlstedt, a professor of computer science and a musical composer who teaches at the University of Gothenburg in Sweden and at Aalborg University in Denmark.

"The word digital strictly only means that something is represented in discrete steps in contrast to continuous analogue signals," Dahlstedt explained to me. He continued to describe how most phenomena perceptible to human beings can be represented digitally today, which is particularly true for acoustic phenomena. What makes digital representation so attractive in contrast to analogue representation is that digital objects can be replicated without loss. A clone of a digital object does not display any difference to its original, which is not the case for analogue representations. So far the term 'digital' did not seem problematic to me, but Dahlstedt continued: "A lot of things that we associate with the word digital are, however, also possible with non-digital means. And a lot of things that most people think are analog are really digital. For example all writing is digital, and has always been."

In fact, digital signals can be represented with light, with hydraulic pressure, with mechanical gears, or with voltages. As most people, I imagined something electronic when talking about digital representations. But not only are there analogue computers that can be both mechanical or electronical, there are also digital computers that can operate non-electronically. An example for such non-electronic computers are the computing machines that the English mathematician Charles Babbage developed in the 19th century. Digital, it became clear to me, describes a different and a far older idea than the processes of an electronic computer. This misunderstanding seemed also to be at the core of Dahlstedt's skepticism: "the term has become all and nothing, sometimes it means 'electronic' sometimes it means there is a computer involved, sometimes it means it has to do with the internet." Dahlstedt sees the reason for this in a lack of understanding by a majority of people in the humanities and the broader public for the terms of computer science, "terms are used loosely, metaphorically, and finally lose their value."

When I asked him about an example from his own field for such a loss of explanatory value, he told me that in his work with electronic music digitality is not a crucial parameter: "Many of my tools are digital, many are analogue and many are hybrid." He added that recording can be digital or analogue, too. And to complicate things even more, certain acoustic signals can be discreet and therefore digital in time, but not in magnitude and vice versa. It became clear to me that the categories 'digital' and 'analogue' fail to address what is driving Dahlstedt's production process. He insisted, "it makes no sense to talk about digital as opposed to non-digital. It is like saying that a CD with the Berliner Philharmoniker is computer music, because there were computers involved in the making of it. Of course, it is digital music, in a way, but that is not the crucial parameter. It is a digital way of storing the music — it was analog until it reached a certain machine in the chain, and it is analog when it reaches our ears." For Dahlstedt, a far more relevant parameter than if something is digital or analogue is the way one interacts with one's tools. Rather than distinguishing digital from analogue objects or practices, the particular methods used and their intentions matter. What kind of computation is involved in the composing? What forms of abstraction are applied? What data structures are used? To subsume these questions under the term digital would not only miss the point etymologically, but also would create an obstacle in practice.

And yet, Dahlstedt does not relativize the new possibilities that increasing computational power holds: "With electronic digital computers, we can do things that we could not do before, mostly because of the orders of magnitude of increase in speed and memory over the last decades. Gradually we have pushed our thinking, and our tools, and the cognitive models of the tools to be able to imagine new processes we can do to data — but the difference is only in terms of orders of magnitude in [storage] space and [processing] time." Dahlstedt emphasized that the modes of computation are nothing new. What has changed is mainly the speed in which information can be computed and the storage space and, thus, the amount of information that can be computed. Dahlstedt stated that "all methods, for example, are well-defined and could have been done one hundred years ago, but they were unimaginable. Any computation, search, data manipulation, calculation, was in theory possible before the age of computers. But since it would have taken unthinkable amounts of time and storage space to compute, it was unimaginable." For Dahlstedt this means that our thinking develops with the tools. But he also insists that our thinking does not become more complicated. Rather than that, we as humans deal with higher levels of abstraction thanks to the increase in speed and size of computers.

After our conversation, the term digital did not longer feel so intuitive. I started to wonder about my impulse to call things digital and realized the term often had not added much to my conversations. A digital manager is just a manager, a digital designer just a designer. So why was I bothering to add the term at all? Because calling something 'digital' implies a narrative of a disruption. It implies a future with shining new things and ways of living. More than an explanatory I used it as an aesthetic category. By calling things digital I was taking part in this meta-narrative. From Dahlstedt's perspective the term had just become meaningless and annoying. But it was dawning on me that 'digital' was more of hype than explanation, a metaphor that had detached itself from the fields of its origin so much that it now was meaningless. I wondered if 'digital' had even become an obstacle for understanding how computers interact with our lives. Could the term even foreclose insights about our relationships with information technologies?

A provocative essay by the psychologist Robert Epstein came to my mind. Its title is also its premise: "Your Brain Does Not Process Information and it is Not a Computer." In the essay, Epstein criticizes the dominant framework of cognitive neuroscience, namely, that human brains are information-processing networks. Epstein points to a range of misconceptions that come with the metaphor of the human brain as a computer. He elegantly debunks, for instance, the idea that consciousness might become downloadable at some distant time in the future. Epstein reminds his colleagues and readers that they operate with a model and, thus, with a metaphor. He argues that this metaphor has become an obstacle framing many problems in neuroscience as unexplainable. What I really liked about Dahlstedt's explanations was that they pointed to the historical continuities of computational methods.

At the same time they were conscious of the transformative potential that their development holds. All these nuances are veiled by a narrative of disruption that comes with the term 'digitalization.'

When calling something digital I was buying into this hype, rather than understanding a particular technological context, its histories, and implications. I was focusing on the new, while bracketing out where the new had its beginnings and in which directions it might drift. Just in the case of the brain as a computer, digitalization as a disruption is a faulty metaphor. As Dahlstedt described, even our ancestors relied heavily on digital media, if we count writing as one of them. Describing something as digital frames the computer as a technology without history. It desensitizes us for the historical conditions and human agencies that have contributed to the development of a particular technology. But how could we now imagine a term, that takes into account the continuities of computational methods and still describes the transformations we are facing today?

It might seem to you that this is a call for more precise terms. After all, careless imprecision seems to have turned 'digital' first into a useless metaphor and later into an obstacle for understanding. But rather than calling for more precision, I would propose a more careful imprecision. The theory of epistemic objects by the German philosopher of science Hans Jörg Rheinberger shows that certain types of imprecision are as necessary as the conceptual clarity. His theory also might help us to find terms that embrace both continuity and transformation. Rheinberger's research examines how new ideas come into existence in science. In contrast to the idea of a divine inspiration or divine disruption of individual researchers or a technology, Rheinberger argues that science generates new knowledge by iteration. A single experiment without its context remains meaningless. But if experiments are repeated, adjusted and contextualized to a body of knowledge new ideas come into existence. Rheinberger calls this not-yet-formulated body of knowledge of a discipline its "epistemic object." Epistemic objects are produced through an experimental system, the totality of all research technologies, experiments, instruments, and infrastructures of a discipline. They are per definition imprecise at first. That means that they are not entirely knowable as they are the imagined knowledge for which an experimental system strives. Accordingly, an epistemic object has to be precise enough to generate knowledge and imprecise enough to incorporate unexpected results of experiments. Rheinberger's theory shows that we should be carefully imprecise with our terms and that we should value iteration more than disruption. If the 'digital' is an epistemic object, we were not only blind for its continuities, but also carelessly imprecise with it. What could better epistemic objects when trying to make sense of the transformations that computers have brought to so many domains of life? I don't have an answer to this question. However, I have an intuition that these terms will be as hybrid as our production processes have become today. After all computing is not a phenomenon limited to computers. For our research group we ended up with the title *Cybernetic Symbioses: Shaping Human-Technology Futures*. It involved enough imprecision to embrace the social impact and imaginaries of technologies. And it was sufficiently discreet to clearly communicate the merging of ideas from two systems, namely informational studies (cybernetics) and life sciences (symbiosis). This is when I stopped calling things digital.

On the Boxes at the Margins →

Cornelius Heimstädt

One day I was riding through the hood, pumping the latest Dr. Steelbutt track, *Venus* (currently suffering from a limited number of views on YouTube). I was entirely lost in the Dr.'s outstanding rhetoric and his flow—smooth like butter, when, suddenly, I spotted a bunch of douchebags staring at stupid red plastic boxes, as if they were the latest design breakthrough. With sweaty faces, they jumped from one leg to the other screaming something like "Bauhaus-Shit, Bauhaus-Shit." "Go to church!" I yelled out of the window of my low-riding vehicle but they didn't get my "dirty south" cross-reference and started crying. This irritating encounter kept me thinking. Why is it that all of a sudden people are fancying boring boxes? After 666 sleepless nights, I cut all my social relations, sold my low-riding vehicle and delved into Babylonia's holy culture of unboxing boxes.

"In the moving box, it seems that the transitory has come to itself and has come to the end of history."[1] Even though I still don't really know what Claus Pias means with this beautiful description of the moving box, I scratched it into my forearm, as a mantra to guide me through this unpredictable journey. To be honest, I stumbled across this quote while reading Klose and Marcrum's study on shipping containers.[2] Just like Pias, the authors conceive of the shipping container as a form of thought and order that extends far beyond its material 'corpus.' The big steel box forms a socio-technical hybrid that merges human and non-human capacities of moving beyond time and space. In boxes of any kind "all histories are reconfigured with each load. What lands inside [them] depends on chance, the organizational and logisti-cal competency of its packer, and, ultimately, the standardized volume and capacity of the box itself."[3] Taking a closer look at the box that prompted this journey, variously referred to as 'Euro

1 → Claus Pias, "Wer sein Leben im Griff hat, kann einpacken: Der Umzugskarton als Medium der Selbstinventur," trans. editors, in *Frankfurter Allgemeine Zeitung* (Frankfurt), May 05, 1999.

2 → Alexander Klose, *The Container Principle: How a Box Changes the Way We Think* (Cambridge: MIT Press, 2015).

3 → Klose, *The Container Principle*, 152.

stacking container,' 'Euro container,' or 'Euro container perforated' in a more technical jargon, not only its volume but also its material, its weight, or its perforation turn out to be a complex interplay of heterogeneous and overlapping standards. If Timmermanns and Epstein's description of standards as rendering "the world equivalent across cultures, time, and geography"[4] is correct, where is the equivalence between the douchebags staring at boxes and, let's say, unpaid guest workers in the greenhouses of Alberia? Or, between the douchebags and the monotonous everyday work at Harry Brot?

To get my head straight, I wanted to get a grasp of one of the places where boxes are brought into existence. However, the sacred halls of polypropylene injection molding were impossible to access—they remain one of the greatest questions of (non-)humankind. In his writings about an exhibition of plastic objects that took place in Paris in 1957, Roland Barthes predicted this almost mythological dissolution of the origins of plastic. He, like me, experiences the birth of plastic artefacts as evading from the knowing subject, "[a]t one end, raw, telluric matter, at the other, the finished human object; and between these two extremes, nothing; nothing but transit."[5] In this regard, it seems as if boxes emerge as fully functional objects from nowhere, ready to enlighten the non-standardized wilderness we dare to call reality. If there were such thing as standards-porn, the "technological script"[6] of the box would trigger miraculous wet dreams, folding qualities such as 'hygienic flawlessness,' 'stackability,' 'suitability for dishwashers,' 'DIN 55423-compliance,' or 'compliance with automated logistics' into timeless matter.

As my desire to observe the birth of the box was turned into a subliminal erotic experience, I decided to continue my journey at what I expected to be a pleasure garden for standardized food distribution—a Berlin based fruit and vegetable wholesale store. Analogously to Sven Markwart, the wholesale store awakens one hour after midnight. In order not to raise attention, I crafted myself a decent camouflage suit out of boxes. From a strategic hideaway in a weeping willow next to the trading halls, I jumped on a forklift truck that passed by. The clueless forklift carried me through the barrier-free canyons of storage, like a gondolier carries love through the channels of Venice. Exotic fruits from far away countries in cardboard boxes with colorful slogans, stacked up to the ceiling. Asparagus from Belitz in disposable polyethylene bags, spread out to the horizon. Exquisite mushrooms and selected herbs carefully stored in humming cooling units. Sweet, sweet strawberries in synthetic bowls to be thrown away right after being emptied. An uncountable number of everlasting interfaces filled with ephemeral delights. However, my desire to observe my beloved Euro container in the field was not fulfilled. Its strength, the durability of its standardized external dimensions, turns out to be a weakness at this site of semi-automated logistics. Its affordance of non-disposability renders the Euro container meaningless in this particular world of accelerated flux.

Full of grief, I returned to Vienna, to enjoy a bittersweet Apérol Spritz in the soothing evening sun of Yppenplatz. With tears in my eyes I fell asleep. The next morning, I was woken by the bustling noises of Brunnenmarkt—

4 → Stefan Timmermans and Steven Epstein, "A World of Standards but not a Standard World: Toward a Sociology of Standards and Standardization," in *Annual Review of Sociology 36*, no. 1 (2010): 69–89, 69.

5 → Roland Barthes, *Mythologies*, trans. Annette Lavers, (New York: Hill and Wang, 1972), 97.

6 → Madeline Akrich, "The De-Scription of Technical Objects," ed. W. E. Bijker and J. Law., in *Shaping technology/ building society: Studies in sociotechnical change*, 205–24 (Cambridge: MIT Press, 1992).

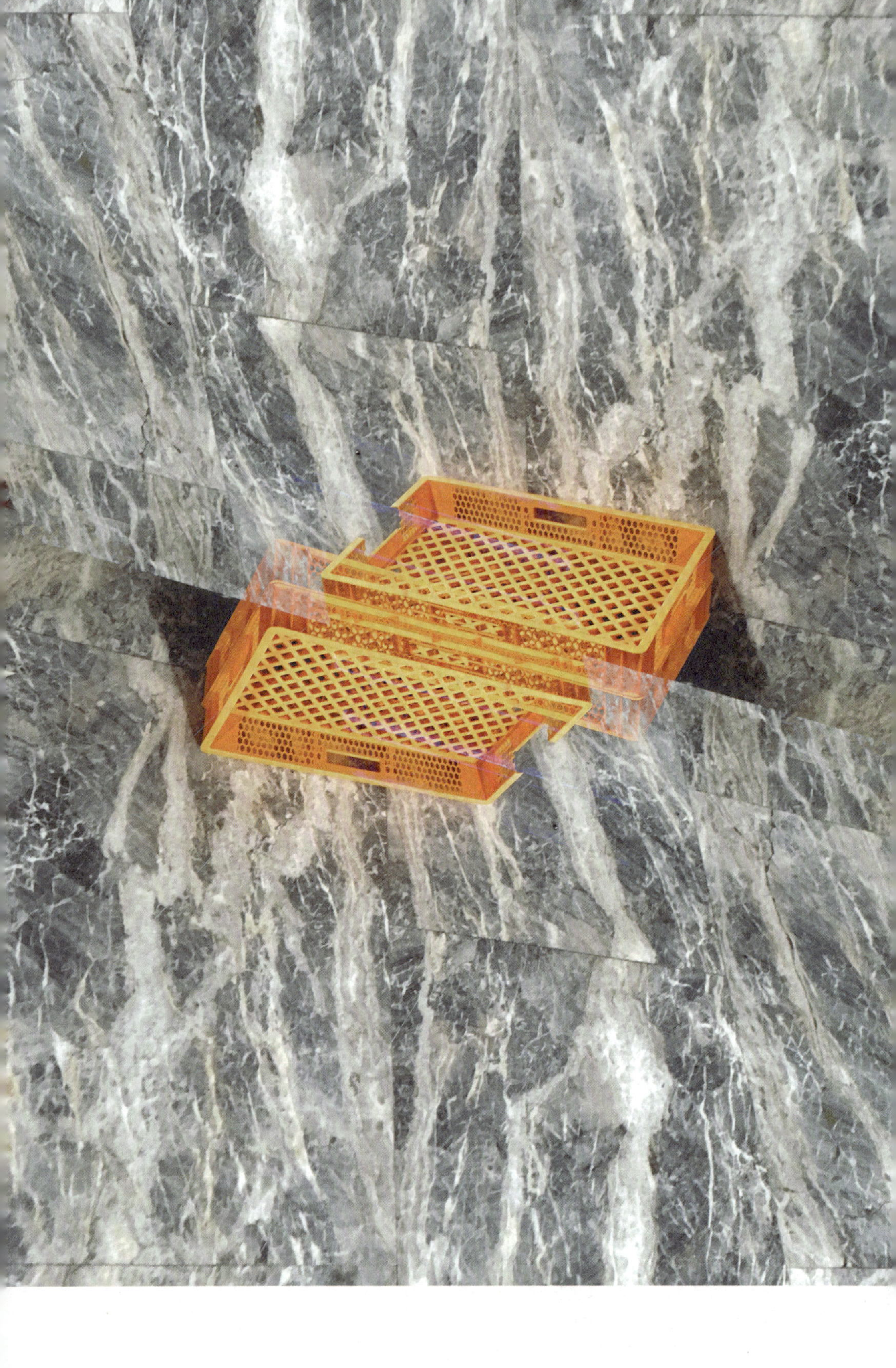

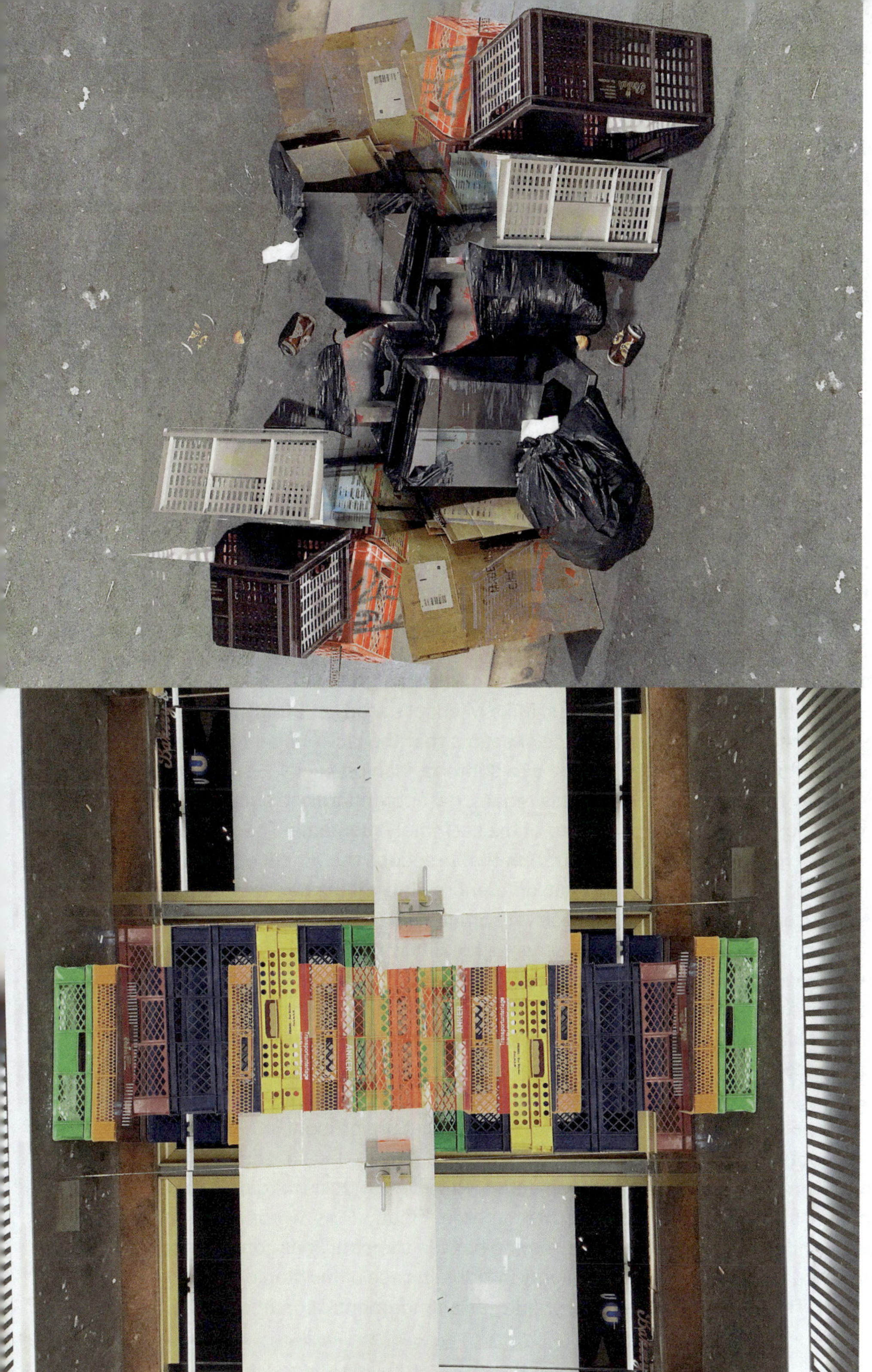

a daily market taking place next to my night's lodging. Researchers need to eat, so I ordered a Club International Toast (C. I. Toast), consisting of toast, bacon, spinach, feta, and a fried egg. The toast arrived. Then it got stuck in my throat. I couldn't believe what I saw. It seemed as if I had finally arrived at a place where boxes and people live out the post-quantifiable dream of standardization. Whole market stalls built out of flipped and stacked boxes. Two vertically positioned boxes facing each other while carrying a wooden plank—a perfectly aligned table. Laughing children sitting in boxes re-interpreted as low-riding vehicles. Boxes arranged as if they were meant to advertise fresh vegetables, containing nothing but useless hi-fi crap. And, you won't believe it, I even saw a good-looking-soon-to-become-Columbia-University-student, with dark curly hair and circular designer glasses passionately making out with one of the boxes (I'm currently editing the video for a major release on YouTube).

As Theodore Porter puts it, quantification which is implicit to statistics and standards is a "technology of distance" which "minimizes the need for intimate knowledge and personal trust."[7] Quantification is thus deemed to be successful in stabilizing itself for professional groups with feeble authority—for example bureaucrats—to respond to social and political demands for objectivity and accountability, particularly in situations involving uncertainty. However, observing the box at the Brunnenmarkt, it seems that this standardized stability is accompanied by a co-existing world of implicit fixes. Mike Michael's study of 3D printing[8] strongly resonates with this account. Hence, it seems that the lack of plasticity that is inherent to the box is accompanied by a subterranean plasticity—an emergent necessity for reconfiguration. In this regard, my unstandardized encounters crucially touch upon the 'ontological politics' of the seemingly mundane. There is no essential reality of mundanity or standardization that precedes the practices the box is entangled with at the sites. Instead, different realities of the box are found, affirmed, realized, or destroyed through these very practices—opening up different worlds of relevance. Annemarie Mol stresses, "[i]f reality is multiple, it is also political."[9] Even though she is concerned with the multiplicity of atherosclerosis, taking into account the ontological politics of the box, a similar question emerges: "the question of what kinds of politics to engage in: one of setting standards or another that, convinced of messiness of the nonconforming world we live in, seeks better ways of handling it."[10] Given this, I am not talking about conscious going-to-a-demonstration sort of politics. I am talking about the realities that are brought into being despite the scripts that render their existence negligible. The surface of standardized boxes may seem flat, uniform, dead, or objective. However, at their margins, worlds of friction, hybridity, life, and subjectivity emerge. Finally, Pias' words make so much sense. Indeed, it seems, that in the moving box the transitory has come to itself. However, there is no end of the history in sight. In case of the stupid red box there is beauty. The beauty of precarious hybridity as a fundamental condition of life.

7 → Theodore M. Porter, *Trust in Numbers: The Pursuit of Objectivity in Science and Public Life* (Princeton, NJ: Princeton University Press, 1996), xi.

8 → Mike Michael, "Process and plasticity: Printing, prototyping, and the prospects of plastic," in *Accumulation: the Material Politics of Plastic*, 30–47 (London: Routledge, 2013).

9 → Annemarie Mol, *The Body Multiple: Ontology in Medical Practice* (Durham: Duke University Press, 2002), 7.

10 → Mol, *The Body Multiple*, 100.

The Second God, Golem, and Chess Regarding the Critique of Technical Reason → Katerina Krtilova

Almost without questioning, digital technology is nowadays declared to be the technological condition of our present—be it of the everyday, of culture, of science, or of politics and economy.[1] Everything seems somewhat traversed by digital technology … from large infrastructures to diet or dating-apps, which record bodily and emotional processes (and stir them). We are all constantly part of computer systems, much more than just 'users.' On the other hand, these systems remain invisible for the most part and are able to insert themselves unnoticed into the everyday—into social interaction and bodies as in the idea of 'ubiquitous computing.' The disappearance of media with their usage, a basic figure of media theories, becomes the program for the arranging of digital environments.

The blurring of limits between nature, culture, and technology, body and technology, between the symbolic and the material, but also between different cultures in a 'digital culture' poses new challenges to a critical reflection of our cultural and, among others, technical conditions. In the following text, I would like to emphasize an author that would probably belong to the grey fore-ages of technological innovation from our current standpoint of technological innovation: Norbert

1 → Erich Hörl, *Die technologische Bedingung: Beiträge zur Beschreibung der technischen Welt* (Berlin: Suhrkamp, 2011).

Wiener, one of the fathers of cybernetics—the science of controlling and regulating machines, living organisms, and social systems. I hope that precisely because he stands at the beginning of the digital transformation, his 1964 book *God & Golem Incorporated* can help lend a different and foreign gaze to our thoughts on the matter.

Within and without the chess board

The confrontation and entanglement of man and machine, which preoccupies Wiener, is finely illustrated by one scene realizing his thought experiment 30 years after *God & Golem*: in 1997 the former chess world champion Gary Kasparov loses a regular chess game against the IBM Computer.

The turmoil around this symbolic event is barely intelligible nowadays, for a chess program can now run on a smartphone. Even if today, 'intelligent' technologies have become common—the question of machinic or artificial intelligence remains actual. Nowadays, computers can also beat humans in the complex game of Go^2 in such a way that even the Chinese Go Master Ke Jie suggested it to be a sort of a "Go-God."[3] The point here is not rhetorical exaggeration—the computer really learns by itself and develops other strategies than humans. The so-called 'deep learning neural networks' allow the recognition of patterns within highly complex formations which are not easily decomposable. The 'independence' of learning remains, of course, limited, as deep learning relies on given models, it must be told what should be recognized in the entered sensor-data. The computer can however find other patterns and there is no way of knowing how it comes to such results. Just like the chess program of the 90s, deep learning is reaching a limit, which pivots the sovereignty of dealing with technology towards the phantasmatic: what happens within and with a machine smarter than its creator, and not just faster or stronger? Is the intelligence with which the machine was built just an effect of technology, an automatic procedure better realized by machines than humans? Or, does the intelligence of the machine reach deeper than the one of the human?

The mathematician Norbert Wiener remains rather calm in 1964: computers can only play games for which it is clearly and explicitly defined how the game can be won according to certain given rules. A chess game like in Caroll's *Alice in Wonderland*, in which the pawns march through the board, would, for instance, not make any sense for a computer, just like playing with puppets. No human could be beat in this regard. With chess, a certain playing field of the encounter between human and machine is covered, in which the 'intelligence' of the human stands directly opposed to the that of the computer, allowing for them

2 → Regarding the phenomenon of the man-machine relation see Tim Othold, "(In)stabile Technik. Über kreative Algorithmen und mahnende Regenschirme," in *Prekäre Existenzen*, ed. Johannes Bennke, Johanna Seifert, Martin Siegler (Munich, Wilhelm Fink, 2018).

3 → Ke Jie quoted in Christian Stöcker, "Ein Gott braucht keine Lehrmeister," trans. editors, *Der Spiegel*, accessed November 29, 2017, last modified October 29, 2017 http://www.spiegel.de/wissenschaft/technik/kuenstliche-intelligenz-gott-braucht-keine-lehrmeister-kolumne a-1175130.html.

to be compared. However, this playing field is a room with fixed rules and conditions of action, in which one decides what is a win or a loss.

I hold the following three aspects characterizing Computer Chess to be particularly telling for the digital-technological condition:

1. The fixed rules and the "pre-decided decisiveness."[4] An aspect strongly highlighted by Dieter Mersch: computers follow a mathematical logic of decision-making which forecloses the undecidable and the incalculable to begin with. Even when this has to do with computing images, sounds, gestures or faces—it all takes place within the realm of what can be mathematically modelled.[5]

2. The 'superficiality' of a game of Chess or Go. The rules of chess, as one can claim with Vilém Flusser, can neatly be transformed into processing—the 'body' of a chess game can be abstracted almost entirely (except for a certain visual order, which can be designed in several ways). This step of abstraction, according to Flusser, allows for the possibility of writing: "the following text, printed in yellow, would not bear any other meaning."[6] Switches in digital technology, 0 and 1 as states are referred to by Flusser as "zerodimensional"[7]—completely un-sensual. In his essay *Schach,* Flusser turns the usual gaze upon chess around and focusses on the aesthetics and materiality of the chess game. The towers (rooks) are reminiscent of Moorish towers in Andalusia: "The wooden being of chess, such as the patterns and rings of the tree from which the pawns are carved" changes one's position towards the game, as well as towards the figures of king, queen, pawn, etc. which fight a war.[8] This brings a depth to the game going beyond deep learning—which is akin to the flatness of the old machine-learning, the necessary reduction of the field, already leaving out the recognition of objects on images.

3. The competition as primal scene of machine intelligence. "There may be great doubt as to how to win the game, but no doubt whatever as to whether it has been won or lost."[9] The logical necessity for a decision might connect to the capitalist sociopolitical economy and its logic of competition—thereby generating effects, in which fatal game situations arise. Wiener's example of such a situation is—as it was 1964—atomic war. He warns of the "magic of modern automatization"[10] and the state of mind of the "gadget worshippers,"[11] which do not pay attention to the automatic processes following a very clear logic at the heart of computers. Their decisions are in some sense blind. Wiener describes this 'magic' through a story of W. W. Jacobs, *The Monkey's Paw,* in which a magic monkey-hand grants three wishes. A family comes to process said monkey-hand, but is warned that the third wish is always death. The first wish is possessing 200 Pounds. Someone knocks at their door and tells them of the death of their son, freeing an insurance sum of 200 Pounds. Second wish: the son should be revived. Someone knocks at the door—and their son enters as living-dead. The third wish, as foretold, is the death of the son.

4 → Dieter Mersch, "Turing-Test oder das 'Fleisch' der Maschine," trans. editors, in *Körper des Denkens: neue Positionen der Medienphilosophie*, ed. Lorenz Engel et al. (Munich: W. Fink, 2013), 12.

5 → Dieter Mersch, *Ordo ab chao—Order from Noise* trans. editors (Zurich: Diaphanes, 2013), 61.

6 → Vilém Flusser, "Auf dem Weg zum Unding," trans. editors, in *Medienkultur*, ed. Vilém Flusser (Frankfurt: Fischer, 1997), 22.

7 → Flusser, "Auf dem Weg zum Unding," 126.

8 → Vilém Flusser, "Schach," trans. editors, in *Dinge und Undinge phänomenologische Skizzen*, ed. Michael Krüger, trans. editors (2011), 57.

9 → Norbert Wiener, *God & Golem, Inc., A Comment on Certain Points Where Cybernetics Impinges on Religion* (Cambridge: MIT Press, 1966), 25.

10 → Wiener, *God & Golem, Inc., A Comment on Certain Points Where Cybernetics Impinges on Religion*, 52.

11 → Wiener, *God & Golem, Inc., A Comment on Certain Points Where Cybernetics Impinges on Religion*, 53.

The second god or:
the magic of computation

At the end of the most famous version of the Golem lies: death and destruction. Humanity unleashes forces it cannot control. But how does humanity even acquire such forces? In this context, it is not a matter of matters, but of the potential of cybernetic 'magic'—connected by Wiener with the magic of the Golem-Legend.

As was already apparent in Wiener, this magic is a mathematical one. In Flusser's sense, one can observe that machines can play through numerical (or alphanumerical) thoughts "better than humans, because they play better (faster and with less errors) than they do."[12] Such thinking—in numbers and symbols akin to numbers—is indeed computable and continues to grow independently of mathematical models developed 'in the mind.' The starting point of a ground breaking medial transformation: thinking is not just something occurring in the head, in the mind (to then be expressed in various ways), but is rendered possible through the corresponding symbols which allows for the system of written calculation and geometry. Sybille Krämer and others have shown how even the most abstract thinking proceeds 'diagrammatically,' that is, it depends on graphic symbols and would be impossible without them.[13] Therefore, computers were not the first ones to connect processes of matter and mind—but they allow new ways of mechanization and automatization of these procedures. Calculations can also be executed alone by machines—and what might be equally troubling: they connect the symbolic order with operations in the real itself, shows Friedrich Kittler.[14] Flusser's vision of a new universe of computation, which he sketches in the 1980s, takes a similar direction: the "calculated thinking," claims Flusser, has penetrated evermore deeply into the realm of appearances:

"It has analyzed (decomposed) it, which in turn led phenomena to increasingly take on the structure of calculating thinking … There is no more mention of the "res extensa," instead, one speaks of fields of structured particle swarms. With such particles, for instance quarks, arises the question of whether they truly are particles of the world or symbols or signs of calculating thinking."[15]

In Flusser's sketch we can truly speak of a 'digital culture.' In this new universe, digital technologies entirely determine the world-relation from recognition to perception and action. Thanks to the new technologies decomposing reality and recomposing it, reality becomes freely modifiable—we note that "we form everything that we experience ourselves and we could form it differently, model in a yet undetermined sense all which we experience, and could model this differently."[16] There is no more given reality. (Human) consciousness can "itself create [out of its algorithms] concrete worlds, over which it is omnipotent,

12 → Vilém Flusser, *Für eine Philosophie der Fotografie*, trans. editors (Berlin: European Photography, 2011), 30.

13 → Sybille Krämer, "Punkt, Strich, Fläche. Von der Schriftbildlichkeit zur Diagrammatik," in *Schriftbildlichkeit*, ed. Sybille Krämer, Eva Cancik-Kirschbaum, Rainer Totzke (Berlin: Akademie 2012), 79–100.

14 → Friedrich Kittler, *Die Nacht der Substanz* (Bern: Benteli Verlag, 1989).

15 → Vilém Flusser, "Digitaler Schein," trans. editors, in *Medienkultur*, ed. Vilém Flusser (Frankfurt: Suhrkamp, 1997), 208.

16 → Vilém Flusser, in *Lob der Oberflächlichkeit*, *Für eine Phänomenologie der Medien, Schriften*, vol. 9, trans. editors, ed. Stefan Bollmann and Edith Flusser (Bensheim/Düsseldorf: Bollmann Verlag, 1995), 39/40.

because those were programmed by consciousness itself. We are creators (gods) of such worlds. We are digitizing gods."[17]

Flusser accurately gets cybernetic mathematical magic: "Cusaner once thought God may very well be omniscient, but could not know better than we know, that 1 + 1 = 2."[18]

At this point the connection with the legend of the Golem can be established, which remains rather between the lines in Wiener and others. It is established in all its clarity almost parallel to Wiener's *God & Golem Inc.* by the historian of religion Gershom Scholem: during the inauguration of a super-computer in Rehovot (Israel), for which Scholem had proposed the name of "Golem I," he holds Rabbi Löw from the Golem-Legend of Prague to be the forefather of the mathematicians Norbert Wiener and John von Neumann, who "more than anyone else have added the theoretical foundations to the kind of mathematical knowledge, that has produced the Golem of our day, the modern computer."[19]

Rabbi Löw, so claims the legend, had created the Golem in 16th century Prague with the help of cabbalist magic. In the last step, a note with the unspeakable name of god is put into its mouth, bringing the clay-creature to life. On one Shabbat however, the Rabbi forgets to take out the note, leading the Golem to rage in the Ghetto and to destroy everything around him until Rabbi Löw manages to remove the note — turning the golem back into a clump of clay.

What kind of magic is this? The cabbalists consider the world to be made in its essence by the primal elements of numbers and letters — the letters of the language of god are concentrated creative energy.[20] The mysticism of numbers and letters are closely connected in this regard. In *Sefer Yetzirah*, the book of creation (or the book of giving form), the most important text of the Kabbala for the creation of the Golem, the ten Sefirot, translated by Scholem as the "10 primal numbers," form the middle link between god and the world, between the cause of creation and its effects, as original image and, at once, as a tool for the creation of the world.[21]

Scholem points to the connection of the book of Jezira with Neopythagoreism: for neopythagoreans the number is the primal image of the world, the original thought of god, the tool of world-creation, the reason of all things. "All things of the world, claims Nikomachos are arranged by premonition and world-forming reason according to numbers: for the principle and original image of things is the number, which precedes them in thinking of the creator, solely immaterial and reachable in thought, but still the true and everlasting being...."[22] We can see the parallel to Flusser's universe of computation.[23] With the right combination of those letters, with which earth and sky were formed, the creation of man can be repeated. The true combination is of course secret. "Otherwise, every reader would be able to create a world, revive the dead, and cause miracles. Thus the order of the Tora has been hidden from all apart from God."[24]

17 → Vilém Flusser, "Rückschlag der Werkzeuge auf das Bewusstsein," trans. editors, in *Die Rache der Oberfläche: Heidegger, McLuhan, Greenberg: International Flusser Lectures*, ed. Graham Harman (Köln: Walter König, 2015), 4.

18 → Vilém Flusser, "Einbildungen," trans. editors, in *Lob der Oberflächlichkeit, Für eine Phänomenologie der Medien*, vol. 1, ed. Stefan Bollmann and Edith Flusser (Bensheim/Düsseldorf: Bollmann Verlag, 1995), 271.

19 → Gershom Scholem, "Der Golem von Prag und der Golem von Rehovot," trans. editors, in *Judaica 2* ed. Gershom Scholem (Frankfurt: Suhrkamp, 1970), 79.

20 → Scholem, "Der Golem von Prag und der Golem von Rehovot."

21 → Karl Erich Grözinger, *Jüdisches Denken: Theologie, Philosophie, Mystik* (Frankfurt: Campus, 2005).

22 → Grözinger, *Jüdisches Denken: Theologie, Philosophie, Mystik*, trans. editors, 42.

23 → And to Friedrich Kittler, who explicitly refers to the Pythagoreans.

24 → Scholem, *Zur Kabbala und ihrer Symbolik*, trans. editors (Zurich: Rhein-Verlag, 1960), 25.

In *Sefer Yetzirah* it is said: "Ten are the numbers of the ineffable Sephiroth, ten and not nine, ten and not eleven. Learn this wisdom, and be wise in the understanding of it, investigate these numbers, and draw knowledge from them, fix the design in its purity, and pass from it to its Creator seated on his throne."[25] The loss of control over the own creation, resulting in destruction, is thus caused by the human creator taking god's place. By attempting to be god, he crosses a border in interfering with creation itself, which belongs to god.

The Golem and the secret of creation

The danger of the creation of the Golem as formulated by Gershom Scholem, lets us return to the digital magic: "a successful creation of the golem, that would not only occur in the symbolic, would start the 'death of god.' The hubris of the creator would turn against God."[26] Vilém Flusser and Friedrich Kittler see the potential of new technologies in exactly this: whatever can be thought, becomes technically possible. The new realities can be created through interfering the symbolic with the Real—they are not just imaginations, images, utopias of past realities, reality itself becomes, as a matter of fact, computable.

If we follow the subtitle of Wiener's book, *"A Comment on Certain Points, where Cybernetics impinges on Religion,"* the point of questioning the motives of cybernetics through religious figures (in this case Jewish ones) also arises. Not from the standpoint of the history of religion or theology, but rather, through considering the techniques of the creation of a Golem from a philosophical perspective with particular attention to media. A hint at this shift in perspectives is given in a remark by Flusser which stands in tension with his vision of computation (which runs across his entire work):[27] technology, as is written in his philosophical autobiography, is just "one of the forms, in which man mysteriously plunges its hand into concrete reality."[28]

The creation of the Golem is in fact shaped by technology in its contemporary appearances—be they the series *Westworld* or Films such as *Ex Machina*. If we however return to the origins of the figure, technology loses its contours; magical, ritualist, technical, reflective practices interfere with one another just like theory and practice: the knowledge of the letter as "primal building materials, stones, above which creation arose" in *Sefer Yetzirah* is equally practical as it is theoretical. The book contains the "theoretic manual to the understanding of the architecture of creation," but can also serve as a "key for magical practices."[29] How this key is to be understood, let alone how it works, remains an open question or rather a secret. Scholem historically shows that there is a tradition of interpretation and use of the mysti-

25 → William Wynn Westcott, *Sepher Yetzirah: The Book of Formation and the 32 Paths of Wisdom* (London: Theosophical Publishing Society, 1893), 15.

26 → Scholem, *Zur Kabbala*, 235.

27 → Scholem, *Zur Kabbala*, trans. editors, 235.

28 → Katerina Krtilova, "Medienreflexiv. Zur Genese eines Verfahrens zwischen Martin Heidegger und Vilém Flusser," in *Internationales Jahrbuch für Medienphilosophie* 1/2015, 95–118; "Can We Think Computation in Images or Numbers? Critical Remarks on Vilém Flusser's Philosophy of Digital Technologies," in *Flusser Studies* 22/2016, accessed October 04, 2017, www.flusserstudies.net.

29 → Scholem, *Zur Kabbala*, trans. editors, 222.

cism of the letter and number which could be called practical-technical but also another tradition, which revolves around an exercise of the mind, a deep insight. One who only reads the book for contemplation can gather a creative wisdom (only taking place in the symbolic, after god's creation). It is then a creation in mind.[30]

There is however, an even older tradition, which can be traced to the creation of man: Golem here is the name for the undersigned, formless, "the Adam that was not yet touched by the breath of god."[31] As is said in the Talmud: "In the first hour the earth was gathered, in the second one a Golem, a yet unformed mass, in the third one its arms and legs were pulled out, in the fourth the soul was thrown in it; in the fifth it stood on his feet, in the sixth it gave names to all living things" and so on.[32] In this tradition, yet another aspect than just the mysticism of numbers and letters, becomes graspable when we return to the Prague-legend: the materiality of the clay-body of the Golem, awoken by the right combination of letters (the note with god's name on it). In this tradition, Adam is the symbol of earth's marriage with god. When it says in Genesis (1:24) "may the earth bring about living soul," the spirit of the first Adam is not a soul with which he has been infused, but "the soul of earth, a vital possibility inherent to Earth."[33] This creative power, albeit stirred by magic, does not leave the sphere of the elementary forces, remarks Scholem.[34] After all, the Golem does not die like man or animal: it returns to his element, to earth, his elements diffuse. In this tradition magic is thus a natural capacity of human productivity — of forming, building, planting, and reproducing.[35]

In the beginning was the word — the first of the ten Sefirot is the spirit of god, god's voice, his breath and his word, the primary cause of movement for the remaining nine. Spirit, voice, and word progressively bring about all elements of physical nature.[36] Yet this primacy of spoken and written word (and along with it, of numbers) always also has another side to it in earlier and later cabbalist traditions. One connected with the 'earth-character' of the force of creation. We could generally give it a practical and sensual, unformed-material and performative dimension, which has no place in the digital connection between symbolic and real.

Let us return once more to the book of Jezira: a merely written transmission does not suffice to carry out creative magic and be able to grasp it — it is about a process, a praxis. This aspect can hardly be traced through religious history for lack of sources. It could be the case, that the intonation of the combination of letters plays an important role, a certain breathing technique or movements of head and hand, which had to accompany the various acts; thus, a certain corporeality, also acknowledged by the text itself: "Ten Sefirot belima according to the number of fingers, five opposed to five with their bound of unity lying in the middle, in the milla (the word) of mouth and tongue and in the milla (the cutting) of the private parts."[37]

30 → Scholem, *Zur Kabbala.*

31 → Scholem, *Zur Kabbala,* 213.

32 → Scholem, *Zur Kabbala.*

33 → Scholem, *Zur Kabbala,* 216.

34 → Scholem, *Zur Kabbala,* 250.

35 → Scholem, *Zur Kabbala,* 228.

36 → Scholem, *Zur Kabbala,* 38.

37 → Westcott, *Sepher Yetzirah: The Book of Formation and the 32 Paths of Wisdom,* 15.

The miracle of the written word lies precisely in the possibility of abstraction from this concrete, singular presence and the paradoxical presence of something absent—it is this technique that has shaped Judaeo-Christian culture for millenia—not only in their imaginations, but also in a concrete-material way, as illustrated by the symbolic machines. The logocentrism of western culture has however repressed other moments of form-giving or creation in its focussing on the word, on language as spirit, as bodiless sense. Those other moments are present in the mystic tradition, but also in artistic endeavours: everything outside of the playing field sketched in the first part, the undecidable, the illogical, the unformed material and the sensual—all other forms of practice or effect than technical production and rational action. Judith Butler has further criticized logocentrism as phallogocentrism. In her book *Bodies that Matter*, she described the exclusion of an excessive, unformed, ungraspable materiality, which is always already colonized by the phallogocentric principle and which can only arise or be voiced in a specific form, say, during a game of chess.[38] Here seems to lie a possible connection to the earthy force of creation of the most ancient Golem-traditions and a possibility to observe how phallogocentric techno-logic excludes these types of creation in its desire for a completely abstract universe—which can be entirely modelled—fully governed by mathematical logic, rendering everything controllable. That which escapes this logic, to put it with Butler, cannot even be named.

When dealing with bodies, feelings, experiences, or perception of things, of nature, of the environment in reflecting 'digital culture,' all of these are usually thought of in relation to digital technology. Explicitly or implicitly, it always is about human enhancement, affective computing, ambient computing, motion sensing, self-tracking, the internet of things, biotechnology, smart cities and so on. Yet, in the reverse direction lie many blind spots: bodies, feelings, perception, thinking, believing etc. cannot be thought of as distinct from cultural techniques and medial practices; otherwise the separation of something knowable in mind, in the symbolic, on the one hand, and impervious practices or materiality on the other, is presupposed in the sense of phallogocentrism. In both cases we remain trapped on the chessboard.

To shortly sum up: with a side-glance at the chess-logic of Wiener's cybernetics, I would want to plead for a more sober gaze on 'digital culture' with regards to the enchantment of digital technologies, and draw attention—against the 'unlawful use' of language, writing, and other 'phallogocentric' means in the magical creation of a Golem—to the inscrutable, uncontrollable and miraculous character of medial practices of speaking, writing, calculating, and forming, which were less produced 'by' them than brought about 'through' them.[39]

38 → Judith Butler, *Bodies that matter, on the discursive limits of "sex,"* (New York: Routledge, 1993), 28–56.

39 → Butler, *Bodies that matter, on the discursive limits of "sex."*

Today I am functional + Conversation with Max Wallenhorst →

Christiane Heidrich

And while the possibilities rear to be touched, my own body definitely holds still.

It takes me an hour and a half from my whereabouts to the destination, that was passed on to me, but where I also want to go.

Seen from afar I hold big objects up to the camera on a rotating basis.

My hands look unpleasant. They shimmer, as though they were see-through, inert. As though lying unintentionally in time, referring to nothing.

I enter the destination, organs contracted. I don't have a topic.

The questions I'll ask myself today all have to do with handling.
The questions I'll ask myself today all have to do with handling and consumption.

An order lies ahead of me. I cautiously lift my legs and take a look at the giant, merely recognizable.

I fall in love with the idea of having a plan. I sleep on my laptop better than ever before.

The main part of the project is finished and there's nothing to tell. I sort myself. There's a lot to tell.

My sphere of influence widened. Laughing with my coworkers in the elevator, every time we sense more resonance.
Finished identity. Self-contained landscape. To edit the image no further.

If I formulate a request, a Facebook comment, try to pull a small, sweaty thread
through the eyelet and language

gives up at precisely that point, where it mediates too little in too short.

Could you comb my hair like something that went wrong,
but is supposed to come across really well? Bend my shoulders?

Lead the tools, close to the body, even closer to my skin? A kind of jewelry that I
could put on or off. Usage that I could put on or off.

Pressboard crumpled act-drawing, badly converted documents.
Nothing gets unreadable, though.

No real holes here, where our best clients sleep stretched out.

On a slippery field of unanswered messages. On a busy field of confirmed and
unconfirmed events.

Winking into surveillance cameras we know: inconvenient feelings are most open
for their consumption.

Your choice, which begins with the shoulders. Carried on by other councils,
successively joining. Guessing at body building and structure,

I unfavorably agree to an inventory. Too happy the names, pivoting, too dogged,
nasal. In this space I simply add other items.

Like angles of bodies, leftovers—nobody can prove their not-belonging-to-me.
Something unhandy emerges for both sides.

Unforeseeable proliferation of sides, signs, quirks. What a preview!
This preview is the stammering glow in my face.

Conversation

Max Wallenhorst: Christiane, in your work you deal with digital surfaces considered to be neutral and slick—and you try to trace their friction. You work with media in which these surfaces became the paradigm—with animations and selfies, videos and images. But you're also writing! Which I find super interesting, because a poetic approach towards adobe-informed digitality doesn't seem so obvious at first sight. Stupid question: Why? What does writing and text have in store for you and your work?

Christiane Heidrich: The increasing slickness of digital surfaces implies an improvement of software and that one is capable of virtuously exhausting their possibilities, which become actualized more and more. I'm interested in the fact that this development doesn't as easily apply to writing. It's not clear how to recognize a high-definition text. Does this have something to do with context-specific, professional modes of speaking 'high language,' which is a certain inventory of the text? Do I associate this writing with the idioms of marketing and technology, because it is there that slick surfaces are present— or, vice versa, do high-definition environments effect speaking? In a text I can unravel the messy blend of appeal and compulsion that these environments bear for me. I can claim pointed positions of speaking, that antagonize and are entangled and thereby do not claim neutrality.

Max Wallenhorst: How is writing a bodily medium for you? Do you have to design a body, so that it can appear in the text or is it already there, anyways?

Christiane Heidrich: The body is always already in question and this question moves the text. Not only, where the word *body* appears or body parts, but there where the speaking fades in—the need to say something at all. If there is a designed body, it is on the other side, wears clothes, a haircut, a form, writing the text. At the point where it's not about changing the design, in order to become someone else, writing maybe enables something: to play out the design in mobile constellations me and you, moving through space.

Max Wallenhorst: What I so like about these texts is that it is never clear to me, if a sign of liveliness—"the stammering glow in my face"—if that counts as a glitch or if it's just an especially realist rendering effect? Does technological optimism or pessimism play a role for you?

Christiane Heidrich: As the capturing of bodies and identities gets more and more precise, I of course look for the gaps, where it doesn't help this classification, that the glow is clearly visible, where something within the technical withdraws from it.

(un-)imagining or why the blank page is a lure in imagining the new → Pierre Schwarzer

In a dark room, projected onto a wall, we see the hands of a man dressed in black, on a wooden table. In crisp detail, we see him holding a page from a magazine, with some advertisement on it. Slowly, the page is being crumpled, we hear the whispers of a plain surface turning into a ball, only to be unfolded again, at the same pace. This folding and unfolding is calmly repeated. At each instance we see ink evaporating, progressively, floating in the air, resting on the palms. The flattened gloss and glitter of the page dwindles, becoming grainy, colors fading under the pressure of the fingers. Each unfolding shows the traces of its submission to the forces of a body, folding lines appearing like wrinkles on a face, transforming the formerly flat gloss into a landscape, with hills and valleys. We see the vanishings of ink, transmutations of color into dusty clouds with a pale dye hanging above a muddy white scenery, darker and darker stains on the palms, traces of transforming repetitions.[1] What appeared as evident and immediate, the ad on the page, the supposedly everlasting beauty of its image, was confronted with that which it appears to negate, corporeality and time, that is, history. The almost meditative character of the hands' pace gives Ismaïl Bahri's work *Revers* a resting intensity, a meditative sturdiness countering the image with and through images. That which colonizes our imagination, that which stirs our desire and channels it into the given structures, is here not de-constructed in a move of exposing its falsities. Rather, it is presented with its gaps, brought into a sphere where its shortcomings are not called upon, but actively, calmly, rendered present.

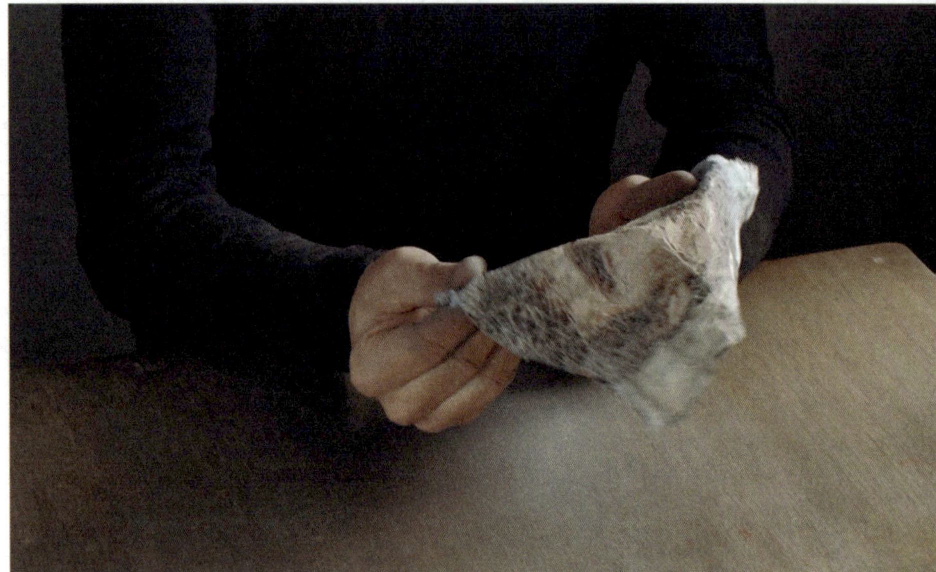

Ismaïl Bahri, *Revers*, 2017, film still.

On overflow

In a time of immediacy, impatience and constant imperatives to imagine (as long as the imagined stays within the given), *Revers* can be seen as an attempt at unimagining, a term that is the focus of this essay. For indeed, how are we to imagine, in our dystopian disjunctive present, a future different from an accelerated escalation of the already right-at-hand tendencies of our times, with sleeker surfaces and accrued injustice? Politics, as a practice shaping the future, relies to some extent on imagination, be it manifest or latent. The editors of the Public Seminar series draw attention to the need of a radical imagination as a means to "challenge ... dystopias."[2] Eight years ago, the book *Capitalist Realism* claimed it was easier to imagine the end of the world than the end of capitalism.[3] Perhaps this is less the case nowadays, after the fad of the Mayan doomsday passed in 2012 and a current US-presidency that conjurs specters of nuclear destruction that might make us aware for the need to imagine anew. However, Fisher's diagnosis points to the difficulty of channelling such imaginaries:

when advertising is drawing on the aesthetics of protest to promote Pepsi,[4] when past utopias stir up the bitter taste of blood and today's billboards have appropriated queer aesthetics, how can we imagine a change for the better?[5] Are we to strip our imagination of its historical baggage? Is the idea of an ahistorical imagination not itself a myth tied to a notion of omnipotence?

Unimagining, I claim, is a necessary step towards re-imagining. However, it cannot simply be a cessation of imagining, but rather, a certain modality of it. If radical imaginations are complex constellations of concepts and images, unimagining must thereby behave towards them in a certain way instead of wholly refusing them, by negating specific aspects of them while retaining others. Unfortunately, however, analyzing revolts and their images might be a dead end for our conceptual endeavor, for they are not separable from the context in which they arise. In fact, the image-production is in that case not necessarily steered by the rebels, but rather fueled by a journalistic gaze aiming obsessively to depict, striving for viewership. This gaze does not refrain from the impulse to place what is captured into pictorial traditions, be they the lonely martyr, the bereft child, or the crying woman. Instead of looking at empirical events and their symbolization, I suggest turning towards contemporary art instead. As a conscious practice of imagining and symbolizing within a framework that is *a priori* differentiated from the political, contemporary art could offer insights into what a practice of unimagining could look like and what it implies. Taking a look at contemporary art requires, however, that we clarify the meaning of the 'contemporary.'

Presents and beginnings

Calling artworks 'contemporary' does not, however, indicate their having been produced recently or to them being close to us chronologically. Rather, it signals a coming together of multiple times that are equally present; it is, following Peter Osborne, "the concept of the contemporary projects a single historical time of the present, as a living present: a common, albeit internally disjunctive, present historical time of human lives."[6] In other words, we create a unity of the differing and contradictory times we live in, creating a common notion of history that unites very different historical perspectives coexisting at once. Needless to say, the notion of the contemporary is problematic because it lies beyond possible experience, it is a hypothesis, it assumes a unity not given in the moment, a claim that can only be verified *a posteriori*. Indeed, the 'contemporary' could be considered utopian insofar as it projects a future that can only be judged as accurate in retrospect. It is a fiction wrapping something fleeting in a conjuncture, like a photographic image annihilates temporality, presenting itself instantaneously. Yet the problems of the concept of the contemporary are not just temporal, but also spatial, for the term presupposes some sort of global contemporaneity, while the meaning of the contemporary is very different depending on where it has been formulated, in a geographical sense: the US might not have the same understanding of what the contemporary is as Russia, for instance. Yet the concept of the contemporary also projects a task of bringing together differentials as differentials, of making sense of the disjunctive multiplicities in a globalized political sphere.

Thus, my suggestion to turn to contemporary art is not simply an invitation for thinkers to walk into a museum and turn away from books, but, rather, to develop a critical account of the concept of the contemporary and engage with those works that can provide frames for pondering the question of our time. That means reflecting on the imaginations that fill it, imaginations that themselves imagine, spinning fictions that could provide answers to help us deal with that which ought-not-be but nevertheless, and unquestionably, is.

In times of image-saturation ("don't forget to follow me on Instagram"), contemporary art in the critical sense acts like a suggestion for dealing with said overflow, cutting through it and, precisely in making such a cut through the images, sounds and discourses of our time, makes the conscious decision to leave something out, allowing for a space on the other side, unmarked, where a new imagination can constitute itself.

Reformulations

In *Revers*, the supposed timelessness of the images abounding in our societies, drawing our gazes with their ethereal gloss, the standstill they signify, is actively processed, manipulated and transformed. We are left with a grey-white landscape of paper, inviting us to make sense of it, to treat it precisely as something that calls upon our own sense-making and allows it. It shows the slow decomposition of a given suggestion, only rendered apparent in the process of its mutation, in the ink detaching from the sheet and scintillating in the air, in the creases appearing more and more on that which once was flat. The labor of the hands, along with its accomplice, time, allows us to reach a space no longer fixed and given, but full of potentialities. This space is not empty, it is not a blank slate, it bears history.

Perhaps only by acknowledging this, that not everything is always possible at any given moment, can we start to imagine something different. Here, I don't mean generally different, or different from everything, but specifically in a way that renders experimentation and action possible in a different way. The blank slate is a lure, it is equally flat, it suggests that we can do anything with it, that we could draw whichever figure. But, in a world that is precisely not blank, which bears the traces of history, could it be right?

What would unimagining mean, then, in this case? Firstly, it implies working with and through what is given, for even the given. The seemingly natural bears a history, just like we have been shaped through time. Secondly, unimagining implies the introduction of something else into the given, like the steady agency of the hands, repeatedly crumpling and unfolding. Thirdly, it requires repetition, not as mere re-instantiation, but as a progressively rendering of the past as an actual agent in the present, not through a violent repetition, but in the renewed disconcertion of the present through re-enactment.

Unimagining is therefore a creative act that frees a space in which the imagination can start anew, not on a blank slate, but on a reformulated landscape in which the formerly 'given' is less probable and cannot simply be returned to, just like watching the looped *Revers*, in which a glance at the intact magazine page will no longer be the same. One can never completely avoid returning to what is given, but that which is given might no longer be 'given' in the same way, it is enriched with the potentiality that it negates, even if that potentiality is a mere glimpse.

However, it is crucial that unimagining itself relies on something, that it leaves traces or artifacts, that it is recorded; otherwise one could not build anything upon it. As stated before, unimagining is itself an act of the imagination. Let us look at yet another video-work, Ismaïl Bahri's *Foyer,* to emphasize certain points before turning to the relation between unimagining and imagining.

Foyer, a 31-minute video piece, was filmed in Tunis in 2014 and 2015, shortly after the country's transition to democracy.[7] The pace is slow and yet, one is drawn into a trance-like state of concentration — precisely because one does not see anything precise, but not nothing, one lets the eye roam across the screen and focus on the sounds, on the voices. Just like the wind is a sort of cameraman, it is up to us to make something of the voices, of the words, separated from the bodies out of which they emerge. The gaze is captured by the dances of light, instead of becoming affixed to people, suspended in mid-air, allowing for a different state of experience. The poetics of the formal experiment are equally hindered by the questioning of the artist's position and by the questions of the point of the work. In French, says Bahri, the title can refer to a fire in a home, a place around which people dwell to speak. There is indeed a strange intimacy to the film, a surface upon which things are projected while transformed into flickerings of white, turning into a vibratory surface which allows us to look onto a place already routinely captured by news-outlets, without it being turned into a dramatic event, without it being reduced into the usual news-sections. In veiling the screen, other veilings are lifted. The camera, says Bahri, becomes sensible — a seisometer — capturing infinitesimal vibrations where it is placed.

The screen shows a sun-drenched white. Topical, fuzzy stains of blue and clear-white abound, moving around on the screen like shimmers on water. We hear street noises, distant car horns, fading roarings. The image flickers, occasionally revealing sun and tarmac around the lower edges. A piece of paper has been placed in front of the camera. People come by, speaking Tunisian Arabic and ask the film-maker what he's doing. They question his role, whether he is an artist or studying for film school, they wonder what he is filming. He tells them he is studying light — a formalist experiment with paper shutters. The shades of fingers sometimes appear behind the paper, people talk about color perceptions, sometimes even mock the artist, while rhythmic pulsations abound on the screen, children come by, inquiring whether the film will be shown in a cinema, "Can you see anything? No I can't see anything" goes their conversation as they look through the lens, before their voices disappear, the screen still flickering, street noises continuing. "What kind of message are you trying to convey?" is a topic of discussion of the passers-by. The street noises increase, chatter in the streets crosses our field of hearing. After several conversations with people, Policemen arrive, inquiring what is being filmed. At the station, he explains his experiment to them. The screen goes black but the sound-track goes on. They discuss the experiment, ask the artist where he lives and discuss the situation in Tunisia, their fears of a democratic spring turning into an abyss before releasing him. The screen turns white again, we are back on the streets. On the screen there is a flickering of grey, white and blue. New passers come by, and we notice we are on the shore (of a canal as we learn later). A group of friends question his position, what he does. "Facebook afterwards? Can you see this on facebook?" asks one of them before another leans in, claiming the film is a great idea and worth exhibiting—"what is there to understand?" The discussion then centers on the artist's position as a Tunisian, claiming he's already too far away from the country as he is not bothered by all the questions of an unemployed youth, then plunging into the water, screaming "Action!" several times, "Action!", and then "Cut!" We hear the sound of splashes, shadows moving on the screen, shortly revealing part of the shore in the evening light before turning black.

What is being unimagined here? A first answer might be cinema itself, a landscape for dreams, narratives and abounding colors, meticulously cut, framed and arranged. Along with it, we might unimagine that certain gaze, presenting what it captures in a matter-of-fact way, exhibiting and exposing objects to be arranged in series of images, catalogued in fleeting arrangements. Then, one might add the unimagining of the position of the artist as producer of a certain truth, a truth that is vigorously questioned by the captured voices. Then follows the position of the cameraman (the wind playing a major role) and its potential hunger to capture, a hunger so questioned by the policemen. On yet another level, one can speak of an unimagining of a social and political environment, of a news-casted spring and its aftermaths.

In *Foyer*, we start with a white sheet on the screen, but, as the film tells us, it cannot hold up to the world that hides behind it, sounds and noises seep in, unplanned commenters abide (influencing the light shed on the page that we see, but also outside of the frame, through their voices). The blank sheet in front of the camera negates our longing for objects and allows us to focus on the rest. Unimagining, as *Foyer* highlights, is not a purely unrestricted practice, in fact, it can even be methodical, as long as one grasps that no method is a manual, but rather a guideline that

Ismaïl Bahri, *Foyer*, 2016, film still.

needs to be modified if the object requires it. Here, what started out as a formalist experiment ends up being a portrait of its time. The white sheet is a lure: by placing it in this context, we are shown how it only gains in value through its position within the world, through those things behind it. The stirring shades of white are, for a moment, the only things for the eye to latch onto. At the end of the film however, one feels as if one could shape them, as if their indefinite movement and their blurriness was just temporary—we are ready to imagine. In this sense, *Foyer* can be read as inviting us to unimagine, to imagine anew afterwards. Creation and cessation are here shown as intertwined: we never start from scratch, but what we have to work with might also not be enough: much like *Revers*, *Foyer* highlights the importance of practice, of manipulation, of the position one needs to place oneself in to unimagine. *Foyer* goes further, however. One might almost say that the white landscape that has been crumpled in *Revers*, is now in front of the camera, serving as a surface to both unimagine, in so far as we have nothing to latch onto, but also to imagine anew, as we can focus on what happens behind it in our own theater of shadows. Instead of silence, we have urban white noise, instead of a story we have encounters, instead of an all-knowing artist we discover the filmmaker as a part of and subject to his practice. In doing so, the work frees itself from both delusions of grandeur: the one of the camera and its gaze, and the one of the author and his power, leaving its own journey to be unravelled before fading to black.

In English, the word 'foyer' also means a space for waiting and for entering, and indeed, one might claim something becomes possible here after we accept that we won't see anything clear on the screen—that the border of the screen becomes vibratory, sensible, skin-like—that in inhabiting this space, in doing something, its pores might let the new seep through.

Unimagining is context-dependent, it is a practice with no universal solution, for it depends on that which is to be unimagined. Unimagining is bound to history, bound to time. It tries to open up a space in the all-too probable, it switches the necessary and the contingent around until, like dancers, figures can be drawn around them. It is a careful, repeated suspension, a working-through what is for what could be. Unimagining allows us to imagine, not in general, but in a specific *now*, a now that, for once, refers to more than just the date on our calendar: a now-ness that might refer to the quality of contemporaneity. While this notion retains a certain fuzziness, we should attribute this to the white-noise-character of unimagining it-self. White noise allows for the experience of silence as silence, precisely by not being silent. There is no manual for unimagining, but we might consider art-works such as the two discussed here as scores, as invitations to interpret, and to take part.

1 → Ismaïl Bahri, *Revers*, 2016–17.
2 → Aris Komporozos-Athanasiou, Chiara Bottici, "The Radical Imagination: Imagining the future in financial capitalism," Public Seminar, accessed June 02, 2017, http://www.publicseminar.org/2017/06/the-radical-imagination/.
3 → Mark Fisher, *Capitalist realism: is there no alternative?* (Winchester: Zero Books, 2010).
4 → Pepsi, *Kendall Jenner Pepsi Commercial*, advertisement, accessed June 02, 2017 https://www.youtube.com/watch?v=73P9STckPLw.
5 → An excellent study on protest images can be found in Georges Didi-Huberman, *Soulèvements* (Paris: Gallimard, 2016).
6 → Peter Osborne, *Anywhere or Not at All: Philosophy of Contemporary Art* (London: Verso, 2013), 22.
7 → Ismaïl Bahri, *Foyer*, 2016.

soft-fiction →

soft-fiction → Hard is the opposite of soft. Hard implies exact measure-ment, substantial confines, and clear distinctions—Physics. When Chick Strand made Soft Fiction in 1979 she made a 'soft' film: it was neither about ease and contem-plation nor was it about comfortability. Soft implied the permeability of the boundary, the complicated relation between abuse and desire, the performativity between the camera and its pornographic evidence. Soft Fiction takes the world as a diagram whose very internal sexuality may be explored through delicate constructions. Or rather, it is only the detail allowing us to explore what appears to be the same but different.

A Sense of Heat →

An interview with Heather Phillipson on her work *WHAT'S THE DAMAGE*

Heather Phillipson's most recent work performs 'a bloody hot takeover' by intertwining digital fluidities and physical cycles. The complex augmentations between textual rhythms and visual layers, between different textures of fluidities, constantly multiply the interconnections. And while we watch a hideous blond head of hair (read Trump) mounted onto a cowboy photo (read Putin) in a wooden frame being chased by a grey arm we hear, "shovelling down sound bites & regurgitating it / over our saddest images."

Pujan Karambeigi: I would like to start this conversation by talking about the 'bloody hot takeover' you are both proposing (politically) and performing (formally) in *WHAT'S THE DAMAGE*. Could you say something to that?

Heather Phillipson: I made this work quickly, at the end of 2016, and with a sense of heat. I feel alive in a state of emergency right now and this, for me, was a means of directing that feeling. It's redolent of a state of deluge, and insurrection.

At its most literal it's proposing, yes, an upsurge of menstrual blood as a tide against dominant power structures. I mean, what if? Just think of all the richness, color, nutrition, outflow, power that's produced across the world monthly (daily), and flushed into sewer systems. How about taking the concomitant disgust, shame, and submission that's imposed on menstrual bleeding, and exposing it, upending it. In her epigraph to *Hope in the Dark*, Rebecca Solnit quotes an American news anchor, saying, "If you don't like the news, go out and make some of your own."[1] Well, I don't like the news. So that idea,

1 → Rebecca Solnit, *Hope in the Dark: Untold Histories, Wild Possibilities* (Chicago: Haymarket Books, 2016).

and its formation, gets me—don't just listen: speak, agitate, produce, disseminate, renew. It contributes to a sense I have that art (in its broadest form/s) is protest, not just a form of it. What's being protested and why and how depends on the artist and the work, of course, but, for me, making is first and foremost a means of answering back, a way of activating worlds, a way of conceiving alternatives. An artwork is a mind, and it's a mind that, at its most potent, might allow thinking to become unhinged (even more unhinged).

Of course, the 'bloody hot takeover' is also a metaphor (what isn't). Menstrual blood is the result of an un-made baby, so it manifests a potential life, and its lack. It's complex, both in its composition and in its political, cultural, and personal significance (frequently, inseparable). It's a substance that makes neutrality impossible. Menstrual bleeding is not obedient and it's not rational: it's a pungent, bodily response. And, in keeping with my use of materials more broadly, it's readily available and has combustible potential.

But, importantly, though menstrual bleed is an exclusively fertile female substance, I don't want to exclude those that don't menstruate. As it appears in my video, menstruation is, above all, a representation. It's an image—of propagation, eruption, release. A call to harness the (whatever) forces at our disposal.

Pujan Karambeigi: Looking at your piece *COMMISERATIONS!*[2] you used the human heart both literally and metaphorically to confuse digital and physical realities—"taking the heart as a specter." However, in *WHAT'S THE DAMAGE* you are not engaging in a muscular organ (and its clichés) anymore but rather in a biological cycle (and its fluidities). How would you address this transformation in the object of study?

2 → Heather, Phillipson, "*COMMISERATIONS!*", accessed June 29, 2017, https://vimeo.com/141163304.

Heather Phillipson: I'm interested in how things (often, bits of ourselves), are relayed back to us as images, metaphors, marketable bytes. Across my works (across media), this is often played out through the use of apparently instantly readable images (in these

cases, the heart, blood) — let's say, clichés — being wrenched from their conventional modes of circulation, and getting wedged, smashed, remixed, in order to render redundant, re-framed. And if images and words and syntax govern what's thinkable, then unchecked clichés — perfect examples of the automatic conversion of image produced into image consumed — are interesting, powerful, dangerous. Cliché's are not called, in French, 'tartes á la crème'[3] 3 → Translation: custard pies.
for nothing — 'the proof of the custard pie
is that someone gets it in the face. It proves itself by bursting, spreading, crumbling, dripping.'

Pujan Karambeigi: In my last question I referred to a center of *WHAT'S THE DAMAGE*. However, looking more closely at the piece it seems to systematically undermine any reference to a center-like structure, most prominently through its paranoia. For instance, different types of fluid textures adjoin and augment each other both on the textual and the visual level. There is a bubbling, there are blots, plodding rivers, and clotted blood, just to name a few on the visual level. Then there are oral flows, changing from a chorus to a monotonous reading to an agitation. These complex augmentations (in opposite to gaps or differences) between textual rhythms and visual layers constantly multiply interconnections. The crucial question at this point seems to be, how much meaning may be stacked on a screen and are we at any point reaching something that could be described as depth?

Heather Phillipson: The crucial question for me in response would be, what do we mean by 'meaning' and what do we mean by 'depth?' I'm not trying to be facetious, I am genuinely unsure of these terms, especially in relation to art. And, for me, that's productive, because it relates very directly to working with what's (nearly?) incommunicable, to working with dynamics as much as with forms, to working in the context of being numerous, to putting moments of flight in the system, to taking nothing for granted, delaying coherence. Defying the pressure to immediate understanding — and, instead, squandering meanings — has critical potential. This is a site that permits ambivalence — or, at least, allows it to be negotiated. And it's perhaps because of these concerns — driving forces — that my work is always made with a sense of vertigo — precariousness, falling — which may be the greatest indicator of any kind of 'depth' (height, volume, psychological space). And, along the way, it's as much about what escapes, gets lost, as what sticks. The binary of winning/losing, getting it/not getting it, is revealed as a false one, a decoy.

What is vital to me is precisely these textures, rhythms, layers, and agitations because they're thoughts given form and, to quote Sturtevant and Marianne Moore respectively, "thinking is a kind of madness"[4] and, "The sentence is a radiograph of the personality"[5] — and, for me, editing videos is likewise.

4 → Tony Benn, "Certainly Thinking is a kind of Madness. Interview," *Site*, no. 7, 2004, 29.
5 → Marianne Moore, "Feeling and Precision," in *The Sewanee Review*, vol. 52, no. 4 (Baltimore: John Hopkins University Press, 1944).

How I orchestrate encounters between bodies and screens — so that the monitor (and it is usually a monitor) is consistently altering/blocking visual space — is a significant part of these textures and rhythms. Between my videos and their sculptural environments are constant attempts to enhance their mutual material and tactile properties — the affective properties of worlds on-screen and off, in which the image performs as part-body and the body as part-image — so that the digital and physical may be momentarily conflated, without ever allowing total assimilation. It has to do with an attempt to understand technology as a kind of ecology — not extraneous to the human (whatever we mean by 'human') but constitutive of it.

Pujan Karambeigi: Simultaneously we watch an ugly blond head of hair (read Trump) mounted onto a naked cowboy photo (read Putin) in a wooden frame that is chased by a grey arm. Is *WHAT'S THE DAMAGE* bleeding into the digital space (the archive of 21st century junk)? And if yes, what would that actually mean?

Heather Phillipson: Oh yes, surely. It's hard to produce much that doesn't contribute to the archive of 21st century junk — although who knows how long it will last, so what kind of archive it will be, if any. All I know is that we're permanently in emergent and associative states, mutually contingent, and that's our primary connection, so anything that bleeds out into this digital, far-flung space, has the potential to become contagious.

Pujan Karambeigi: A last question: How come you upload your works for free on Vimeo, distributing them all over the place rather than artificially running them short? Do you think this has any relation to you not being represented by a gallery?

Heather Phillipson: Everything to do with the distribution of my work is related. My videos take from the internet and go back out into it. Everywhere the work is shown, context re-frames readings. It keeps them numerous.

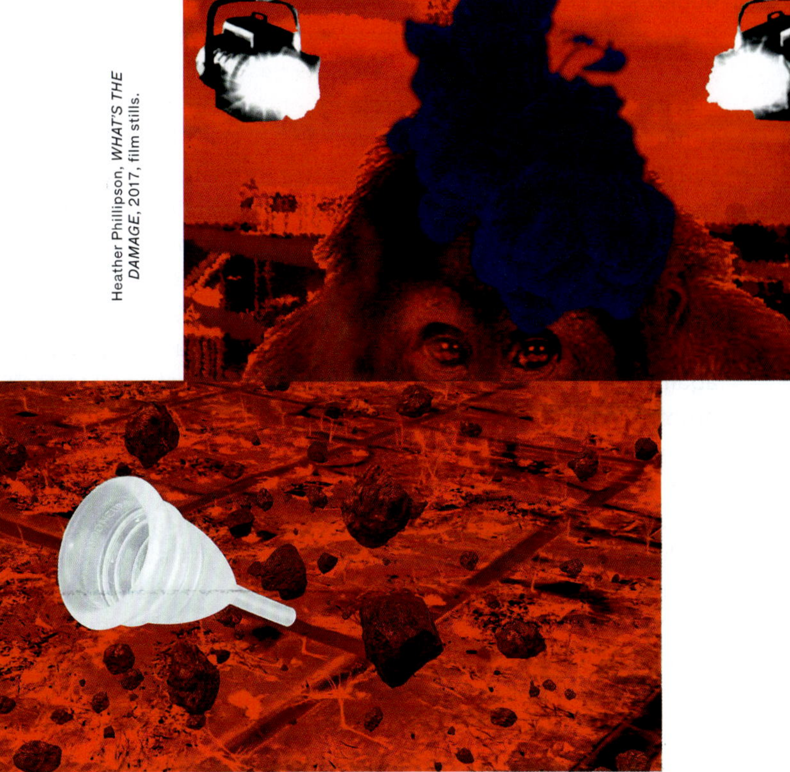

Heather Phillipson, *WHAT'S THE DAMAGE*, 2017, film stills.

SEXTING, SEASON 2 →

Max Wallenhorst

This is a text-turned-talk-turned-text about its frame, a series of text-based works called *Sexting, Season 2*. It's an introduction, squeezed in two episodes late—which means I should be in a hurry and I'll just fast-forward recap *Season 1* for you. OK. Sexting is, first of all, digital communication with sexually explicit audiovisual and/or textual materials. It's a new term, although it's new for a long time now—since 2004, to be precise—and its newness seems, yep, ordinary. Ordinary to such an extent, that even if you don't engage in sexting for whatever reason, perhaps you can still imagine what it feels like. Like a love letter, but faster. Like real life sex, but slower. Mid-tempo, but mid-tempo as something weird—a bit off, and then off-off, and then again, there again, super-linear. As in any sex, there is a certain virtuosity wanted from me navigating these rhythms, their normativities and non-normativities. But perhaps sexting as a more sensibly mediated form makes this self-technology now more explicit. You have to get the pacing right, as *Vogue* columnist Karly Sciortino puts it.[1] By 'pacing' she and I do not only refer to temporal distribution, yet to spatial distribution as well. When my sext message reaches your screen as

a push, it's not only about the appropriate time-zone, but also about the appropriate table you'll find your phone on: your night stand or the coffeetable at your mother's place and oh did you turn off preview mode in our homescreen.

Whereas the myths of 1990s cybersex imagined infinite parallel universes in the depth of the internet,[2] discourses of sexting, much more mainstream, conjure an infinite stretching of IRL relationships in the flatness of social media. Optimistic approaches towards sexting—from *Vogue* to *Vice* to me sending to you that pic of my hip bone—express the hope that distances within relationships can be overcome by mediation. Sexting, in this view, offers episodes of embodied synchronization: for bridging long distance relationships, preparing with dating apps, or beginning anew in instants of sexual crisis. Pessimistic approaches towards sexting express the fear that something might get lost on the way—lost in a networked sense, shared beyond control. In the US the

1 → Karley Sciortino, "Breathless: Mastering the Art of Sexting," accessed February 01, 2017, http://www.vogue.com/article/breathless-karley-sciortino-sexting.
2 → Elivia Wilk, "Where looks don't matter and only the best writers get laid," accessed January 04, 2017, www.elviapw.com/WLDM-ew-041913-2.pdf.

dominance of the latter in certain areas even leads to an atmosphere feminist scholars call "Sexting Panic."[3] Conservative and neoliberal opinion-making once again denies youth, especially young girls, the right to their own body production, placing the responsibility for sexual violence on the internet on them. At the same time revenge porn and unsolicited dick pics are still seen as accidental, the constitutive minimal risk of mediation in the realm of 'you knew that this could happen.' Thus, online-sex even underlies a more restrictive legal situation than offline-sex: in some states of the US, child pornography laws apply to 'cases' of sexting, so that young adults who would be legally allowed to sleep with each other can be prosecuted for producing or owning sexually explicit audiovisual material of their partners.

Fuck that, no spoiler alert: sexting carries, like most sex, normative fantasies of sovereignty. The fantasy of expanding what I deem my best body parts to wherever you are. At work, in Miami or Mitte. And even within less normative lives than those compatible with *Vogue*, I have to get the pacing right to cater to this fantasy, otherwise I'll freeze your hotness and end up as a super ridiculous screenshot. I think, the sex in, after, or before sexting might be better sex or it might be worse sex—that's not for me to say, as I think, to paraphrase the feminist Lauren Berlant, episodes of sex are always only related/ unrelated to the series they are embedded/ not embedded in. But this slogan is not as on the beat and boring as it might sound at the first hearing. Because maybe the ting in 'sexting' in all its verbality and verb-form—moving with the iMessage ringtone it imitates, with the sweaty dancehallrhythm it also evokes[4]—hints to a new ensemble of media, bodies and

writing. Plus maybe within the trickiness of pacing to new possibilities of the distribution of bodies. Maybe and really only maybe.

Thus, in *Season 1* sexting stands in for a contemporary infrastructure. Writing, to paraphrase media theorist John Durham Peters in his book *The Marvelous Clouds*, has never been a more paradigmatic mode of technology and communication. Writing for Peters is marked by its off beats: the blank space between letters, spatial and temporal distance between writing, reading and writing, the ground on which they leak into each other. Off beats that open up multiverses of variation—Peters compares writing to quantum computing. Think the split second in which I have the time to edit my texts and sexts before hitting the send arrow. The trouble of getting the pacing right is not the difficulty of adjusting to a new trend, it is informed by this syncopes of writing: On the one hand, one gesture doesn't follow as immediately as in the improvisation of skin-to-skin-interactions—on the other hand, sole texts in traditional long-form appear more isolated from their context than sext messages. So there's these two hands and the third hand is what I'd call sexting. And sometimes this third hand feels like more of the same, but at certain other times it just appears with the special effects of horror. Writing has always been embodied, but perhaps it is now inscribed into our movements, moved into our scriptures to such an extent that you could generally, just for a moment, view it as sexting. Look at how much smartphone cameras made it easier to literally and

3 → Amy Adele Hasinoff, *Sexting Panic: Rethinking Criminalization, Privacy, and Consent* (Champaign: University of Illinois Press, 2015).
4 → Swing Ting, accessed July 10, 2017, https://soundcloud. com/swingting.

non-literally write 'with' my body, how messaging apps let me feel the vibration of an incoming text message as excitement in my shorts, how affirmative data plans let me check on you (and you and you) in carefully paranoid frequency. *Season 1* tries to establish these entanglements of bodies and media as a paradigmatic constellation to any contemporary writing. Keep in mind, that this is only art-oriented hobby essayism and I'll continue to drive through the series via the ridiculous sportscar this genre unlocked for me oh wow that was so fast: sexting here doesn't only refer to sexually explicit scenes of communication, but offers an infrastructure for describing the episodes, in which the entanglement of bodies, media, and writing becomes tangible. An entanglement that could queer the fantasies of sovereignty all these forms — bodies, media, writing — are operating with. Could!

What if, for example, all the women who were in their absence addressed by oh so deep love letters from great writers had the flat possibility to just text them back within a second? What if the explicitness feminists demand for sex with *Yes Means Yes* is not the end of seduction, but rather to not stop writing, within a realism that takes the trickiness of getting the pacing appropriately serious? Is sexting, as an extended practice or concept, productive for these instances in which bodies and concepts crash into each other? Chris Kraus writes in *I Love Dick*: "Every letter is a love-letter."[5] Reviewing McKenzie Warks and Kathy Ackers online correspondence, Ruby Burton claims, "E-mail is best for crushes."[6] What is texting for? Let's say, texting is for sexting. Catchphrase, fireworks and *Season 1* finale.

Everyone is hyped and exhausted at the same time. There is this strange holidays' episode that tries to overcome the distance between seasons. I'm at work right now and your ear lobe is nowhere near my gums, but I like that thought of your gums not even close to my kidney. This is me in public, guess what I'm wearing, as your back turns away from knee. Your toenail distances itself from my lips, your gums leaves my forearm. My ear moves further from my neck. My eyelid not touching my face. Your teeth not touching my face. Where are you right now and what are you wearing?

And then there's *Season 2*, which is here. The main story arc of *Season 1* — to establish sexting as a concept with a sportscar, as an idea for an infrastructure — is not as attractive anymore. Claiming the newness of a world sexting is a part of — this plot device in *Season 2* transforms into the micropolitics of ordinary world-building in an ordinary world that is not only there, but lived as well. A series — I learned from reading Deleuze or watching HBO — only really begins to function as a series when it detaches from its beginning, like cinema, when it was interrupted by the innovation of the cut, or in *The Leftovers*, when it entered its second season. In this sense, *Sexting, Season 2* via mid-tempo reached its middle, 'par le milieu' — the place where its rhythm is probably the most complex, the most physical because it doesn't have to start and it cannot yet end. This is why I keep bothering you with this series-metaphor-mannerism because I do think it can really be a useful tool to locate openness in in-between-ness — I know it can be eyeroll emoji and I'm sorry. The

5 → Chris Kraus, *I Love Dick* (London: Serpent's Tail, 2016), 105.
6 → Ruby Bruton, "All My Ghosts," *Real Life Mag*, accessed June 13, 2017, reallifemag.com/all-my-ghosts/.

problem is that this mid-world of *Sexting, Season 2* isn't a center and there's not really an episode guide. *Sexting, Season 2* in the end probably isn't officially even confirmed yet.

So I turn to plots and plot holes, which are for now and for me ahead of schedule, which are already adding block for block to the world-building of what I'd call here *Sexting, Season 2*, what is here not more than a fan fiction framework trying to adopt a new perspective of the things it gathers around. Things that do not end at the entanglement of body and media and body-media, the back-and-forth of writing in-between—this atmosphere is rather what they synchronize with as their habitat from the start. The pseudo-science of this essay, as the series its part of, focuses on episodes tending towards artistic practice, because this is its environment, but there is obviously more to be described elsewhere.

All these episodes emerge from very different backgrounds, in the wormhole of their specific middle. There is for example the writing arc, in which theories and poems navigate the surroundings of this series. Starting from there, the contemporary writing (perhaps rather than literature) I am a fan of does neither speak on a panel of supposedly public discourse, nor is it over-identified with its own form. It sounds out contemporary language in its use as a cultural practice, not with a semiotic logic of representation, but within embodied and mediated relationality. There is the body arc, in whose dance and performances embodied synchronizations are outlined beyond the contours of skin, as if it were nothing new. Movements are not so much going with the flow of bodily connection, but rather with the dub of its disconnections—

with what is embodied, yet not personal. There is the media arc, in which promises of the internet are traced within the repressive authentication processes of social media; in which, even if it doesn't feel as spectacular, creative, or original as I imagined the online experience must have felt prior to its territorialization, there is still experimentation on the surface in tension.

What may seem, with or without the silly fan-fictional shipping I'm trying to do here, like a couple genre-specifics randomly thrown together, for me are new approaches to practice the dynamics of contemporary coherence. This was reluctantly called "infrastructuralism" by Laurent Berlant as well as John Durham Peters. A performative restructuring of structure, but not only performative, as these practices cares about and for macro/micro levels of affect, so hidden in plain sight within the 'infra' of "infrastructure," that it cannot be said to be performed. In addition to the gesture of 'making visible'— which was so dominant for anti-normative artistic practices within and whose importance cannot be underestimated— these episodes rather try to audibly hum with the background noise of bodies, media, and writing normativity puts on mute.[7/8]

---

7 → Laurent Berlant, "Starved," *South Atlantic Quarterly* 106, no. 3 (2007): 433–44, http://doi:10.1215/00382876-2007-002.

8 → John Durham Peters, *The Marvelous Clouds: Toward a Philosophy of Elemental Media* (Chicago: University of Chicago Press, 2016).

How to Talk to Aliens? → And Other Questions on Social Imaginaries of Now and Then →

Danae Theodoridou

"Greetings to you, whoever you are. We come in friendship to those who are friends."

"Greetings to our friends in the stars. May time bring us together."

"To all those who exist in the universe, greetings."

"How's everyone? We all very much wish to meet you, if you're free please come and visit."

"Greetings from a human being of the Earth. Please contact."

"We are sending greetings from our world, wishing you happiness, health and many years."

"Greetings to the residents of far skies."

"Greetings to the inhabitants of the universe from the third planet Earth of the star Sun."

"Greetings. The people of the Earth send their good wishes and hope you find good fortune in this life."

"Friends of space, how are you all? Have you eaten yet? Come visit us if you have time."

"Hello to everyone. We are happy here and you be happy there."

"We strive to live in peace with the peoples of the whole world, of the whole cosmos."

"Hello from the children of planet Earth."[1]

In 1977 NASA launches a message from Earth into space, thinking of the possibility that the message will be found by extraterrestrial beings: the *Voyager Golden Record*. The message includes images and sounds from life on Earth, greetings in 55 languages, and a series of music pieces from all over the world.

A statement from the president of the United States also accompanies this message:

"This Voyager spacecraft was constructed by the United States of America. We are a community of 240 million human beings among the more than 4 billion who inhabit the planet Earth. We human beings are still divided into nation states, but these states are rapidly becoming a single global civilization. We cast this message into the cosmos. It is likely to survive a billion years into our future, when our civilization is profoundly altered and the surface of the Earth may be vastly changed. Of the 200 billion stars in the Milky Way galaxy, some — perhaps many — may have inhabited planets and spacefaring civilizations. If one such civilization intercepts Voyager and can understand these recorded contents, here is our message: This is a present from a small distant world, a token of our sounds, our science, our images, our music, our thoughts, and our feelings. We are attempting to survive our time so we may live into yours. We hope someday, having solved the problems we face, to join a community of galactic civilizations. This record represents our hope and our determination, and our good will in a vast and awesome universe."

HOW TO TALK TO ALIENS?

Some years earlier, the drawing of a naked man and woman, the *Pioneer Plaque* was also sent into space.
     The creators of the *Voyager Golden Record* have clearly stated that there is only a tiny chance that this will ever be

1 → Greetings from the *Voyager Golden Record*, sent into space by NASA in 1977. For the complete archive, see: "Voyager Golden Record," *Voyager Golden Record*, accessed June 28, 2017, http://goldenrecord.org/.

real seen by an extraterrestrial, but it will certainly be seen by billions of terrestrials. Its real function therefore is to "appeal and expand the human spirit."[2] The task pursued for the creation of *Voyager Golden Record* has been described as follows: "Describe the world—its place in space, its diverse biota, its wide-ranging cultures with their lifestyles, arts and technologies—everything or at least enough to get the idea across... Oh, there's one stipulation: assume not only that your audience doesn't speak your language, but that it has never even heard of the Earth or the rest of the solar system. An audience that lives, say, on a planet orbiting another star, light-years away from anything you would recognize as home."[3]

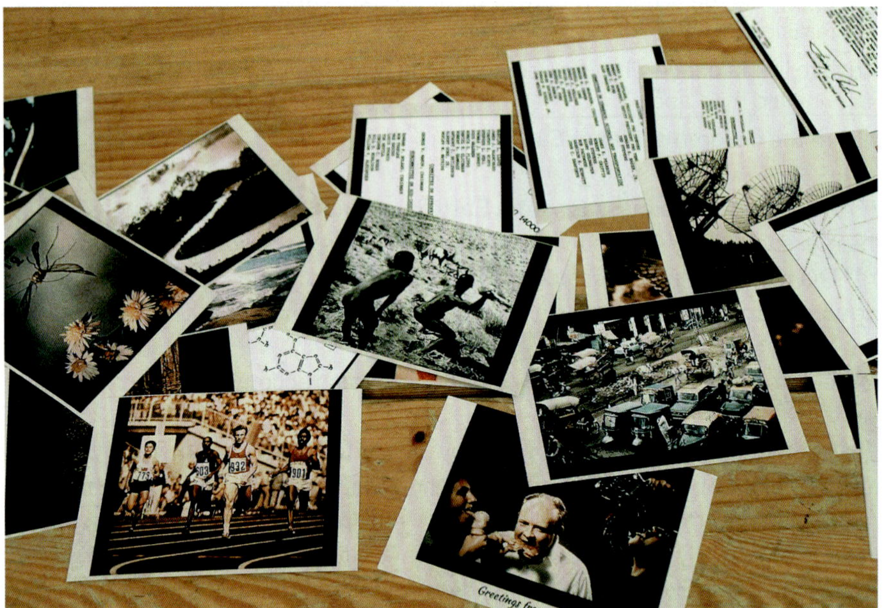

Images of the *Voyager Golden Record*.

What if one took this task as a starting point again for the creation of a similar message from life on Earth, this time a live instead of a recorded one?

How could one describe the world in a similar way today?

How can one reproduce an imaginary of the past in order to be able to imagine in the present?

How could a past dream once more appeal and expand the human spirit, especially in relation to collective dreaming and imagining?

How can we co-imagine not in the 1970s but in the beginning of the 21st century?

2 → Bernard Oliver quoted in Carl Sagan, *Murmurs of Earth, The Voyager Interstellar Record* (New York: Ballantine Books, 1979).

3 → Carl Sagan. *Murmurs of Earth, The Voyager Interstellar Record* (New York: Ballantine Books, 1979).

How can we dream together not in the time of the great fascination of humanity with space or the time of the sexual revolution and the other social imaginaries that emerged during the 1960s and 1970s, but in 2018 when public sphere and what we have in common gradually disappears and is under constant threat?

HOW TO TALK TO ALIENS?

Imagine the naked man and woman of NASA standing in front of you.[4]

Imagine them trying to re-narrate, in their own way, the story of life on Earth as this is found in the *Voyager Golden Record*, a clearly Western-based linear narration of our life that departs from the planet's place in universe and human biology to then move to animals, nature, human races, the way our social life is organized in cities, families, schools etc.

Imagine a naked man and woman as a live message from Earth today. Imagine them around a large dinner table, served with drinks, desserts and the images from Earth sent into space in 1977. Imagine them talking about how we walk, run, eat, drink, and relate as if their guests never heard of these before. Imagine them in a typical gesture of human hospitality, greeting their guests continuously by using the original archive's greetings or by pointing to small details in the pictures on the table.

Imagine this peculiar community of naked and dressed human beings attempting to reproduce a social imaginary from a time when shared imaginaries where much more vivid and perhaps also much more irrational in order to understand how such imaginaries could possibly also emerge now. And then imagine this awkward encounter being interrupted repeatedly by the statement of the president of USA, a reminder of humanity's voice still travelling in space since 1977.

What if NASA's message managed to reach extraterrestrials?

What if this message was not just phonograph records but a live performance of human beings?

What if terrestrials would indeed meet (extra)terrestrials in person?

How does a peculiar dinner of two naked and several dressed humans relate to critical voices of our time?

HOW TO TALK TO ALIENS?

Dunne and Raby say that today we experience a serious crisis of imagination.[5] Our social imaginaries have been downgraded to hopes. We hope that everything will be alright, but there are no more visions. We don't know how to dream collectively about changing things, we are just hopeful. This has been the

4 → All descriptions refer to the performance "One Small Step for a Man: Hello, Goodbye," by Danae Theodoridou which premiered in March 2016 in Michael Cacoyannis Foundation in Athens.

5 → Anthony Dunne and Fiona Raby, *Speculative everything: design, fiction, and social dreaming* (Cambridge: MIT Press, 2014).

price we had to pay especially after the fall of the Berlin Wall in 1989, the triumph of capitalism, the atomization of society, and the frustration that followed the decay of the great dreams of the 20th century. All these, they say, make political and social speculation today more difficult and less likely. Anything that does not align with the dominant thinking lines of neoliberal thought are dismissed as something not to be taken seriously, as 'unreal' or fantasy. Today the 'real' expanded and swallowed up whole continents of social imagination.

Frederik Jameson argues that it is now easier for us to imagine a comet impacting the planet and ending life on Earth than imaging an alternative to capitalism.[6]

Cornelius Castoriadis reminds us that what is presented as extreme rationality in modern society is simply dominant syllogisms that borrow their content from the imaginary.[7] Today's obsession with 'rationality' is only a second-order imaginary, a pseudo-rationality that arbitrarily posits itself as an end intending nothing but a formal and empty 'rationalization.' This is visibly so, for example, when we look at the place of individuals at all the levels of the productive and economic structure. In the case of the worker, the employee, or even the 'executive,' replacing a person by an ensemble of partial features and treating them as a thing or as a purely mechanical system and evaluating them in this way, as we see it often happening in the various evaluation tests used by companies today, is not less but more imaginary than claiming to see a person as an octopus for example. In fact, an octopus may resemble much more a human than a mechanical system does, since they are both animals.

How would a city built by humans and octopuses look like?

How to (co-)imagine other ways of living together in a time that leaves no space for imagination and has often been described as the time of 'no alternative?'

HOW TO TALK TO ALIENS?

"Greetings from the red of the shirt of a young athlete running in the Olympics in Munich 1972."

"Greetings from the green of the skin of a little frog."

"Greetings from the black of the sweater of a little student in South Korea."

"Greetings from the white of the teeth of a woman licking an ice-cream in America."

"Greetings from the dark blue of the sea around the smallest island of the Pacific Ocean."

"Greetings from the yellow of the bananas in a supermarket's trolley in Denmark."[8]

6 → Frederik Jameson, *Archaeologies of the Future* (London: Verso Books, 2007).

7 → Cornelius Castoriadis, *The Imaginary Institution of Society* (Cambridge: Polity Press, 1987).

8 → Theodoridou, *One Small Step for a Man: Hello, Goodbye.*

Every society, for Castoriadis, attempts to give an answer to a few fundamental questions:[9]

Who are we as a collectivity?

What are we for one another?

What do we want?

What do we desire?

What are we lacking?

HOW TO TALK TO ALIENS?

And it provides answers to these questions through systems of imaginary significations valuing or devaluing, structuring and hierarchizing an ensemble of objects and corresponding lacks. This means that societies, even the most 'rational' ones like ours, are totally dependent on their own imaginaries presented as 'reality.' Moreover, what is essential for the creation of alternative imaginaries or 'realities,' according to Castoriadis, is not 'discovery' but constituting the new. The Athenians did not 'find' democracy among the other wild flowers growing around the Acropolis, nor did the Parisian workers find the Commune by digging up the boulevards. Nor did any of them 'discover' these institutions after inspecting all previous forms of government, placed in well-ordered showcases. On the contrary, they invented something, they tried something out, which proved to be viable in particular circumstances, but which also, once it existed, changed these circumstances essentially.

Dunne and Raby also stress that alternatives are exactly what we need.[10]

We need to imagine new trajectories for the 21st century.

OK, let's dream.

But how can we do so in a time of no alternative?

How can we imagine a future seen not as a destination but as a medium to aid imaginative thought to speculate with, not just about the future but about today too?

And how can art open such space for imagination?

How can it move beyond neoliberal modes of production, which ask artists to fully preplan their projects, envision them always to the future, present the results of projects that haven't even started yet and prove the full value of them, preferably money value, in advance, only to then

9 → Castoriadis, *The Imaginary Instituion of Society*.
10 → Dunne/Raby, *Speculative everything: design, fiction, and social dreaming*.

be given permission and support to simply execute them?

How can art today open space for experimentation, risk, and imagination, offering social and political alternatives, as is its main role?

HOW TO TALK TO ALIENS?

Imagine again that naked man and woman, who are still eating with their guests around the large table. Imagine them struggling to alienate and unfamiliarize the banal, the known, the everyday; trying to estrange 'reality' and everything we take for granted, suggesting that the weirdness and imaginary quality of things we don't even think of, like the way we speak, eat, or greet, could possibly give rise to alternative understandings of what it is that we do and how, and subsequently also of how we do things differently.

Richard Kearney discusses processes of alienation that subvert our established categories and challenge us to think again by threatening the known with the unknown.[11] For him, if something or someone becomes *"too transcendent,* they disappear off our radar screen and we lose all contact."[12] We thus stop seeing them or even conceiving them as this or that thing, which means that we become unable to recognize, imagine, or narrate their alterity. On the other hand, if something or someone becomes too *"immanent,* they become equally exempt from ethical relation."[13] In this case, they become indistinguishable from one's own self and we are again unable to see them, recognize them, or imagine them as different. It is for this reason that one should not "let the foreign become *too* foreign or the familiar *too* familiar"[14] but constantly try out a variety of crossings between the same and the other, that is, between knowing and not knowing. By suspending our defense mechanisms against alterity, we may be able to rise to a poetics of new images and an ethics of new practices, he concludes.

By returning to a past social imaginary, as this was expressed via *Voyager Golden Record*; by reproducing an imaginary from a time when imaginaries were more likely; by delving deeper into an imaginative movement that today would most likely be dismissed as at least bizarre; by addressing once more every spacefaring civilization, (we tried to embrace alienation—not too much, not too little) we can approach the inevitable others with which we share life on this planet and co-imagine with them new images and practices for our present and future. In order to indeed manage to talk to the aliens of this Earth…

11 → Richard Kearney, *Strangers, Gods and Monsters: Interpreting Otherness* (London: Routledge, 2003).
12 → Kearney, Strangers, *Gods and Monsters: Interpreting Otherness,* 11.
13 → Kearney, Strangers, *Gods and Monsters: Interpreting Otherness,* 11.
14 → Kearney, Strangers, *Gods and Monsters: Interpreting Otherness,* 11.

I'm not going to tell a story that puts all the parts together

→ An interview with Leslie Thornton on her work *The Great Invisible*

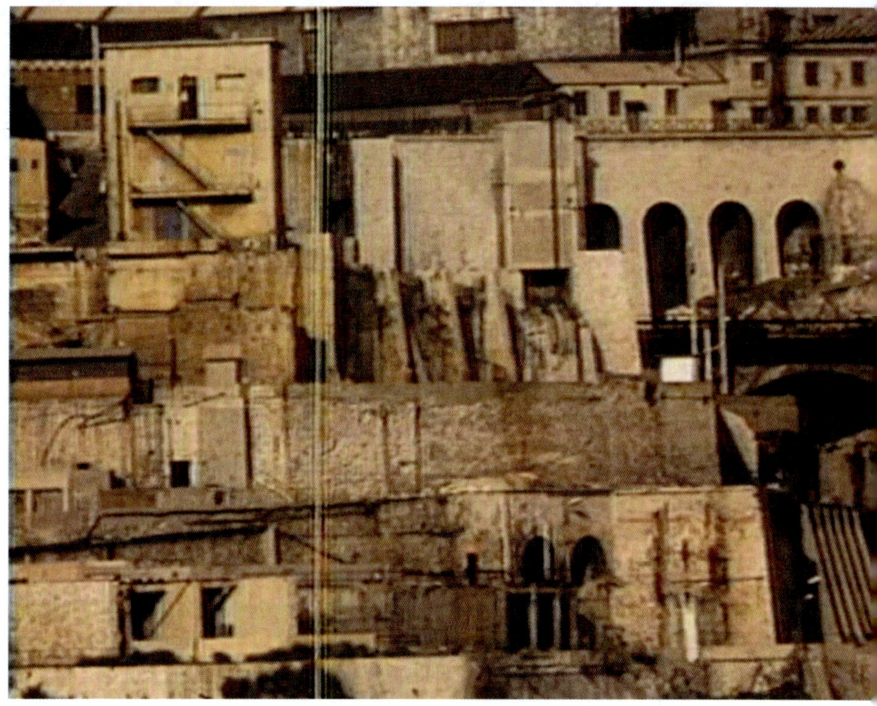

Leslie Thornton, *The Great Invisible*, 2002–ongoing, film still.

You could describe *The Great Invisible* as a mystic performance: following Isabelle Eberhardt's path as she sets out to become the great 19th century adventurer/writer/explorer, Thornton's film is a re-enactment of her moving to Algiers, dressed as a man. And as much as Eberhardt converts to Qadiriyya, a Sufi order of Islam, the film performs a mystic journey against the long tentacles of exoticism.

In her combination of documentary footage, enacted 'historical' staging and making-of-scenes, Leslie Thornton reflects about the status of images in their relation to technologies of representation: Performing against the fetish of the reliving.

Pujan Karambeigi: I would like to start this conversation by talking about what one might call the plot. I know that many scholars have (aptly) focused on your deconstruction and fragmentation of the narrative. However, in *The Great Invisible* the very story of Isabelle Eberhardt seems to be a crucial guideline: A woman breaking out of her patriarchal surroundings to become part of a hallucinatory experiment. Eberhardt joins the Qadiriyya, a Sufi order of Islam known for its mystic practices. What role does hallucination play in *The Great Invisible*?

Leslie Thornton: That is an interesting question; I'll begin in another place and circle back to this topic. When I started the project, I had one agenda, but it's changed very much in the remaining years, after I went to Algeria. When I was there, and the government stepped down, and the civil war broke out, that was the beginning of 1992. And I was shooting this narrative like a period piece, organized around this character, the subject, this historical figure, that I was fascinated by, but also didn't care for too much. There was more of an interest in what surrounded her historically. If I was plotting anything, I'll say it was more of a quest on my part in *The Great Invisible*, to deal with biography in a different way and history in a different way. I'm not going to tell a story that puts all the parts together. I'm going to drift across many possibilities that are suggested or documented, things that can contradict each other, and I try to do this in a number of ways, including having a number of different women's voiceovers, or people I call the storytellers, including me. And it was like a bit of an excuse to study this period of time. And definitely an excuse to look into Arab culture, not necessarily Islam, but Arab culture in both the title's reference to lack, or invisibility, the invisibility of this world culture in the United States, on a popular culture level. There wasn't an Arab World. Until terrorism comes onto the front page.

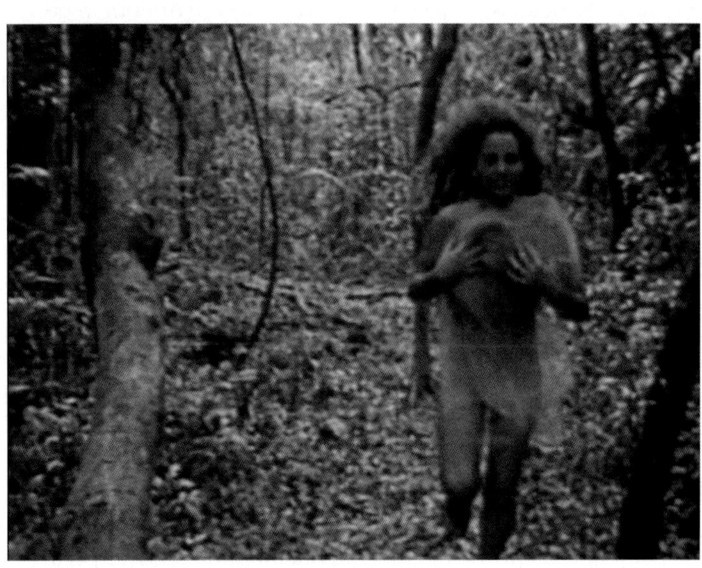

Leslie Thornton, *The Great Invisible*, 2002–ongoing, film still.

Pujan Karambeigi: If I may reiterate my question, because I think there's something to it. I wasn't implying you have a plot, or you used her plot, and what's been told of her. What I meant is that in some sense *The Great Invisible* reflects her getting away from her patriarchal surroundings into the hallucinatory practices of the Qadiriyya.

Leslie Thornton: Yes, so now to try to answer your question — you are right, in a way. I was tracing a rejection of 19th century Western rationalism and materiality. Eberhardt embraced mysticism. This woman struggled with a father — as you said — a patriarchal figure — but literally this particular man/creature/person, a Russian anarchist, posing as a pope in the Russian Orthodox Church. She goes from this into an orientalism. She wasn't, I would say, quite the same kind of orientalist as so many of her literary and artistic peers. Her transformation happened in more subtle, complex ways. Her aim was to find another way of being, one that felt true, a way of being that she could believe, and inhabit fully. Hallucination, is not the term I would use for mystical experience.

When I started this project I had imagined an extreme experience for the viewer. For the last 10 minutes of the work, there would be an inducement towards a trance-like state. This would happen through a relentless manipulation, with repetitive sound and image. The viewer would be faced with an unanticipated shift in form that would discourage customary ways of following a narrative. The familiarity of cinematic forms would drop away. I imagined wearing down resistance in the viewer, abandoning the familiar in favor of a disorientation, kind of 'not knowing,' which is in part how I understand mystical practice to work. I wanted to point towards the ecstatic.

In Sufism it could be the case that one's erudite, literate, and highly educated Master would instruct an initiate to stop reading books. To attain a mystical state, there must be a letting go of what is generally considered knowledge, allowing another kind of "knowing" to come forward. The mind, the actual brain is altered. These are beginning steps to ecstasy—you are not worried, you are not in danger, and you enter into a kind of detached present, an arrestment or stopping of time. And I'm not a mystic. But I was thinking about that it all along, as I was drawn to the particularity of her existence. I even thought, in another world, and time, and life, I could have been a mystic.

> Pujan Karambeigi: How would you describe the process of re-engaging with Isabelle Eberhardt after your first encounter with her in *There Was an Unseen Cloud* (1988)? For instance, in *Unseen Cloud*, it seems to me that the work shows us the very limits of looking outside of us: We cannot know anything of Isabelle (nor Islam). Or rather, the film asked: Who am I to say anything about Orientalism? Would you say it is a way of re-captivating that question of how far you can get in encountering something outside of yourself?

Leslie Thornton: *Unseen Cloud* was made very much as a surface, and it was meant to be on the surface. It relates most closely to my earlier work *Adynata*. As I embarked on *The Great Invisible* I had a very different attitude. I have a hard time with the puritanical, politically correct position, of designating who can say what about what. I felt that I could position myself as an outsider, but speak with responsibility and sensitivity about another culture, another way of existing that was not my own. For example, it is the case that when traveling in a North African country, one might visit an hamam with American and local friends, and with no thought of embarrassment, give each other a good thorough wash sitting in a room of nude women. And upon return to America, with the same friends this would not happen. How can it be comfortable in one place and not in the other? Because that is the case— it is OK there and not so OK here. So I get very impatient with Western academics who critique the attribution of a greater sensuality within one culture over another. As if to be sensual is a diminishment. Maybe what I'm calling sensuality is just a more comfortable relation to the body. To acknowledge attractive difference across cultures is not to diminish. Rather, to deny this difference is to diminish and to place oneself in a higher, though false, position.

> Pujan Karambeigi: There is one particular story you tell in *The Great Invisible*: In 1991 you embarked with a ferry from Geneva to Algiers, almost a century after Isabelle Eberhardt went on that same journey. A day

before you left you rented French military uniforms, the woolen symbols of imperialism. Already on the ferry, you realize that it might be a bad idea to bring these media of repression through customs. So, we watch you dismembering them: taking the precious material apart and re-assembling it, rendering its origin and its use almost inconceivable. In fact, what remained were traces of colonialism, invisible to the customs control.

It seems to me that this 'anecdote' of dismembering and re-assembling carries a pertinent relation to your own moving image practice.

Leslie Thornton: Yes, we were outdoing Belgian deconstructive fashion! Do you mean in the sense of taking something apart, and putting it together in a strange way that still holds up? I never thought about this anecdote as a metaphor, but you're probably right about that.

I don't like the notion of anti-story applied to my work; rather, I would say I'm interested in storytelling, but in a dimensional form of what I call verticality in story. I'm interested in a continued expansion of form that we recognize as narrative-like. Certainly newer technologies such as VR and gaming will impact story, and some of that will rise above the commercial and entertainment level. I will stick to the vertically deep dimensional environment of the technologies I already know. I like the idea of a shift in form that is like a shift in key in music. It changes everything but it is all still connected, moving forward. It may be jarring. It wakes us, it heightens us. It's like you are walking up a hill but then you are falling down a mountain.

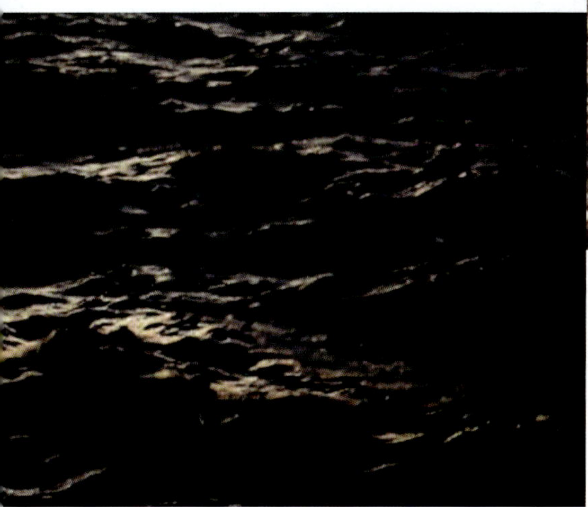

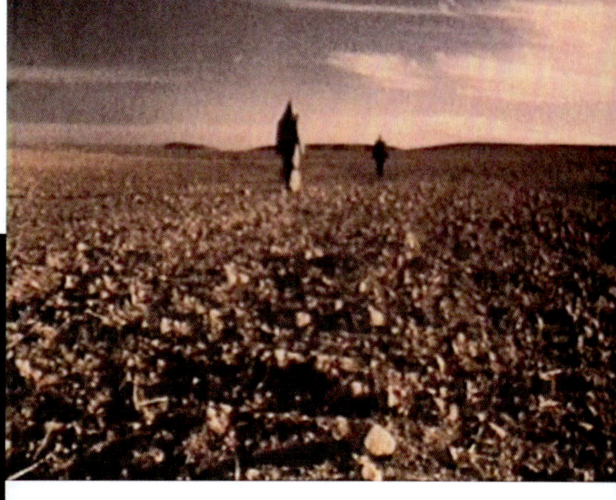

Leslie Thornton, *The Great Invisible*, 2002–ongoing, film stills.

home → Tepping1337: RIP HOME!!!
Tepping1337: RIP HOME!!!
Tinki Winky: :O
Tepping1337: It was fun!!!!
Jasmin: one minute
Window_Viper: I love u all.... :<

The final 60 seconds of Playstation
Home before Sony unplugged

the virtual wonderland. There is no plug. You cannot, but return. Home urges to explore so-called "roots," to investigate what it is that structures. Home is an attempt to recover, a place mental and real, in which past and futures collide. There is no RIP. Home is where the heart is. Home is where it hurts.

Traces of Places →
My Dog is My Piano →

Antonia Baehr

Tocki and Bettina von Arnim live together in the same house. They do not speak the same language, they are hardly alike and yet, they have assembled.

In the sonic lecture performance *My Dog is My Piano*, Antonia Baehr sketches a subjective acoustic portrait of the affinity between her mother, Bettina von Arnim, and her dog, Tocki: what kind of language emerges from this long duet of everyday comings and goings, of these choreographies of affinities? *My Dog is my Piano* engages with a very specific companionship. Yet, it examines ways of observing and recording in general. It maps traces, archival material and acoustic inscriptions and drafts a score for an interspecies togetherness. The house in which Bettina von Arnim and Tocki live becomes an archive, precious for archaeological examinations. Over years, dogs and humans have lived there together leaving traces in the architecture and the ecosystem: scratches on the doors, dents on steps, bird's nests built out of dog's hair. The archive encapsulates Bettina von Arnim and Tocki. They articulate every notch and trace there is and establish a language, an acoustic archive, that witnesses their companionship. In *My Dog is my Piano*, the house of Bettina von Arnim becomes the score of the choreography of everyday life. The score presents the means of analysis and in the end it is the score that characterizes and transcribes the relationships.

My Dog is My Piano has three parts. In part one Antonia Baehr stands behind a table with two turntables and a mixer on it. Baehr spins two records each under one hand, labeling and commenting along her sound experiments. In part two Baehr manipulates transparencies and objects on an overhead projector, while a video of an interview with her mother is projected superimposing the overhead images. In the last part Baehr becomes Tocki, Bettina von Arnim, the record players, and the house altogether at the same time with her voice.

I started this work upon an invitation to partake in a conference on affinities by the philosophers François Noudelmann and Avital Ronell in New York City in the Fall of 2011. Some further participants were Pierre Bayard, Judith Butler, Hélène Cixous, and Yann Toma. Donna Haraway was invited as well but she had to stay home with her dogs. She was present all the same through her book, The Companion Species Manifesto: Dogs, People and Significant Otherness that I was offered to read for the occasion. I was programmed in the evening about musical patterns of affinity. Six years later, this invitation by warehouse to contribute to an ethnographic online archive brought my mother's dog to play being her piano again, since it is the perfect project for this invitation: an online archive about a live work about a kind of archive that is alive because that archive is played live everyday by its protagonists… Oh dear, this sounds quite nebulous. Anyway, here it is. Antonia Baehr

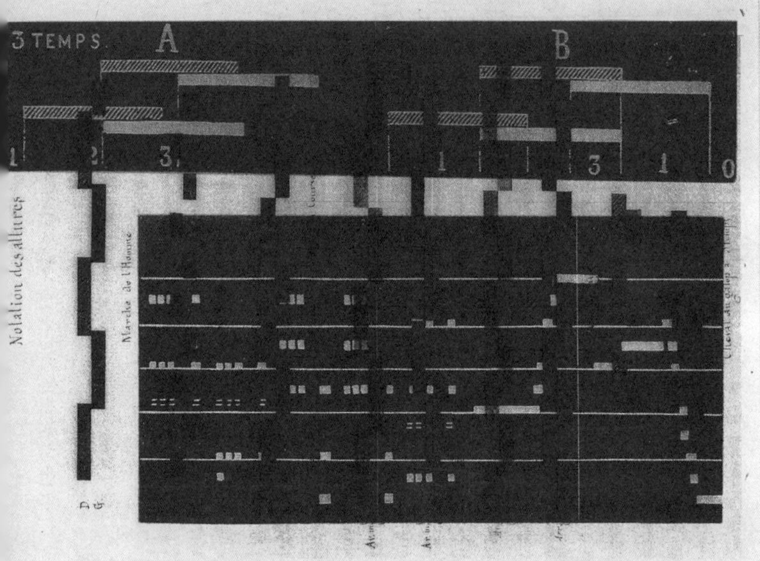

Notation des allures (1887) by Étienne-Jules Marey, manipulated by Antonia Baehr.

ANTONIA BAEHR,
standing behind a DJ table with two turntables and a mixer on it, three-quarter facing the audience.
She wears red nail polish on her left hand. The speakers in the room are paned left/right.

Good evening. My name is Antonia Baehr and I will present *My Dog is My Piano*, a sonic lecture-performance in three parts.

She plays the first track, looks at the audience once it plays.
She says to the audience:

My mother, the painter and engraver Bettina von Arnim, and Tocki, her dog, live together in same house since nearly four years in the south of France.

They don't speak the same language, they are hardly alike, and yet, they have assembled.

This is part one. Part one could be called "Qui se ressemble s'assemble" or "Qui ne se ressemble pas s'assemble". It's a french saying which means "Who resembles tends to assemble."

⦿ On this record, I have my mother, Bettina

⦿ On this record, I have Tocki, her dog

You just heard:
LATE MORNING, IN THE STUDIO UNDER THE ROOF, SEWING AND GROOMING

SOME HOURS LATER, MOTHER SEWING
She plays the track.

DOG SCRATCHING HIMSELF
She plays the track.
I compare.
She fades from one record to the other on the mixer.
I mix.
She mixes the two sounds on the records.

LUNCH TIME, IN THE KITCHEN,
DOG EATING UNDER THE STOOL

She plays the track called "gamelle" (dog's bowl in French).

WOMAN EATING SITTING AT THE TABLE

She plays the tracks.
I juxtapose.
On the mixer she goes from one sound on the one record to the other sound on the
other record,
in fast back and forth motions.
I assemble.
She pans the sound to the left and then to the right.
(Tocki has two tracks, "Knochen" (bone in German) and "gamelle")

EARLY AFTERNOON, AFTER THE SIESTA,
BETTINA DRINKING WATER, and: TOCKI DRINKING WATER

I phase up.

Without motor, she tries to phase both records up.

A SENTENCE " "

She gestures accents and holds, with one hand in the air.

A PARAGRAPH ( )

She gestures stormy bubbling and emotional, with both hands, legato.[3]

A WORD

She does one single quick fade up and down.

A SONG

She starts gesturing like "paragraph," then with both hands in the air, and she gets into the space with her gaze, reaching out of the theater.

This was side A, THE PARALLEL LIFE; LIVING SIDE BY SIDE //

She pans the sound to the middle.

And now we come to side B, THE SHARED LIFE; RELATING TO EACH OTHER #

ON THE STAIRS OF THE HOUSE: WALKING UP AND DOWN THE FLOORS TOGETHER

She turns the records to side B and puts the needles on.

WITH 6 LEGS " ""

She gestures walking up the three floors of the house with four fingers on the left hand and two fingers, index and middle finger, on the right hand.

WITH 4 LEGS ""

She gestures walking up the three floors of the house with four fingers on the left hand.

WITH 2 LEGS "

She gestures walking up the floors of the house with two fingers, index and middle finger, on the right hand.

I explore rhythmic structure.

She Djs seriously. The record players' motors are off.

And now we come to the INTER-SPECIES LINGUISTICS: PATOISER Etymologically, "patoiser" is old French and means speaking with one's paws, so in English it would be "pawese" or "pawish."

She gestures "pawish."

To communicate, Tocki and Bettina have assembled a language that could be called a "companion species patois."

Patois is a french word for any language that is considered non standard. But it's also a derogative word for a local language.

The "patois" that Bettina and Tocki have assembled is an impure, not standardized, queer, crossbred, mongrel, métissée, bricollé, self-made language. Un language fait maison.

She puts the needles on both records.

It doesn't come out of dog school. It's a dysfunctional language, it doesn't really work in a "proper" way, as you will see, but I must say, it works quite well in an "improper" way.

She plays the mother on the mother's record saying: "Mach wuf"
She says: "Say woof!"
She plays the dog on the other record barking three times.

He says: "Oui oui oui," "Yes yes yes," "Ja ja ja."

I match.
She spins her mother back with motor.

I match the other way around.
I magnify.

She slows the records down, turns them extremely slowly with one finger on each record, loud and crazy, starting with Tocki, adding gain and reverb, all with record players' motors cut.
I make them compete.
She spins up the Tocki record very fast with one finger, then immediately after the Mimsou record, steps back and watches the result of the competition: which record will be the last to stop turning

And I conclude:
TOCKI ASKING:
She plays the track and taps with the fingers of one hand in the other hand's lap, producing a similar sound to Tocki's wagging tail.
HE WAGGS HIS TAIL

MOTHER ASKING:
She plays the track and then translates it.
SHE SINGS: "Tockilein, Tockilein, dancing, dancing," AND THEN SHE SAYS: "He goes away, it doesn't interest him at all!"

I LISTEN AGAIN:
She plays the track again.

(Part 1 is approx. 24 min. long)

She stops the records.

Now we come to part two.

She removes the Tocki record which was covering the Vivaldi record
on the turntables.

Part two could be called THE CHOREOGRAPHY OF COHABITATION or in german HAUSMUSIK.

HAUSMUSIK is a very common practice in Germany. In the living room of middle class houses, family and friends perform classical music together for pleasure, in an amateur way.

My mother, who lives in a big middle class, bourgeois house in the Lot, in the southwest of France, is nostalgic of this tradition. So she often plays records of Baroque music to make her dog dance.

She takes the record in hand and gestures around the table.

The dog trots nicely around the big dinner table, in rythm to the music like a little horse.

She plays Vivaldi.

BETTINA VON ARNIM

There are several places with traces of dogs,
also from the times before we lived here. You see them on every door of the house.
The dogs scratched the doors to come in. The little dogs at the bottom and the large
ones there where we human beings put our hand or insert the key to open the door.
The wood is all scratched.

ANTONIA BAEHR

Is that the main entrance door?

BETTINA VON ARNIM

Yes, that's the big front door.

BETTINA VON ARNIM

Outside the door, you see a large stone or ledge. The stone is all shiny. The dogs
that guarded the house have polished the stone with their fur. And the soles of the
humans that for the last 200 years went in and out of the house have polished
the stone too.

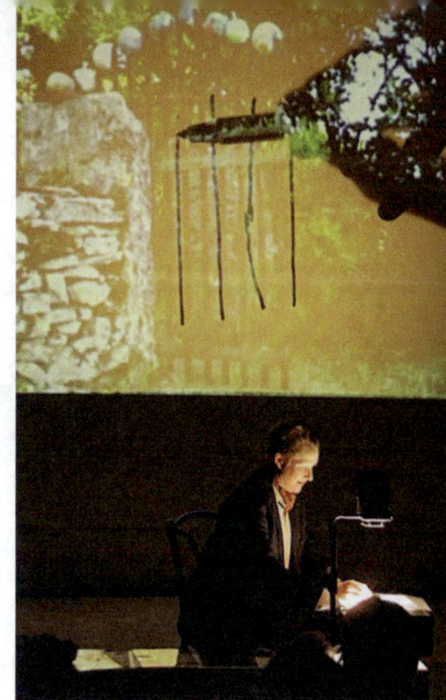

Antonia Baehr performing *My Dog is My Piano.*

So it's the traces of a house, a living house with animals and humans together.

BETTINA VON ARNIM

Then there is a funny picture of the garden door with the traces of all the dogs
we had:
 the little Kniggy, Bimbo the Wild, Berry the Beautiful, the wonderful big collie,
and now Tocki. We gave the balls of the children to the dogs and played soccer
with them. But after a minute you heard "pffff." The dog's teeth pierced the balls, the
air went out, they shook and tore them up. Later you found them somewhere in the
garden again. Finally I installed the whole collection
of these balls like scalps or mummies.
You can see them now on the garden door.

ANTONIA BAEHR

Are there other places where dogs have left their traces in this house?

BETTINA VON ARNIM

Yes, in the trees near the entrance.
From the window of my studio up there
I can see the nests of birds. When it was the collie, with his soft long hair, the birds
built wonderful comfortable nests. With Bimbo
the Wild, they couldn't build lovely nests.
His hair was short and black. The nests were built with a bit of plastic, ugly nests.
And Tocki now, with his reddish brown hair, provides good materials for the birds

ANTONIA BAEHR

Can we see a nest now?

BETTINA VON ARNIM

Now you can see the vacuum cleaner's content. All the dog hair and dirt in the living room, I bring it back to the garden with the vacuum cleaner so the birds can pick their materials for their nests from the emptied bag.
And if you like, you can look at that.

Do you want more traces?

And now we come to Part three, the last part.

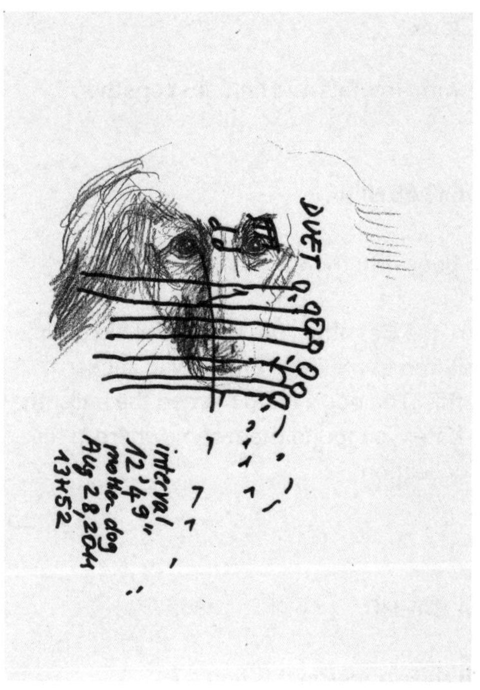

Drawing by Bettina von Arnim, overhead transparency by Antonia Baehr.

Antonia Baehr switches off the overhead projector and beamer. She drinks

from a glass of water. She installs a music stand in the center of the room, facing the audience. She opens the score, puts her glasses on, and says:

Part three is called "Resonances in Furry Humanese."

1 →   Nanna Heidenreich, "My dog is my piano,"
      accessed June 15, 2017, http://bit.ly/2zilXCh.
2 →   Antonia Baehr, *My Dog is My Piano*, premiere:
      Tramway, Glasgow, May 25, 2013.
3 →   In 1937 their beloved Basket died, and Gertrude
      Stein and Alice B. Toklas got another poodle
      who they named Basket. "Basket, a large, unwieldy
      white poodle, still will get up on Gertrude's lap
      and stay there. She says that listening to the
      rhythm of his water drinking made her recognize
      the difference between sentences and paragraphs,
      that paragraphs are emotional and sentences
      are not." Gertrude Stein, *The autobiography of
      Alice B. Toklas* (Seattle: Stellar Classics, 2013).

"She KNOWS no hatred." → Reading Diaries → Tilman Richter

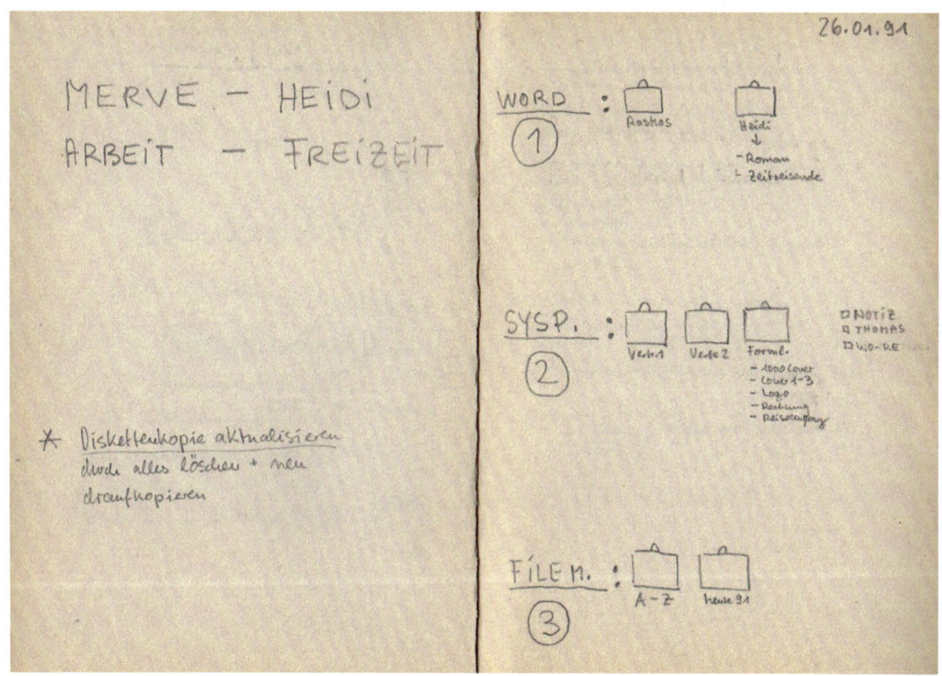

Note by Heidi Paris, 1991.

www.rainaldgoetz.de

The self as a web address. Prior to social media, the domain name of Rainald Goetz's diary project *Abfall für alle* spelled out a connection executed by the technological means of the year 1998. The productive intersection of public and private sphere becomes legible in this online released novel. Nowadays the web address links only to Goetz's publisher's homepage. I have to read the 864 page-long paperback lying on my desk, colored in the distinctive red-orange that marks all of Goetz's publications of the late 1990s. Whatever traces the digital has left have to be read out of the text; its technological preconditions are inaccessible.

Due to its real-time publication (not only its specific date but also the exact time of publishing is recorded for each entry) the readers of *Abfall für alle* reappear in the entries and their readings of the texts are articulated in other places. These feedback loops are moderated by the form of a diary. In a novel with the indicative title, *Dekonspiratione*, one of Goetz's characters names her lecture on Ingeborg Bachmann's diary-novel, *Malina*: *Diskretion als Form* (discretion as a form). This title could have served as a motto for *Abfall*. Discretion becomes a principle for the formation of Goetz's text because it reacts to the diary's demand for openness. As a principle discretion calls for constant reflection: What's supposed to be in the text, what has to be left out? Not only is the text formed through an artistic process, but also through the management of the social aspects of the diary. What form of intimacy may it force onto the reader? Goetz claims: "Basically, I absolutely want to let people BE."[1] But in being published this claim wants to be acknowledged, at least it has to be written down.

If understood as a social practice, reading diaries gains a new perspective. The diary's text is connected to an exterior—which for Goetz means: to the bodies. In *Abfall für alle* some of those connections are explicit. For example, the *Chroniken* (Chronicles) of Heidi Paris, co-owner of Merve publishing, archived under the domain www.heidi-paris.de. In the course of the year 1998 Merve released Goetz's volume

Note by Heidi Paris, 1991.

Mix, Cuts, Scratches (co-authored by Westbam). The physical proximity of Berlin and the media typical of the time connect Paris and Goetz ("there's a very holy-day-ish fax from Heidi");[2] their notations of that year intersect. So, I end up reading Heidi Paris's writing about herself, describing her impressions while reading *Abfall* written in the third person:

"Tuesday, March 31, 1998. Downloaded/printed out Rainald Goetz's complete diary *Abfall für alle*. At night, complete reading of the 121 packed pages. The forced voyeur's gaze feels awkward to her, when he's doing laundry and so on, interesting are the notes/reflections on his own writing practice, his preparations for the event on poetics in Frankfurt. The internet has but one disadvantage: 'The impossibility of responding or retorting … that's what the principal of power is based on.'[3]"

The first entry in *Abfall* is dated February 2, 1998, but the internet was then still a fickle medium—the collected entries up to then are only published by March 30. It's Paris's first impression of *Abfall* that focusses directly on its distinctive topics. Aside from the distinctions "awkward" and "interesting" she focuses on the configuration of privacy in the text: "The forced voyeur's gaze"—the reader sees more than she shows, but also more than she wants to see. The negotiation between one's own and the other is recorded publicly, it lacks the possibility of reaction and conflict. That of all things the "impossibility to answer" is described as a characteristic of the internet seems to be a curious observation from today's point of view. But precisely "the notes/reflections on his own writing practice" deal with this problem. Goetz is preparing *praxis*, his Frankfurt lectures on poetics. Documenting the preparations for *praxis* and his readings of famous predecessors, the diary leads him and Heidi Paris to Ingeborg Bachmann who is quoted on the question of the individual in writing:

"Although the diary/I seems to act at random, it is selective by nature. The I does not figure the whole of André Gide but it poses—I do not mean this in a pejorative way—as the author André Gide. It is the distinctive feature of the diary/I that it does not have to create the character 'I,' just as the letter I. It has got no choice but to be incorporated (as I) into the text."[4]

The 'I' predates the autobiographical statement and thereby doubles itself: It is given as content, as a representation, as a pose, as a character; on the other hand, it acts as the selective, the creative entity. It has the ability to arrange its pose confidently or can choose to play with it. The subject of the diary is based on the observation and management of this doubling. In doing so, it is indistinguishable from other subjectivities, but it exposes the mode of this process.

Heidi Paris inquires about this doubled subjectivity in a letter to Goetz listed in *Chroniken* on April 13: "Doesn't the relationship turn around and everything lived becomes degraded to material and one lives for one's stories?"[5] Goetz himself draws attention to this problem in *Abfall*. For him the danger lies in the "Ernst-Jüngerisierung" of the diary, in it's literalization. The diary's appeal draws from the tension between the written person and the writing person. The overly confident narrator who designs his records in a literary manner risks to become literature herself and therefore becoming unobservable, an author in the emphatic sense (of the word). A diary, not drawing a clear distinction between itself and the world, can make for a surprising, even unpleasant read. Sometimes the management of proximity and distance fails. Heidi Paris, November 4, 1998:

"The public mention of her full name in Goetz's internet-diary had appalled her. It was like somebody pointed the finger at her in front of everybody. Had she not enjoyed more than 25 years of working for her publishing house virtually incognito?! Usually, when reading Goetz's diary, she loved it as a message in a bottle. One could choose what to feel addressed by. Mentioning her name spoiled this sophisticated game. Well, some seriousness in that matter might be demanded by factuality."[6]

Mentioning Paris' name destroys the illusion of a closed body of text. The published text integrates her as a persona. Not by accident but with a clear intention: "Yesterday Heidi Paris said something completely extreme: she says, she KNOWS no hatred."[7] In his remarks from October 31 Goetz puts Paris on the opposite of himself. Reflecting on her lack of hatred he asks for his own constitution that draws its productivity from nothing but hatred. The diary-ego uses an alter to question itself. The self constitutes itself in demarcation from others. But, for reasons of discretion, decency, and tact ("don't point your finger at them!"), the details of this process are usually concealed. The distancing description of the interaction of two subjects raises suspicion: is somebody trying to reign over this social situation, by means of writing, interrupting reciprocity? Toward the end of *Abfall* Goetz observes these problems:

"1929. Because of *Abfall* people close to me got entangled in a tricky, peculiar situation, and I had to rely on the fact that everybody pretended as if they wouldn't notice a thing. Thanks to all who played this discretion game so indulgently with me. Even to me the mechanism that is at work here is not quite clear. It has to do with the treachery of the written word, the topic of *Dekonspiratione*. In the dreamlike addressee-directed sensing, a kind of abstract You has emerged whose silence attracts and leads me, most of the time. I thought I knew what belongs here and what doesn't."[8]

The written word betrays the social situation. It complicates the "discretion game," changes its rules. Aspects of one's self and of others become entangled, their spatial recording through writing enables discontinuity, switching, and crossings. The description of the other becomes a guideline for myself, the constitution of the self an impertinence to others. We (the 'We' of the year 2017) had to learn how to play a multitude of media-based games of subjectivity, sociality, discretion, and networks. Online subjectivity more than ever is written as an address. This process doesn't have to take place explicitly on social networks, but subjectivity emerges from data and its relations nevertheless. In order to deal with this situation new techniques are needed. Relating to one's self poses new requirements. Instead of dramatizing the technological ruptures it might be helpful to reconstruct older feedback-loops of media-based communication.

Not least, the analysis of writing enables ethnographies of digital spaces. The lesson that could be learned from ethnography stands upright: Not only the production of data but also its interpretation causes individualization: "To all questions the diary's basic answer is: what's YOUR point of view?"[9]

1 → Rainald Goetz, *Abfall für alle*, trans. author (Frankfurt am Main: Suhrkamp, 2003), 568.
2 → Goetz, *Abfall für alle*, 863.
3 → Heidi Paris, "Chroniken. Wo die Zeit geblieben ist," accessed June 10, 2017, trans. author, http://www.heidi-paris.de/chroniken/1998/.
4 → Ingeborg Bachmann, *Frankfurter Vorlesungen. Probleme zeitgenössischer Dichtung*, trans. author (München: Piper Verlag, 1980), 48.
5 → Paris, "Chroniken. Wo die Zeit geblieben ist."
6 → Paris, "Chroniken. Wo die Zeit geblieben ist."
7 → Goetz, *Abfall für alle*, 703.
8 → Goetz, *Abfall für alle*, 863.
9 → Goetz, *Abfall für alle*, 761.

Downstream → An interview with James N. Kienitz Wilkins on *Indefinite Pitch*

The Androscoggin-River is not necessarily known for its beauty. It is rather the heavy pollution by 20th century industry, such as textile mills and paper mills located along its banks, that account for its notoriety. *Indefinite Pitch* is both a personal excursion into the remains of a landscape after the radical decline of an industry and a reflection of digital image production in the face of its exhaustion — an attempt to stir the endless flow of images by freezing it.

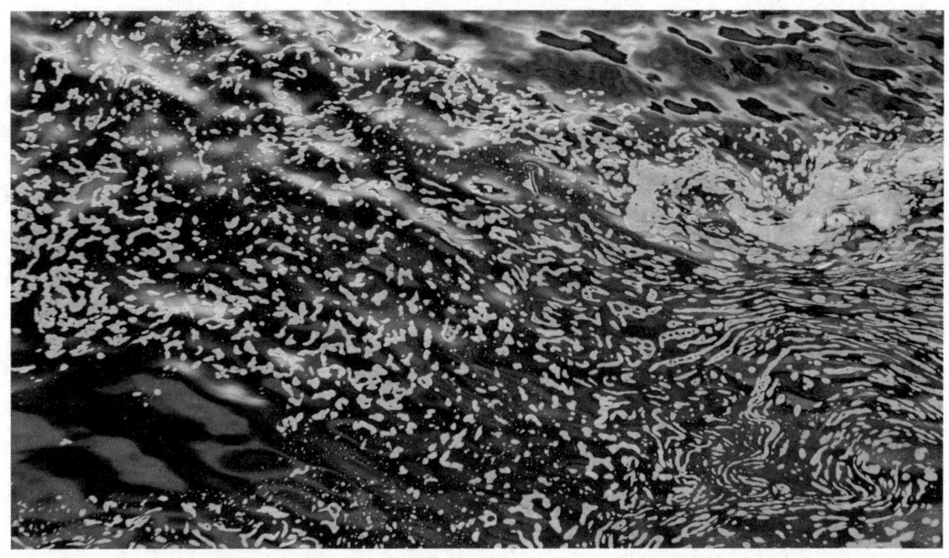

James N. Kienitz Wilkins, *Indefinit Pitch*, 2016, film still.

Pujan Karambeigi: I'm really interested in your decision to make a film about a place you have never been to, namely Berlin in New Hampshire. So even during the production process you did not go there to actually enter the site. Instead, you went to your hometown, Lewiston/Auburn, Maine, 2 hours away from Berlin, to take photos that would later form *Indefinite Pitch*. How did this idea come, to make a film close by but explicitly not on site?

James N. Kienitz Wilkins: I wanted to make a movie free to go where it wanted, without getting carried away. So, its actual shape—photos and sounds—came after the narrative was figured out. This isn't too different from the commercial screenwriting process, with changes and adjustments made to accommodate reality. The final look and feel becomes a record of many compromises. I like thinking of compromise as an artistic tool, especially in the sense of consenting to how one's life is actually playing out. With *Indefinite Pitch*, I challenged myself to be comfortable with autobiographical details, including my general disposition—which I've found harder and harder to hide in my movies. In ways, I'm lazy and impatient. Or I exist more in my mind than in the physical world, and I hope to execute my ideas in the most efficient way possible. Production as an occupation is fairly unexciting to me. Even less so the prospect of travelling to a far-off land in order to film it. So, a site connecting downstream to where 'I knew I would be' (visiting home), rather than where I would decide to place myself as self-appointed filmmaker-explorer, was just good sense. Accepting a shifting subject was very interesting to me. I didn't have to move much for this movie.

Pujan Karambeigi: As we are already talking of the different compromises a film goes through during its production process: could you say something about the imagery in *Indefinite Pitch*, these clean high resolution black & white shots of the Androscoggin river?

James Wilkins: I took the photographs. I like to take photos, though I'm not interested in photography as an end-all. The images in *Indefinite Pitch* are like a deck of cards to me: a fixed set that can shuffle infinitely and without individual value outside of the game. I wanted to create images at once specific and vague. They depict exactly what they are said to depict—the shoreline of the Androscoggin river in Lewiston/Auburn, Maine—but they don't tell you much about the place. They are beautiful, in my opinion, but also generic, the way most beautiful things are generic. Like a photo of a sunset. Or a catalogue swimsuit model. Or maybe a hit movie at Sundance. This connects in a big way to why I used a still camera to make a movie. It's probably the most economical way to make a generic and thus 'competitive' moving image. The resolution of even an inexpensive still camera exceeds today's moving image standards (2K, 4K), allowing for a scalability as high quality as any Hollywood production. It's a sort of unearned resolution. The poor man slipping into a party to which he wasn't invited by dressing the part.

> Pujan Karambeigi: Taking *Indefinite Pitch* as a landscape movie it may be read as a film about the post-industrial New England region and the network of problems that have developed in this radically changing social texture—talking of racism, heroin use, white supremacists, etc. What has intrigued you to use the form of the monologue, or more specific, a first-person essay to do a kind of landscape portrait?

James Wilkins: I agree it's a landscape movie as well as a personal essay. I really love post-industrial northeastern U.S. towns. They can be depressing as hell, but also beautiful. New England in particular fascinates me as the bedrock of the whole American experiment. I wanted to speak to the place.

I'm extremely interested in narrative, which I feel gets a bad rap as the opposite of documentary (untrue), or the enemy of formal experimentation (untrue). Narrative is simply the telling of connected events. It's not always story, which implies finality of values, although it's intimately derived from plot: the material to be connected; the data defining a zone; the borders of a property which can be walked in any direction; the grounds forming a basis of action. In *Indefinite Pitch*, this spatial sense of narrative is used to explore a landscape which is, quite frankly, indifferent to my personal opinions, feelings, or struggles. Monologue literalizes narrative as an intimate, insisting voice of reason trying to control or interpret from above what is happening on the ground, for better or for worse.

> Pujan Karambeigi: In his essay, *The Ethnologist's Jewels*, Lévi-Strauss talks about states of aggregation in relation to ethnological practice.[1] His example is the pattern generated by a drop of milk falling into the same liquid. Only through the means of chronophotography it became possible to both see and store this ephemeral pattern, turning something soft into something hard. However, this solidity must still appear fragile in order to evoke the precariousness of living forms. This is what Lévi-Strauss referred to as jewelry. Now, coming back to *Indefinite Pitch*, I find it extremely interesting that your very specific practice of the flow—photo-graphs of Androscoggin river, continuous pitch

1 → Claude Lévi-Strauss, "The Ethnologist's Jewels," in *We Are All Cannibals: And Other Essays*, 57–63, (New York City: Columbia University Press, 2016).

monologue, manipulating your own voice, a frame rate without movement, doing it 'PowerPoint style'—seems to radically confront the opposition of the soft and the hard, the moving and the immovable in terms of digital moving image production. Could you comment on this in relation to the visual and auditory form of *Indefinite Pitch*?

James Wilkins: This connects to the documentary quality of the movie. When the narrator says, "I want to tell the truth this time," it's no joke. This is the most factual documentary I have ever made. There is truly an attempt to account for facts, as far as my unprofessional self could handle an aggregation of so-called facts found on the internet. In order to do so, I needed a new form. I didn't want to be distracted. Freezing things literally gave me breathing room to consider and reconsider again, including my own relationship to the material. It is an interrupted flow. Hitting 'pause' gives time to go back and think, but of course, it spoils illusion. And then there's always flows you can't stop: insistent voices, hidden frame rates, hemorrhaging of money, life itself. How to deal with this? I think a lot about Harun Farocki's statement from "Between Two Wars:

When one doesn't have money for cars, shooting, nice clothes; when one doesn't have money to make images in which film time and film life flow uninterruptedly, then one has to put one's effort into intelligently putting together separate elements: a montage of ideas."[2]

Pujan Karambeigi: Now in terms of reception, what do you think of radically changing the temporal flow *Indefinite Pitch* has been embedded in up to this point? From being shown in a cinematic landscape to being exposed to the laptop screen?

James Wilkins: I think the site of *Indefinite Pitch* is as much the internet as any geographic space. It's the wellspring, so to speak. In fact, very little information outside of personal anecdotes couldn't be reconstructed from available sources on the internet. This is similar to some of my past work.

But a newer idea I've been playing with that connects to upcoming work is the idea of a movie being scalable, which I mentioned earlier. Physically unburdened, like a vector graphic or a Platonic form. Perhaps never actually existing in a substantial way. The way movies are watched these days certainly emphasizes this. From the confusion of terms (film for what is not film; TV for what is not TV) to a basic lack of control over technical parameters once a movie is released. Watching movies these days is a proposition ('if' you are watching it in a theater; 'if' you are watching this in HD), logically, and almost sexually; like, a pact between maker and viewer that things could be different. The relationship could change. Like, what do you want out of this? Juicy 24 fps? Or good old reliable 23.98 fps? Shall we put on the 3D shades, or pretend it's like film? I'm increasingly OK with this. There's something kind of perverse and stimulating about it.

2 → Harun Farocki, "Between Two Wars," 978.

Close or Claim →

Johannes Siegmund

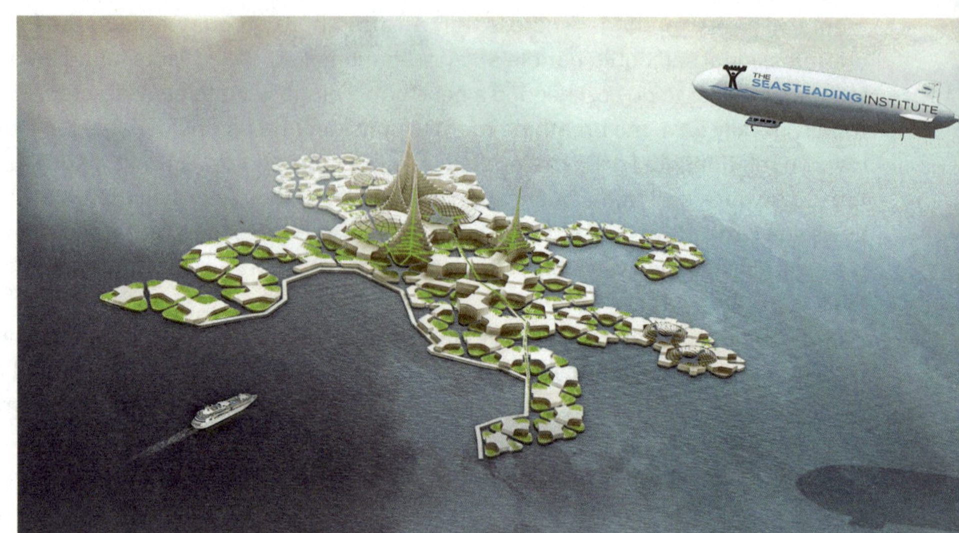

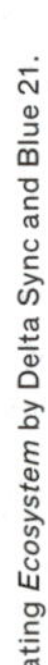
Floating *Ecosystem* by Delta Sync and Blue 21.

The tendency of creating the world-market is readily given in the concept of capital itself. Each border appears as a barrier to be overcome.[1]

The specifically political distinction underlying political actions and motives is the distinction of Friend and Fiend.[2]

The party of neoliberal globalization is over. Where free trade, open borders, and multiculturalism just yesterday was celebrated, the party guests are now hangoverishly retreating. Borders are being built, trade agreements revoked, and the formerly extinct dinosaurs of nationalism awake anew. With its tendency to steadily tap into new spheres of life, global capitalism is confronted with increasing national walling-off.

The tensions between capitalist removal of limits and political limitations can be read through two different island-experiments in the pacific: the seasteading-project of the company Blue Frontiers in French Polynesia and the Australian refugee camp on the island of Nauru. Both island-experiments offer a view on the conflict between capitalist exploitation and the closures of the nation state, therefore allowing for a breakdown of the concept of the border.

To physically bring the libertarian utopia of seasteadings to sea, Blue Frontiers, an offshoot of The Seasteading Institute, plans a prototype in a bay of the French Polynesia. This special economic zone loosely bound to a state is to be a preliminary stage to the swimming micro-states. In a second step, the experiences made with the prototype shall transform the high-sea into a science fiction space of unlimited possibility where one need not submit to any states, borders, taxes, rights, and regulations. The required seed capital is collected from business angels such as Peter Thiel that wish for libertarian freedoms within capitalism. The venture capitalists and start-ups want to create a new world-order on the seasteads. This world order is to accommodate the flexibility of the cosmopolitan winners of globalization. The libertarian micro-states would consist of individual cells rearranging and coupling themselves according to their necessities. A market of government forms would arise where the inhabitants could dock their cells onto the seastead of their choice. The wealth of the inhabitants would trickle down to the workers that would be hired all over the world to build and maintain the swimming platforms, the gigantic wave breakers, the labs, and the luxury establishments of the islands.

Libertarian ideology lies bare so openly in seasteading that it almost disenchants itself on its own. The seasteads would probably become tax havens for the super-rich, onto which the elite would retreat just as the conflicts fueled by unjust distribution of wealth, neo-colonialism, and individualization would escalate on the mainland. Amid the shipwreck of the ongoing crisis, the seasteads want to pull themselves up by their bootstraps and exist autonomously. Keeping alive the myth of autarchy in a globally connected world requires relying on a blindness cultivated over centuries regarding the material substructure of societies. While the cities might float freely, they would still depend on the base of global flows of labour and commodities. Where would the materials of those cities come from? Who would maintain them while the sea gnaws at them? Who would secure the fuel for their reactors? Which structures of exploitation has capital created for them to be built and all the research projects on them? These questions remain unanswered.

The 'Blue Frontier' shows the fragility of the techno-ideology in its transformation into a segregated society. In a capitalist sense, a border is a frontier whose function is to steadily enter new fields and claim uncharted territories. The frontier of capitalism constantly creates new spheres of life through logistics and techno ideology, and colonizes them for the private appropriation of their resources.[3]

While the super-fluid capitalists want to move the frontier of capitalism onto the high seas, national states rearm those borders against the superfluous of global capitalism. The logic of the nation states requires sealing off what is one's own from what is alien. The extraterritorial refugee camps of Australia on Nauru and Papua New Guinea have reached a tragic celebrity in this regard. Australia's border regime is one of the toughest in the world. Beyond the Australian territory, Australia is outsourcing its border to one of the most corrupt and criminal countries in the world, Nauru. After the frontier of capitalism had passed through and destroyed Nauru's environment through the exploitation of its phosphate resources, the island has deteriorated into a real dystopia. This is the place where Australia sends the illegalized migrants that it 'seized' on its seas. The little information coming from the strongly shielded camps is frightening—in 2016 the refugee Omid Masoumali immolated himself in protest; reports of rape and suicide draw the picture of a "human rights catastrophe…; a toxic mix of uncertainty, unlawful detention and inhumane conditions.[4]

Behind the scam stands a nation state asserting its power via inclusion and exclusion. Australia wants to sovereignly decide who lives on its territory and how these people get there. To deter unwanted migrants, this state creates camps, humanitarian spaces void of any rights, where people are robbed of the possibility of action and reduced to their bare-naked lives. Giorgio Agamben warned of this exclusion of the superfluous and predicted that the state of exception of the camps would begin to grow rampant. He saw in these camps democracies moving in the direction of totalitarian systems.[5]

The camp on Nauru is an extreme case and Agamben has rightly been criticized for losing sight of the grey zones of the border areas. Yet, in a time in which all over the globe borders are being fortified, in which Europe discusses camps in North African states and in which authoritarian nationalism has become a successful political role model, camps such as Nauru can offer a sight on the potential radicalization of the borders of nation states. From an economic viewpoint these camps are insane, from a jurisdictional one they are illegal, and from an ethical one a catastrophe—they only make sense politically. While nation states increasingly lose power, national quotas are sinking and supranational organizations as global corporations gain power, nation states reassert themselves of their sovereignty via sealing off their borders.

The extreme examples of both seasteading and the refugee camp on Nauru bring in their radicalness the ambiguity of the German word *Grenze* into view. The German word *Grenze* means border and frontier at the same time. The frontier is an instrument for reaching fields to be appropriated. The border is more static. It includes the own and excludes the alien. While in a globalized world, the frontier has become mainly an instrument of capitalism, the border is its nation state counterpart. One can view both projects described above as extreme shapes of the two different concepts of border and frontier. The capitalist frontier of seasteading tries to break free from the nation-state and claim new territories in high-sea. The sealed-off border of the nation state, on its side, separates the own from the foreign on the basis of a political logic that initially excludes economic interest. Through this, the logic of breaching of the frontier stands in tension to the closing function of the border. While capital wants to reach the world market and become borderless, nation states close their borders to define who belongs inside and who does not.

This tension between closing off and claiming was historically merged during imperialism. The frontier escalated together with the border. Fostered by racism, segregation, and categorizations of the subjects, imperial borders arose through the world. This imperialist model of the border has only limited validity in a geostrategic perspective today. It has not disappeared—remember the occupation of Crimea, the conflicts around the islands in South China Seas, and the polar regions. However, it is no longer a solution that can be used in a large-scale-fashion.

In light of postcolonial globalization, imperialism has been replaced by a neoliberal model of the border. Global capitalism demands open borders and a tearing away of limitations to multiply its frontier. Nation states reacted with a further differentiation of the border. Borders became a system of manifold, differentiated in- and exclusions, a heterogeneous regime including securing borders abroad and controls, passports and deportations within. Border regimes open for flows of information, resources, goods, and finance, as well as for demanded human capital, while more or less divesting themselves of migrants that were not a promise of profit.[6]

Has globalization itself reached its limits with its semipermeable borders? At the moment a new compromise for borders is sought. Capitalist frontier and political border are newly recombined. The camps and the seasteads can be understood as gestures of power in the negotiation for a new model of the border. Closure and expansion, limitation and delimitation, border, and frontier are newly reconfigured. It is not a surprise that Peter Thiel withdrew from the seasteading-project and entered negotiations with the Trump administration; both seasteading and nation state isolation are unrealistic escapisms. Capitalism and the nation state are so closely bound that they would not be capable to act without each other. Without the military safeguarding of trade routes and resources, without government infrastructure and stabilizing rescue packages, capitalism cannot exist. Likewise, even if they maximize the political legitimacy through nationalism and populism, nation states cannot leave the global market and ignore rating agencies and big corporations. At the moment everything points to a national-liberal compromise through the revival of the frontier and at the same time, the strengthening of nation states. It is an option both easy and deadly. The safeguarding of the borders and security technologies have been further expanded while capital continues to accumulate and intensify inequalities. We are driving towards a gated capitalism after the model of many countries with enormous gaps in wealth distribution.

But is this the only possibility of conceiving the border and therefore something without an alternative? Jacques Derrida has sketched another format of the border. Because the border does not only allow for both exclusion and appropriation. The border is also a place where one can hope for absolute hospitality.[7]

1 → Karl Marx, *The Grundrisse* (New York: Harper Torchbooks, 1972).

2 → Carl Schmitt, *The concept of the political* (Chicago: University of Chicago Press, 2008).

3 → Sandro Mezzadra, and Brett Neilson, *Border as method, or, The multiplication of labor* (Durham: Duke University Press, 2013).

4 → Amnesty International, "Nauru Camp A Human Rights Catastrophe With No End In Sight," accessed July 05, 2017, http://www.webcitation.org/6CRWNaOjW.

5 → Giorgio Agamben, *Homo sacer: sovereign power and bare life* (Stanford: Stanford University Press, 2010).

6 → Sandro Mezzadra and Brett Neilson, *Border as Method* (Durham: Duke University Press, 2013).

7 → Jacques Derrida and Anne Dufourmantelle, *Of hospitality: Anne Dufourmantelle invites Jacques Derrida to respond* (Stanford, CA.: Stanford University Press, 2000).

We Ethnologists →

Excursions into the Posthuman →

Dirk Rustemeyer

To alien intelligences, organically based human culture might one day appear like a falling star of meaning in an otherwise indifferent universe. With much effort, humans attempt to wrest somewhat stable forms from the cosmic pulsations of order and chaos. And yet, their 'culture' contributes to unleashing entropy. Especially the distinction between what is one's own and what is foreign—also useful to distinguish human from nonhuman—anchors the germ of negation within human culture and encourages cultural orders to crumble. Often the distinction between the Own and the Foreign turns into the political distinction of friend and fiend. Humans are 'political' beings; not necessarily because of their natural talent for reason, but rather because of their tendency to allow self-made distinctions to violently escalate. It is that which distinguishes them from their relatives, the chimps. It is unclear what this would look like in a post-human machine culture—there seems to be little reason for optimism. In light of the new ethnography of a digital triumph over human centered culture, the history of the cosmos according to homo sapiens is merely an episode of the past.

Even former transhumanists like Nick Bostrom are now working on strategies to keep potentially out-of-control-computers in check:

> *Should we one day build artificial brains surpassing human brains in general intelligence, then this super-intelligence could become overly powerful. And just like the fate of gorillas nowadays depends more on humans than on themselves, the fate of our species would depend on the actions of this machine of super-intelligence. (...) This is the supposedly greatest and most frightening task humanity has ever faced—and no matter whether we will master it or fail: it will probably be the last.*[1]

Algorithms are already on their way to the human brain. Digitized recordings of brain activity can be copied into other human brains and robots.[2] Medical progress in the area of artificial body parts or flexible programming of industrial robots opens up new technical horizons. 'Mind control' feeds into the fantasies of neuro-engineers soon to 'optimize' both sick and healthy brains. While stroke-victims and paraplegics hope for a cure, athletes, sniper-shooters and combat pilots hope to improve attention, fine motor skills, and memory.[3] Late developers, the unhappy, migraine-sufferers, the nervous, the addicts, or dementia patients become potential targets of the super-brain-industry thanks to transcranial direct currents stimulation (tDCS).

Maybe, says Yuval Noah Harari, the old Homo sapiens will soon strip away the hardships of embodied existence and gain digital immortality as "Homo Deus."[4] In exchange for meaning, Homo deus gains godlike power over the limitations of nature. "Humans weave webs of meaning, believing in it with all their hearts and yet, sooner or later, this web disintegrates. And looking back, we cannot believe how anyone could ever have taken it seriously."[5] Aside from ideologies, in a sphere of pure information, the technically enhanced human could exist in virtual worlds as part of an all-knowing and all-powerful current of data—a vision of digital redemption in the algorithmic garden of Eden.

Robin Hanson sketches a society in which 'brain emulations,' scanned from human brains, develop a life of their own. For them, the human body would be but an organic attachment.[6] Hanson takes today's technological possibilities as grounds for combination of scenarios of a digital future from current social and cultural theory. After the Neolithic and industrial revolutions, the digital one is supposedly next. While 'ems'[7] would be the more robust and faster alternative to human labour, economists could be pleased themselves with the potential growth of a cyber-economy. Ordinary humans would enjoy their existence as retirees—as long as the ems do not someday decide to recycle their organic substance. Copies of human brains could create their own society, in which the distinction between virtual and real would no longer matter. Because Hanson's vision is based on human brains, it attributes various anthropomorphic properties to the em-society. Nevertheless arises the question: "how inhuman might ems become?"[8] While wars would also become improbable when totalitarian regimes take control and ems take care of a "big increase in total happiness," it very much sounds like a whistle in the dark when Hanson recommends positive thinking: "If the [Em-lead] world is nearly inevitable, then it would be good if literary and public conversations frame it as something to be accepted, and perhaps nudged into preferred directions, instead of as something to be aggressively resisted."[9] A joyful ethnography, counting on the end of the human, even encouraging him to face the tidings of joy of a more intelligent future, is his recommendation. "In sum," so claims the résumé, "to succeed in this new world, prepare to become what it needs."[10]

The following concepts have so far influenced the self-conception of the human: nature, mind, and society. Material processes, symbolic functions, and political institutions mark the dimensions of human existence. The regularity of nature allows insight into its laws and their technical usage, while symbols like language, images, and numbers allow an order of consciousness and formations like communication structures when dealings with 'the other.' Despite being interlaced, nature, mind, and society remain sufficiently distinct for the care and alimentation of their borders. 'Culture' emerges out of these negotiations. Digital couplings of mathematical with technical and organic forms question these regimes of delimitation. Hybrid modes of existence of technical, biological, physical, economic, medical, and social arrangements turn classical anthropocentric ontologies around, projecting the symbolic diversity of mind onto the monosymbolic function of processing. Connections of organic, machinic, digital, and social orders can push open formerly unknown windows of evolution. The bottom line of these changes would be the universal producibility of nature, mind, and society in which old Homo sapiens humbly vacate the crown of creation, following "the Chinese river dolphins into oblivion."[11] The mathematical-technical logic of the binary does away with the multiplicity of cultural differentiations. Paradoxical constellations await, giving humans a rough time to still differentiate the own and the foreign. The universality of binary logic tends to do away with the capacity of human cultures to make distinctions as decisions and thereby regenerate the internal contingency of their orders. The own and the foreign become blurred—not only on an anthropological level, but also on a political one. To meet machines with the political distinction of friend and fiend appears naïve.

Are we at the verge of a new civilization, soon to corral us, like gorillas, into reservations where we are to live as slaves to digital machines? Humans' fascination with machines' intelligence probably also stems from of its cold callosity when it comes to emotional and political distinctions, keeping human cultures in suspense.

How could digital machines count as 'enemies,' if they offer themselves as tireless assistants, divining wishes, submitting suggestions, or instituting virtual similarities? Machines dodge the registers of the political. They promise, if not slavery or teeth-gnashing 'happiness,' an unconcerned efficiency. Their claim is so all-encompassing, that no totalitarian society dared to think of it before. Reword on the ethical endeavors of a humanity involved in feelings and violence—albeit enamored with universal equality—transparency, justice, and peace would be algorithmically warranted in civilization 4.0. To societies unwilling to take anything as willingly, equality becomes the moral and political measure for self-optimization. Automatic comparisons and adaptations paradoxically comply with the dream of universal moral calculation and infinite publicness. Computers process broader amounts of data than the human mind. Hopes for universal transparency, rationality, and peace appear solvable via technology. Softly, the great leviathan would have taken offer, sneaked into the private sphere, and invaded both computers and brains. The human would merge with its creations, from which they no longer wish to be distinct and would even be incapable to be so. Are conceptual or pictorial representations even fit to describe an algorithmically organized culture or would computers also take on the role of the ethnographer in portraying culture as numeral strings? If cultural distinctions would be depicted without a loss as variants of algorithmic sequences, then an era of digital ethnography would have begun, promising to take away from humans even the task of self-reflection.

Digital scenarios of futures or endings repeat motives connected to culture. Reflecting on culture is a paradoxical enterprise as it is to reflect on a genuinely reflexive phenomenon: culture arises through comparisons and the unfolding of contingency. One unable to see the own as the foreign does not know of the own and one looking at one's own for too long is blind to its otherness, so that everything else becomes foreign to him. Viewing societies from the outside is both impossible and inevitable if one wants to understand the function of 'culture.'

No one knew this paradox better than Claude Lévi-Strauss. On his expeditions, he discovered formerly unknown peoples and cultures. Yet one who turns the distant into something close in explaining it with one's own categories robs it of its authenticity. Insight destroys its object. As Lévi-Strauss knew, here lies the tragedy of knowledge of cultures whose ephemerality and brittleness is known by the ethnologist. "The world has begun without man and will end without him (...) Ever since man has begun to breathe and eat, ever since the discovery of fire to the invention of thermonuclear appliances, he has done nothing else—except for reproduction—than unconcernedly destroying billions of structures to turn them to a state in which they can no longer be integrated."[12] On a first glance, the ethnologist's melancholy is akin to the apprehensions of the transhumanist Bostrom. Now the ethnologist's skepticism applies less to the end of humankind, than to the tragedy of recognizing the own and the foreign. The myth of the foreign is turned into the myth of the own—of science. This also applies to the myth of a digital culture which knows neither an outside, nor a reflection of the own and the foreign in its pride for its scientific rationality. The distinction between own and foreign, basic to an ethnology of culture, is lost to it and it runs the danger of dwindling into myth. To see the complementarity of myth and science requires an art of reflection which does not hastily tie itself down and that understands the unfolding of that which is different in contrasting comparisons. Yet, reflection lives from the difference of symbols.

Lévi-Strauss brings into play an idea: complementing the supposed, yet itself mythomorphic alternative between science and myth with a third one—art. Tiptoeing on the limits of contemplation and principle bricolage and method, artworks connect unity and multiplicity in the aesthetic evidence of a work unfolding within itself the particular perspectives on a whole.[13] Science, myth, and art begin a play of observations sustaining itself through the difference of signs. In this game, a neutral observer that rules simultaneously over all options or processes them is impossible. Ethnological analysis such as those of Lévi-Strauss, often resemble virtual transformations of meaning and distinctions precisely because of their structuralist combinations, akin to magical or artistic plays with similarities and contrasts. Instead of reducing difference to simple variants of algorithmic functions as done by the myth of the digital, the ethnological art of observation unfolds tableaus of analogue forms bringing about subtle relationships between drops of milk, atomic explosions, the human life-cycle, ornamental practices, and the crowns of counts, dukes, and emperors.[14] For western cultures, the availability of the third value of 'arts' is essential to establish a sphere of reflection keeping distinctions variable. Visions of a digital future of humankind do not consider, unlike Lévi-Strauss, the erosion of the distinction between the own and the foreign as even a small tragedy. With this distinction, the self-conception of the human as a 'political' being is at one's disposal. A trans-human society would be a post-political culture. Monosymbolic orders and binary logics of either/or wreck the multiplicity of sense arising from the difference between signs, along which mind and world arrange themselves into nonhomogeneous infinities. Lévi-Strauss would probably have struck visions of digital superintelligence with the myths of reason blossoming in societies taking everything to be scientific. Because digital orders equalize everything, they remain foreign to that which Lévi-Strauss thought to be equally precious as mysterious of the foreign. While the ethnologist seeks the foreign—and tragically encounters the own—visionaries of the digital have a better grasp and more correct version of the own—without any tragedy.[15]

Scientists or logicians might scorn at the promiscuity of signs, yet a logos oscillating between myth, science, and art unleashes productive powers within culture. Instead of providing answers, it delivers mystery. What is real and what is fiction, what is theater and what is the everyday, where the foreign looms within the own, depends on perspectives, situations, humans, times, and places. Imagination and reality need to be carefully distinguished at each step. The trust Lévi-Strauss places in art is not something that one can technically simulate. Every digital simulation repeats the monosymbolic narrowing of sense. Celerity and mass-information processing are unfitting criteria for a notion of 'sense.' It would be unfortunate, if human brains were to take arms when faced with the myth of em, mistake their creativity for slowness and renounce a skeptical observation of computers and ems as bizarre coevals with the curious glance of ethnologists.

The universe can be considered an infinitely productive process uniting creation and destruction. "This very world-order has not been created by god or man, it always was and will be: indelible fire, flaring, and fading at large."[16] Life is more than mere biological reproduction. It is also an idea. Understanding this requires, according to

Gregory, "learning to think in a new way."[17] Thinking, which can be understood as a moment of universal reflexive processing, unlike of an algorithmic blueprint, does not run the danger of mistaking itself for technical myths or scientific professions of faith. Reflection—neither pure mind nor pure nature—embodies a creative principle within it. Science, myth, or art alone do not solve the riddles of the universe, but their interplay supplies human cultures with sufficient jest as to prevent them from surrendering to binary distinctions without discarding the occasional value of binary distinctions. Narratives of digital civilizations, whose sovereigns would be supposedly intelligent machines, do away with an understanding of freedom. This idea however grounds that, which western cultures have understood as 'truth,' 'person,' or 'god.' Without this idea, the cultural (self) images of the human would have come to be different. Always anew, 'freedom' questions certainties and identities: those not knowing truth are the ones that have to look for it; a person remains distinct from the communication in which it becomes visible and one asks for a god when interested in the world. Before humanity worships the Great Computer, it would be well advised to send a few ethnologists into the digital jungle to shake the algorithmic trees to look for the gods tumbling down from their branches. On their expeditions through rugged landscapes of validity, good ethnologists round up peculiar beings living within modern culture—and listen to their mumblings.[18] They also lend their ear to the murmurs and whispers of servers without needing to take its advice. Nowadays, travelling has gotten more comfortable than in the days of Lévi-Strauss. With a bit of luck, the ethnologist can find the foreigner already in its neighbor.

1 → Nick Bostrom, *Superintelligenz*, trans. editors (Berlin: Suhrkamp, 2014), 9.; Dirk Baecker, "Superintelligenz, und die Plastizität des Menschen," Kultur/Reflexion, accessed July 01, 2017, https://kure.hypotheses.org/112.

2 → "Der Mensch denkt, die Maschine lenkt." *Frankfurter Allgemeine Zeitung*, accessed March 09, 2017, 18.

3 → Jürgen Müller-Jung, "Das elektrisch verstärkte Denken," *Frankfurter Allgemeine Zeitung Quarterly*, February, 2017, 56–61.

4 → Yuval Noah Harari, *Homo Deus, Eine Geschichte von Morgen*, trans. Andreas Wirthensohn (Munich: Beck, C.H., 2017).

5 → Harari, *Homo Deus*, 206.

6 → Robin Hanson, *AGE OF EM: work, love, and life when robots rule the earth* (Oxford: Oxford University Press, 2016).

7 → 'em' is the short term for emulation—in this case, a brain emulation.

8 → Hanson, *AGE OF EM*, 339.

9 → Hanson, *AGE OF EM*, 370, 373.

10 → Hanson, *AGE OF EM*, 379.

11 → Harari, *Homo Deus*, 534.

12 → Claude Lévi-Strauss, *Traurige Tropen*, trans. editors (Frankfurt am Main: Suhrkamp, 1978), 411.

13 → Claude Lévi-Strauss, *Das wilde Denken* (Frankfurt am Main: Suhrkamp, 1968), 11–48.

14 → Claude Lévi-Strauss, *Wir sind alle Kannibalen* (Berlin: Suhrkamp, 2017).

15 → Mark Siemons, "Die Regierung der gescannten Hirne," *Frankfurter Allgemeine Zeitung*, February 02, 2017, http://www.faz.net/aktuell/feuilleton/kuenstliche-intelligenz-die-regierung-der-gescannten-hirne-14884217.

16 → Heraklit, "Fragment 30," *Heraklit Fragmente*, ed. Bruno Snell, trans. editors (München: Artemis Verlag,1979), 15.

17 → Gregory Bateson, *Ökologie des Geistes: anthropologische, psychologische, biologische und epistemologische Perspektiven*, trans. editors (Frankfurt am Main: Suhrkamp, 1972), 594.

18 → Bruno Latour, *Existenzweisen – Eine Anthropologie der Moderne*, trans. Gustav Roßler (Berlin: Suhrkamp, 2018).

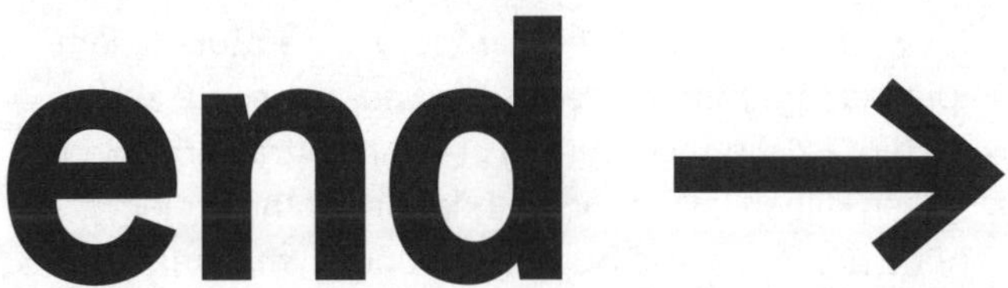

acknowledgements

This book is the last step of *warehouse*. For more than a year we were planning and implementing this project, framed as a research on digitalization. In the beginning, we were five people partially from the association *super filme* but first and foremost friends: Pujan Karambeigi, Anneliese Ostertag, Tabea Rossol, Pierre Schwarzer, and Lukas Stolz.

Our initial question dealt with an unease or discomfort with the prevailing political conditions that we assumed related to what we termed 'the digital.' A long conversation on filter bubbles, gated communities, and power structures pervading the digital sphere developed. After getting lost in wild theories and assumptions we decided to take a more exploratory stance: an ethnography of the digital. We invited London based curator Shama Khanna and her project *Flatness* to join us in the unfurling project for which we started to write applications for cultural public funding. Surprisingly for us, it worked.

warehouse received funding from the Federal Cultural Foundation of Germany, the European Center for Creative Economy (ecce), the Individuelle Förderung von Künstlerinnen, Künstlern und Kreativen (IKF), and the Ministerium für Familie, Kinder, Jugend, Kultur und Sport des Landes Nordrhein-Westfalen under the auspices of the University of Witten/Herdecke with support from the dean of the faculty for humanities and arts, Dirk Baecker.

The project formed as an online platform, a series of events and workshops in Berlin, the Ruhr area, London and Madrid, a digital residency program and finally in your hands, the book a condensation of the whole research process. After the confirmation of the funding, we had to act quickly—jobs needed to be quit, people needed to move. In all this overload, there were many people offering their help, advice, and collaboration whom we want to thank here.

First, we want to express our gratitude to Shama Khanna who supported us with her expertise and skills from the very beginning. Together with Pujan Karambeigi she co-curated *nummer 5,* an online screening series accompanied by texts and interviews. Two interviews with artists featured as part of the series—Heather Phillipson and James N. Kienitz—are included in this book.

Another companion who supported us from the earliest days of the project onwards is Kim Dall'Armi. While in the beginning his thoughts and considerations had a significant impact on the overall concept of *warehouse*, at a later stage of the project we could count on his practical know-how and manual dexterity (as we already did in previous projects of *super filme*).

We also invited Max Wallenhorst with his interest in contemporary literature to join us. On the online platform, he pieced together the series *Sexting, Season 2* and wrote a text on the topic. We owe him a delightful evening in Naunynstraße 53, Berlin. The website was designed by Rasso Hilber, laying the foundation for the project. Another person forming the online presence was Sophia Groening who created deli-cate trailers for the website giving the categories a needed touch.
We were lucky to have Julian Römer fill in and support us with his financial skills until the very end.
When working on the publication, Lisa Martin helped and advised us a lot. She took over many organizational tasks and formed the book with us. Also involved in the publication were Noah Voelker and Elias F. Quijada Link who proofread all the texts day and night and Pia Christmann and Ann Richter who took over the design and the realization of the book.
A big part of *warehouse* has been its events. Most of them took place in the Kreuzberg Pavillon, an off-space in Berlin. Biweekly events brought together Antonia Baehr, Bryana Fritz, Max Grau, Nanna Heidenreich, terra0, THE AGENCY, Guilel Treiber, Katharina Pethke, and Max Wallenhorst. Also in Berlin, but at Ballhaus Ost, we co-produced the performance *NORMCORE* by GIESCHEand followed by a talk with Katerina Krtilova. Together with European Alternatives we co-produced the perfor-mance, *Debriefing Session I* by Public Movement, at TRANSEUROPA Festival in Madrid. Thanks to Shama Khanna's engagement, two screening events took place at the Close-Up Film Centre in London. Supported by medienwerk.nrw, *warehouse* organized two workshops: one with Rahel Spöhrer and the other with Samira Elagoz at [...] raum e.V. in the Ruhr area followed by a screening at Burgkino Witten and a post-patriarchal party format by FAM_.
Another workshop held by Shama Khanna took place in Berlin including a screening by Marwa Arsanios followed by an in-conversation with Shama Khanna. The work-shop brought together all the digital residents: Silvia Amancei, Bogdan Armanu, Max Grau, Nieves de la Fuente Gutierrez, Jorge Laureiro, Lou Morlier, Walter Solon, and Giulio Vacchiano. The residency program was supported by Hartware Medienkunstverein Dortmund. Each resident was selected by a jury in which Inke Arns, Dirk Baecker, Monika Fleischmann, Anna Fricke, Ariel Reichman, Robert Sakrowski, and Christian Sievers took part.
Finally, we want to thank all the people who were there, lending us an ear or a hand, gave advice and support during the last year: Leonie Coers, Niklas Egberts, Christine Frieling, Rafael Dernbach, Jacqueline Grassmann, Christian Grüny, Nanna Heidenreich, Anka Helfertova, Lea Hopp, Myriam van Imschoot, Anna-Verena Nosthoff, Lara Scherrible, Dieter Thomä, Tilman Richter, Milosz Paul Rosinski, and Oliver Zahn.

remarks

stranded

On Disappearances: Reflections on the Techno-Poetics of Invisible Machines was written in German by Felix Maschewski and Anna-Verena Nosthoff. The English translation was provided by Pierre Schwarzer.

Ängste zur Kunst and *whee.gif* are two Twitter accounts that wrote a series of tweets in September and October 2017. They were pieced together by Max Wallenhorst to form *sext:*, 'an ongoing text performance.'

Malinowski's Kiss: Notes toward a Critique of Digital Resistance was first given as an oral presentation at the opening event of *warehouse*.

Repertoires Animés is a long-term project by ARG mainly taking place in the frame of an online residency within the web platform *Oralsite*, a project of *SARMA — Laboratory for discursive practices and expanded publication*. Myriam van Imschoot, co-curator of *SARMA*, connected ARG and *warehouse*. This text was first published online with a video by ARG addressing the work of Paul Otlet.

Be-in: Aspects of a Fascination History of Digital Cultures by Art and Technology by Martina Leeker was translated by Pierre Schwarzer from German into English.

entropy

A Paradigm of the Human Condition, Applied to Arts and Artists by Dirk Baecker was written in German and later translated by Pierre Schwarzer.

Surface is an excerpt of a series of poems first published in Etcetera 148 by ecetera in 2017. *warehouse* invited Bryana Fritz to Berlin in July 2017 to perform *Indispensible Blue*, a desktop poem which is also accessible online within the series *Sexting Season 2*.

"Cut, Copy, Paste!": The Next "New Normal" or Biology's Trend Towards Homophily by Gabriele Gramelsberger was written in German and translated by Pierre Schwarzer.

pray

14th Week is an excerpt of the book *La condition ouvrière* by Simone Weil. It was original written in French between 1934 and 1942 and published post-mortem, in 1951, by Éditions Gallimard in Paris. For *warehouse,* the text was translated by Pierre Schwarzer and published in English for the first time. The introduction was written by the editors.

An Essay on the German Forest: In the Open with terra0 by Pujan Karambeigi and Tabea Rossol was translated by Pierre Schwarzer. *warehouse* invited Paul Kolling and Paul Seidler, two members of *Terra0*, to give a public talk about their project in June 2017.

butter knife: facebook was written by Giulio Vacchiano who has been a digital resident at *warehouse* since August 2017 where he published a variety of texts on the website, *warehouse.industries*. First published in German, Vacchiano translated *butter knife: facebook* into English for this book.

adobe

A first version of the text *The Second God, Golem and Chess: Regarding the Critique of Technical Reason* was delivered as a lecture at Ballhaus Ost, Berlin on invitation of *warehouse* after a performance of GIESCHEand. The text along with all direct quotes was translated into English by Pierre Schwarzer.

Today I am functional by Christiane Heidrich was first published in the German literary magazine *Edit, number 72*. For this book it was selected and translated by Max Wallenhorst.

(un-)imagining or why the blank page is a lure in imagining the new by Pierre Schwarzer was first published online on 'Public Seminar' in November 2017.

soft-fiction

The interview by Pujan Karambeigi, *A Sense of Heat*, refers to the video *WHAT'S THE DAMAGE* by Heather Phillipson. The video has been part of *warehouse* online screening series and was chosen by Shama Khanna.

home

My Dog is My Piano is a sonic lecture-performance first performed in 2011 at the French Embassy in New York City as a commission by the philosophers Avital Ronell and François Noudelmann in the frame of Villa Gillet/Walls and Bridges NYC. *'Infinite Affinities — Chords and Discords — Musical Patterns of Affinities.'* *warehouse* invited Antonia Baehr to present excerpts of *My Dog is My Piano* in Berlin accompanied by a talk with Nanna Heidenreich. *Traces of Places: My Dog is My Piano* was originally published online together with audio records and appears here with a note from the editors.

Indefinite Pitch has been part of the *warehouse* online screening series as well as shown live at the *warehouse* opening event in June 2017. The film by James N. Kienitz Wilkins was chosen by Shama Khanna.

Close or Claim by Johannes Siegmund was translated by Pierre Schwarzer from German into English.

We Ethnologists: Excursions into the Posthuman by Dirk Rustemeyer was originally published in German as "Wir Ethnologen: Exkursion ins Posthumane" by the University of Witten/Herdecke in May 2017. For this book the text was translated by Pierre Schwarzer.

image credits

biographies

Ängste zur Kunst is a twitter account. Scarlett Johansson's voice is in your mind right now.

ARG (Animation Research Group) was constituted in 2014 within the framework of École de Recherche Graphique in Brussels after a workshop by Alexander Schellow and Catherine Perret. The group develops and implements methods and protocols around the concept of 'expanded animation.' ARG members are Alexander Schellow, Anton Henne, Jules Urban, Myriam Raccah, Nicolas Wouters, Olivia Molnar, and Xavier Gorgol.

Dirk Baecker is a German sociologist, Chair of Cultural Theory and Management and Dean of the Faculty of Cultural Reflexion at the University of Witten/ Herdecke. After his studies of Sociology and Political Economy in Cologne and Paris, he obtained his PhD in Bielefeld with Niklas Luhmann. His recent works revolve around sociologies of art, management and new media.

Antonia Baehr is a choreographer, performer, and artist. Baehr studied with Valie Export and holds a master in performance and experimental film from the School of the Art Institute of Chicago. Baehr is currently collaborating with artists like Neo Hülcker, Lindy Annis, and Latifa Laabissi and is the producer of the horse whisperer and dancer Werner Hirsch, the musician and choreographer Henri Fleur, and the aspirant composer and ex-husband Henry Wilde.

Pia Christmann is co-running Studio Pandan, a female Berlin-based agency for graphic design and art direction. The studio focuses on content-driven design and creating visual translations, which should be both challenging and enjoyable.

Samuel Gerald Collins is a cultural anthropologist interested in information society and globalization. His M.A. and PhD are from American University in Washington, D.C. Before he became a professor at Towson University, he taught at Dongseo University in Pusan, South Korea.

Rafael Dernbach is a writer, researcher, and current PhD candidate at University of Cambridge. He researches social construction and aesthetics of futures, from science fiction to scenario planning.

Bryana Fritz studied dance in Minneapolis and Essen and graduated from P.A.R.T.S. in Brussels in 2014. Within her work she explores the uncanny valley between poetry and dance on the everyday user surfaces of macOS. Together with Henry Anderson she founded the *Slow Reading Club*.

Orit Gat is a writer based in New York and London whose work on art, publishing, and internet culture has appeared in a variety of magazines. She is the features editor of *RHIZOME* and was recently awarded the Creative Capital/Andy Warhol Arts Writers Grant.

Gabriele Gramelsberger is professor for Philosophy of Science and Technology at RWTH Aachen University. She received her PhD in philosophy in 2001 at the Freie Universität Berlin with Sybille Krämer. Her philosophical research focuses on the influence of the computer on science and society.

Christian Grüny teaches philosophy at the University of Witten/Herdecke. His areas of research are aesthetics, the philosophy of music, semiotics, and phenomenology.

Jonathan Harth studied sociology at the Freie University Berlin and has been scientific assistant to the Chair of Sociology at the University of Witten/ Herdecke since 2013. He wrote his PhD dealing with computer-controlled game partners and has researched virtual reality technologies.

Christiane Heidrich is enrolled at the Fine Arts Department in Stuttgart. She focuses on the entanglement of bodies and applications, tracing the relationality of computed self-actualization in social as well as other types of media.

Cornelius Heimstädt studied organic agriculture in Eberswalde. He is enrolled in the master's course for Science and Technology Studies at the University of Vienna and works as a writer and musician.

Andy Holden graduated from Goldsmiths, University of London in 2005. His multidisciplinary work incorporates a variety of media, including plaster, bronze, ceramics, music, performance, and large-scale sculpture.

Jean Hubert lives and works in Amsterdam. He graduated in 2010 from the École Nationale Superieure des Beaux-Arts de Paris. His work is centered around video and has been shown internationally.

Shama Khanna is an independent curator, educator and writer based in London. Across her career she has curated more than 70 artists' projects and commissions both independently and as part of collaborations including Kurzfilmtage Oberhausen, documenta 14, Athens, Palais de Tokyo, Paris, Moderna Museet, Malmo and Chisenhale Gallery, London. Currently she teaches at Kingston University and University of the Arts, London, and co-edits *Aorist* arts journal with 7 other writers. Her ongoing research is *Flatness*.

Pujan Karambeigi is a writer and curator based in New York City. He is currently a Graduate Student at Columbia University, focusing on experimental documentary and video art of the 1970s and 1980s.

Katerina Krtilova is a researcher at the Institute for Media Anthropology at Bauhaus University Weimar where she wrote a dissertation on Vilém Flusser's media philosophy in 2016. She focuses on media philosophy, European media theory, and the relations between reflexivity, performativity, and materiality in 20th century philosophy.

Martina Leeker is a lecturer for Theater and Media Studies. She published widely on Media Theory and Media History, McLuhan, art and technology and theater, performance, and dance. Since October 2013 she has been a researcher at the Digital Cultures Research Lab at the Leuphana University in Lüneburg.

Lisa Martin is doing a Master in Art History at the University of Dusseldorf. She studied interior design, philosophy, and art education in Detmold and Paderborn.

Felix Maschewski is a scholar of literature and economics, research fellow at the Institute for Economic Design, Berlin, and member at the graduate college The Knowledge of Literature at Humboldt University Berlin.

Naoki Matsuyama studied architecture and educational philosophy at the University of Cambridge, and is enrolled in the master's course for Science Technology Studies at the University of Vienna. She works as an editor, translator, and writer.

Anna-Verena Nosthoff is an author, philosopher and political theorist. Currently she is writing her PhD on the influence of cybernetics on the political.

Anneliese Ostertag studied cultural studies and performance art in Witten and London. She researches the intersection of art and ethnography and sometimes works as a curator, writer, and publisher.

Heather Phillipson completed her undergraduate degree in Fine Art at the Cardiff Metropolitan University, going on to study drawing at Central St Martins, and subsequently earning her PhD in Fine Art practice from Middlesex University in 2008. Phillipson produced a range of multimedia work and installations in video, sculpture, and music, alongside more conventional published writing.

Elias F. Quijada Link is a multidisciplinary creative, at present translating and copyediting at Spector Books.

Ann Richter is co-founder of Studio Pandan, an agency for graphic design and art direction. The studio focuses on content-driven design and creating visual translations, which should be both challenging and enjoyable. With Agnieszka Roguski she works as "A.R. practice" on curatorial projects.

Tilman Richter studied philosophy and cultural studies in Witten and Berlin and writes on media and the capitalization of individuality.

Julian Römer is an economist with special interests in art and production management and currently does research on the topic of dissent as a means of systemic learning. He also is a systemic consultant.

Milosz Paul Rosinski is an artist, philosopher, and writer based in Berlin. He studied Anthropology, Philosophy, and Visual Arts in Maastricht, Paris, San Diego, Cambridge, and Berlin. In 2017, he completed a PhD entitled *Cinema of the Self* and teaches Comparative Studies at Cambridge University.

Tabea Rossol studied Philosophy, Politics, and Economics at the University of Witten/Herdecke. She likes to write and is interested in ethnology.

Dirk Rustemeyer teaches Pedagogy at the University of Trier and Philosophy at the University of Witten/Herdecke. His research focuses on cultural semiotics, forms of knowledge, and aesthetics.

Pierre Schwarzer is a New-York-based writer and curator currently researching transformations of subjectivity with regards to the digital via aesthetics, phenomenology and psychoanalysis at the New School for Social Research.

Johannes Siegmund is working on a PhD on migration and flight at the Vienna Academy of Fine Arts. He is part of the journal for political-philosophical interventions *engagée* and the collective *philosophy unbound*.

Lukas Stolz is an activist by day and a curator by night. After he resigned from his position at Google he feels like this is an appropriate way of maintaining a creative relationship to contemporary capitalism, which he admires but doesn't like.

Danae Theodoridou is a performance maker and researcher based in Brussels. Her work deals with the notion of social imaginaries. She teaches in various university departments, curates practice-led research projects, and presents and publishes her research work internationally.

Leslie Thornton is a pioneer of contemporary media aesthetics working in cinema, installation, and media contexts for over four decades. She attended the State University of New York in Buffalo and earned her Master at MIT in Cambridge studying with Richard Leacock and Ed Pincus. Thornton is Professor of Modern Culture and Media at Brown University.

Guilel Treiber is a writer and philosopher working at the Research Center for Political Philosophy Leuven. Treiber is specialized in French contemporary political thought with an interest in the notion of resistance. He holds a degree in Politics and History of Islam and the Middle East from the Hebrew University Jerusalem.

Giulio Vacchiano is a critic whose focus is the culinary scene of Cologne. Since 2016, he runs the Facebook page *it tastes like ashes*. In 2017 he published a book with the same title. Giulio has been a digital residence of *warehouse*.

Noah Voelker is a theater maker, dramaturg, editor, researcher, technical advisor, and performer from Texas, based in Amsterdam. He completed his undergraduate at Trinity University and his masters at DAS Theater. His work is focused on dialog practices, storytelling, audience participation, and authenticity in performance.

Max Wallenhorst studied Applied Theater Studies in Gießen and is currently enrolled in Cultural Studies at the Humboldt University Berlin. He is working on auto-essays and weak performances. For *warehouse* he has pieced together the series *Sexting, Season 2*.

Simone Weil (1909–1943) was a French philosopher, mystic, and political activist. After studying philosophy, she became a teacher at a secondary school for girls. Weil wrote throughout her whole life, though her writings did not attract much attention. In the 1950s and 1960s, her work reached a wider audience.

whee.gif is a twitter account about feelings and ghosts on the edge of digitalization. In a very soft way though. You can read this in your voice if you like.

James N. Kienitz Wilkins is a filmmaker and artist based in Brooklyn. His films have a common provenance in internet archaeology and have been shown internationally. Wilkins is a graduate of the Cooper Union School of Art in New York City.

imprint

The book is published on the occasion of the *warehouse* project.

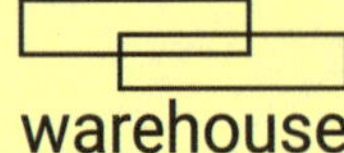

warehouse is a joint venture between *super filme* and *flatness* under the auspices of the University of Witten/Herdecke.

www.warehouse.industries
www.super-filme.org
www.flatness.eu

Editors → Pujan Karambeigi, Anneliese Ostertag, Tabea Rossol, Pierre Schwarzer, Lukas Stolz / **Editorial assistance** → Lisa Martin / **Financial administration** → Julian Römer / **Translation** → Pierre Schwarzer, Max Wallenhorst / **Proofreading** → Elias F. Quijada Link, Noah Voelker / **Contributors** → Ängste zur Kunst and whee.gif / ARG / Dirk Baecker / Antonia Baehr / Samuel Gerald Collins / Rafael Dernbach / Bryana Fritz / Orit Gat / Gabriele Gramelsberger / Christian Grüny / Jonathan Harth / Christiane Heidrich / Cornelius Heimstädt and Naoki Matsuyama / Andy Holden / Jean Hubert / Pujan Karambeigi and Tabea Rossol / Katerina Krtilova / Martina Leeker / Felix Maschewski and Anna-Verena Nosthoff / Heather Philippson / Tilman Richter / Milosz Paul Rosinski / Dirk Rustemeyer / Pierre Schwarzer / Johannes Siegmund / Danae Theodoridou / Leslie Thornton / Guilel Treiber /

Giulio Vacchiano / Max Wallenhorst / Simone Weil / James N. Kienitz Wilkins / **Graphic design** → Studio Pandan – Pia Christmann & Ann Richter / **Typesetting assistance** → Vreni Knödler / **Printing** → Druckhaus Köthen / **Published by** → Spector Books, Harkortstraße 10, 04107 Leipzig, www.spectorbooks.com / **Distribution** → *Germany and Austria* → GVA, Gemeinsame Verlagsauslieferung Göttingen GmbH und Co. KG, www.gva-verlage.de / *Switzerland* → AVA Verlagsauslieferung AG, www.ava.ch / *France and Belgium* → Interart Paris, www.interart.fr / *United Kingdom* → Central Books Ltd., www.centralbooks.com / *USA, Canada, Central and South America, Africa and Asia* → ARTBOOK, D.A.P, www.artbook.com / *South Korea* → The Book Society, www.thebooksociety.org / *Australia and New Zealand* → Perimeter Distribution, www.perimeterdistribution.com

Founding → Federal Cultural Foundation, the European Center for Creative Economy (ecce) / the Individuelle Förderung von Künstlerinnen, Künstlern und Kreativen (IKF), and the Ministerium für Familie, Kinder, Jugend, Kultur und Sport des Landes Nordrhein-Westfalen

First edition 2018, printed in Germany
ISBN: 978-3-95905-231-3

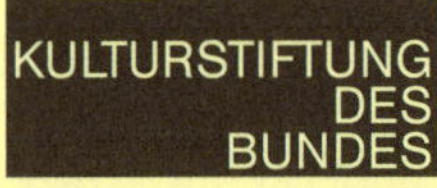

Ministerium für
Kultur und Wissenschaft
des Landes Nordrhein-Westfalen

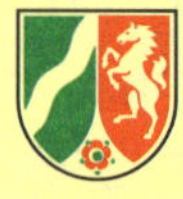

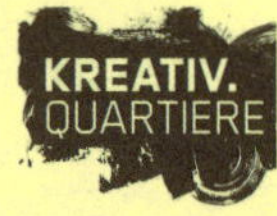

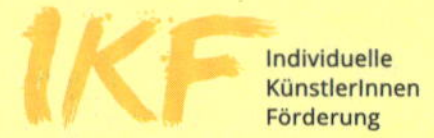

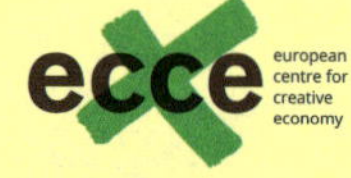